Byron York

The Vast Left Wing Conspiracy

The Untold Story of How Democratic Operatives, Eccentric Billionaires, Liberal Activists, and Assorted Celebrities Tried to Bring Down a President—and Why They'll Try Even Harder Next Time

CROWN
FORUM

NEW YORK

Library of Congress Cataloging-in-Publication Data
York, Byron.
The vast left wing conspiracy : the untold story of how Democratic operatives, eccentric
billionaires, liberal activists, and assorted celebrities tried to bring down a president—and
why they'll try even harder next time / Byron York.—1st ed.
Includes index.
1. Liberalism—United States.   2. Democratic Party (U.S.).   3. United States—Politics
and government-2001.   I. Title.
JC574.2.U6Y67   2005
324.973'0931—dc22   2005000749

ISBN 1-4000-8238-2

Printed in the United States of America

Design by Robert C. Olsson

10 9 8 7 6 5 4 3 2 1

First Edition

For Marty

CONTENTS

The Vast Left Wing Conspiracy

Pushback

The New Movement That Changed Politics

"We have to fight back. We *have* to fight back."

It was the night of November 1, 2003, one year almost to the day before the presidential election, and Al Franken, the anti-Bush comedian and soon-to-be radio host, was addressing a crowd of left-leaning activist, political, and media types gathered at Washington's International Spy Museum. They had come to celebrate the opening of a new liberal think tank, the Center for American Progress, founded by former Clinton White House chief of staff John Podesta. The Center would be dedicated, at least in part, to what Podesta called "pushback" against the Right—that is, to launching daily attacks on the Bush administration and fighting conservatives sound bite for sound bite on television and radio. The prospect made Franken very, very happy.

"Thank God you're doing this," he said to Podesta, before declaring once more, "We have to fight back." As Franken spoke, Podesta stood to one side, acknowledging the praise, while a few feet away, Senator Hillary Rodham Clinton nodded in agreement. Later, she, too, would thank Podesta for his efforts, urging the crowd to take up political arms in what she called the "war that we're engaged in with the other side."

Franken's words were an almost perfect statement of the mood on the Left as the 2004 presidential election approached. Franken, Podesta, Mrs. Clinton, and their allies believed that for years the Left had been "too nice" in the fight against what they called the Republican attack machine. And in starting an institution devoted to pushback, they were just part of a far larger movement to drive George W. Bush from the White House. Their effort would make history, in part because it raised more money than has ever been raised to defeat (or, for that matter, to elect) a single politician—literally hundreds of millions of dollars. But more important, the movement was unprecedented in the degree to which its leaders organized themselves, used technology, coordinated with one another, and transformed liberal anger at the president into actual action. There was the Internet activist group MoveOn.org, the enormous contributions of the anti-Bush billionaire George Soros, the massive pro-Democratic voter turnout effort led by the new organization America Coming Together, the films of Michael Moore, Franken's Air America radio network, and more. Together, they made up what would become the biggest, richest, and best organized movement in American political history.

Of course, in the most immediate sense, that movement failed the night George W. Bush won reelection. But in a larger sense, the new activists of the Left had a profound impact on the way politics is conducted, an impact that will likely be felt for years to come. Simply put, they changed the rules of the game. By circumventing the old political party structure and coming up with new ways to raise money and to reach voters—who would have thought, for example, that movies would play such a high-profile role in a campaign?—they ensured that future campaigns will not look like those of the past.

And it was all done extraordinarily quickly; the activists built their network in little more than eighteen months. Forty years ago, a small band of conservatives, stung by the defeat of Barry Goldwater, came together to create what became the modern conservative movement. From that beginning, it took decades for conservative leaders to achieve meaningful power at all levels of government. Today's Left is bigger and better funded than conservatives were decades ago, and though Democrats did not win in 2004, this left-wing movement—and the foundation of new institutions on which it rests—seems poised to exert even more influence in coming campaigns.

YOU'RE ANGRY, I'M DESPERATE

Why did they do it? It is tempting to ascribe the Left's activism entirely to anger—anger about the Clinton impeachment, anger about the 2000 Florida recount, anger about the war in Iraq, and, in some cases, anger at the look on George W. Bush's face or the way he walked. And indeed, that was an important motivation for many people. But there was more to it than that. The anger directed at President Bush was concentrated mostly on what might be called the emotional wing of the movement—MoveOn, Franken, Moore, and their supporters.

On what might be called the professional wing—America Coming Together, the Center for American Progress, and other groups run by experienced Democratic politicos—the dominant mood was *desperation.*

As the 2004 presidential election approached, the professionals felt they had been the victims of a double whammy—not impeachment and Florida, but rather the 2002 congressional elections and the newly enacted McCain-Feingold campaign finance law.

First, the congressional elections. A decade earlier, after the 1992 elections, Democrats controlled the White House, the House of Representatives, and the Senate; the House had been theirs for forty straight years. Even when the party famously lost both houses of Congress in 1994, Democrats still held the presidency. In 2000, they lost both the White House and Congress but regained control of the Senate after just a few months when Senator James Jeffords left the Republican Party. It was not until 2002, when Democrats lost the Senate, along with the House (again), while remaining out of power in the White House, that party leaders had to face the bleak realization that they controlled nothing in Washington.

"I think it was clear, particularly by what I think was a disastrous strategy in '02, that something needed to be done," Podesta explained to me one morning a few weeks before Election Day 2004. "We're sitting there with no real power, a kind of weak voice in Congress, and the incapacity to put forward an alternative agenda." What needed to be done, as Podesta and others saw it, was to organize. Liberals had never organized on a grand scale in the past, Podesta told me, because they had never really needed to. After 2002, they did.

Not long after the 2002 voting, several of the Democrats who would become leaders of the new movement—Ellen Malcolm of the powerful political action committee known as EMILY's List, Steve Rosenthal, who had spent years with the AFL-CIO, and former top Clinton aide Harold Ickes—held a decidedly downbeat dinner meeting at a restaurant in Washington's Dupont Circle neighborhood to confront what seemed like an almost hopeless presidential campaign in 2004. "We started talking about the need to figure out, first of all, how to beat the Bush juggernaut, which, at the time, nobody thought Democrats were going to be able to win," Malcolm told me later. "We thought that Karl Rove [the president's top political advisor] had a strategy to beat us on the money so badly that . . . they'd get the whole [election] over by summer."

That prospect was daunting enough, but the liberals' job was made even more difficult by the other half of the double whammy, McCain-Feingold. The law, which Democrats had long supported, went into effect after the 2002 elections. It forbade unlimited "soft money" contributions to the political parties, just as a reform in the 1970s had outlawed unlimited contributions to politicians themselves. Under McCain-Feingold's "hard money" limits, in any election cycle an individual donor could give a maximum of $2,000 to a particular candidate, $5,000 to a political action committee in the same period, and $25,000 to a party. That was it.

The new law had a brutal effect on Democrats, who, contrary to their image as the party of the little guy, had come to rely heavily on big checks from supporters in Hollywood and other liberal enclaves. Republicans, on the other hand, despite their image as the party of plutocrats, had always received large numbers of small contributions that would not be affected by the new limits. In the months after McCain-Feingold took effect, the two parties' fortunes went in opposite directions.

In February 2003, for example, as the presidential campaign began to dominate the political conversation, the Democratic National Committee took in $2.5 million from individuals— all in limited, post–McCain-Feingold amounts. The Republican National Committee collected $9.5 million. The Democrats' two congressional campaign committees, House and Senate, took in a total of $1.4 million from individuals during that month. The Republicans' two committees collected a total of $9.4 million. Add everything up, and the Democrats took in $3.9 million in a month in which Republicans collected $18.9 million.

McCain-Feingold was often described by its supporters as a measure to reduce "the influence of big money in politics." It sounded nice, but the people who had given seven-figure checks to the Democratic Party were not going to stand by while their team was slaughtered by Republicans in the fund-raising race. So they found other ways to give, settling on the nominally nonpartisan "527" groups, so named because of the subsection of the Internal Revenue Service code that provided for them. Though 527s were nothing new—several had been in operation in the 2002 election cycle—they became particularly important in the post–McCain-Feingold world because they were still allowed to accept unlimited contributions. Soon, the anti-Bush money came pouring in, and any notion that 527s were nonpartisan was buried under all that cash.

Perhaps the key moment in the massive redirection of money from the Democratic Party to the 527s came on July 17, 2003, when a group of Democratic activists and consultants met with George Soros at his beach home in Southampton, New York. Angry at George W. Bush's foreign policy, and determined to use his fortune to remove the president from office, Soros had commissioned two teams of political consultants to find the best ways he might get involved in the presidential race. Those consultants, in turn, brought along Malcolm and Rosenthal, who were then assembling America Coming Together.

At the luxurious home, known as El Mirador, the consultants introduced Soros to something called "voter contact," a new way of targeting potential Democratic voters. They discussed which states would be most receptive to their efforts. And—I learned through interviews with participants in the meeting—they showed Soros portions of a top-secret Republican voter turnout plan, authored by Karl Rove himself, which, one consultant told me, had been made "unintentionally available" to Democrats. Soros was fascinated.

After seeing the entire presentation, Soros made a decision that changed the course of post–McCain-Feingold politics. First, he decided to give tons of money—he and a few friends pledged to contribute $23 million, a figure that would grow significantly over the next year. But perhaps more important, Soros greatly expanded the reach of the planned effort. Malcolm told me she and Rosenthal had initially planned to work in just a few key battleground states. Soros told them to go for it all. "He pushed us into doing all the states," Malcolm told me. "And he was right."

Soros's relationship with America Coming Together suggested that the new campaign finance rules had actually *increased* the influence of big money in politics. By giving directly to "independent" groups rather than to the party itself, big-ticket donors could influence campaign strategy and tactics more directly than they ever had previously. The fact that Soros essentially shaped ACT's plan, then gave the organization the money to execute it, is a telling example of how the new political world worked: Outside activists and moneymen, some of whom had previously operated on the edges of the Democratic universe, became mainstream power figures.

And the power was concentrated in very, very few hands. According to federal records compiled by the nonpartisan tracking group Political Money Line, in the 2004 race the largest part of the funding for pro-Democratic 527s came from just five people. Soros gave $27,080,105. His good friend and partner in supporting the 527s, Progressive Insurance chairman Peter Lewis, gave $23,997,220. Hollywood mogul Stephen Bing gave $13,952,682. And Herbert and Marion Sandler, friends of Soros and the founders of Golden West Financial Corporation, gave $13,007,959. Together, that came to $78,037,966—more than the $75 million in federal funds that John Kerry and George W. Bush each received to run their entire post-convention campaigns. And the grand total spent by Democratic-supporting 527s in the drive to defeat Bush topped $230 million—nearly two and a half times the amount spent by Republican-supporting 527s.

Throughout the campaign, there would be reports that the 527s were, in essence, writing their own rules. Critics accused them of illegal "coordination" with the Kerry campaign— which was forbidden by McCain-Feingold—and indeed it appears that some of that was going on. In the course of my reporting I also discovered something equally important that went largely unreported in the press: America Coming Together, the biggest and richest of the 527s, developed elaborate accounting ruses that allowed it to, in effect, launder large soft-money contributions into hard money to use in any way it pleased. But in the end, the larger problem was that some activists on the Left simply did not take the new campaign law very seriously.

In June 2004, I went to a dinner in Washington put on by the liberal organizing group Campaign for America's Future. The emcee for the evening, the anti-Bush gadfly Arianna Huffington, made a running joke of McCain-Feingold, one that the audience—which included George Soros himself—joined in on.

Huffington, who had been an outspoken supporter of reform, reminded the crowd that the Campaign for America's Future was forbidden by law from advocating the election or defeat of a specific federal candidate. But she said that despite the law, she wanted to talk about a certain president of the United States whom she would refer to as "Buddy." No names, please—that would qualify as a partisan attack. "Buddy," Huffington said, "lied about the weapons of mass destruction" in Iraq; he "would not appear before the September 11 Commission"; and he "wanted to repeal the bill of rights except the part about guns."

"Just between you and me, and not speaking for anybody but myself in a completely nonpartisan way," Huffington concluded with a smile, "Buddy is in need of a loooooooong vacation, so let's give him one on November 2!" Later, she expressed the hope that "we could get Buddy back to Crawford, not in a squeaker but in a landslide."

After Huffington spoke, New York attorney general Eliot Spitzer, a rising star in Democratic politics, played along with the joke. "Somebody said about Buddy, he is Richard Nixon without the competence," Spitzer told the crowd. "Buddy doesn't get it."

It was all quite amusing, and the crowd loved it. Huffington and Spitzer had toyed with the principle of nonpartisanship that lay at the heart of campaign finance laws, and the message was: Isn't this silly? We don't really have to live by these rules, do we?

THE ILLUSION OF A MAJORITY

Those were the professionals. But much of the energy behind the new activist Left—the energy that produced MoveOn, *Fahrenheit 9/11,* and liberal radio—was the work not of political professionals but rather of impassioned newcomers to the political realm.

These people and groups went about their politics in determinedly untraditional ways. MoveOn, for instance, funded by big money from Soros along with thousands of small donations from its Internet members, created a virtual anti-Bush community across the country. Michael Moore made the most successful overtly political film in history. Director Robert Greenwald made polemic documentaries for distribution on the Internet and in home screenings.

Some were influential, and some weren't, but all were animated by an unshakable core belief: that they represented the true majority of Americans. "Spread the word: we're the majority," MoveOn political chief Eli Pariser wrote to supporters in 2002. "We are the majority," Moore often told audiences. "We are the country, but they control it," Al Franken wrote in his best-selling book *Lies and the Lying Liars Who Tell Them.* Such statements were based on a mixture of a selective reading of polls, a little provincialism, and a lot of hope. But they helped fuel a movement.

Indeed, in retrospect it appears that some of the work of the new liberal activists conjured up the *illusion* of a national majority that ended up fooling even its creators. For example, when MoveOn came up with a campaign to promote Moore's *Fahrenheit 9/11*, it asked members to see the movie during the first weekend of release, and to bring as many friends as possible. The goal was to convince the media, and through them the country, that *Fahrenheit 9/11*'s success represented "a cultural referendum on the Bush administration and the Iraq war," as Pariser put it. A big turnout for the opening would be cited as evidence of widespread, passionate opposition to Bush.

The plan worked. "This is a red-state movie," Moore exulted after *Fahrenheit 9/11* premiered in June 2004. "Every single state that Bush won in 2000, it was the number-one film in it. . . . I'm sure when the White House read that this morning, that was one of their worst nightmares come true." Television, newspaper, and magazine reports echoed Moore's—and MoveOn's— theme. "You would have expected Moore's movie to play well in the liberal big cities, and it is doing so," *Time* magazine wrote. "But the film is also touching the heart of the heartland." A national movement—or so it appeared—was under way.

Yet a few months later, when I began to look into where *Fahrenheit 9/11* had done well, and where it hadn't, a radically different picture began to emerge. With confidential audience information provided by a source in Hollywood, I was able to examine every market area in the United States and determine where the movie did better than might be expected, and where it did worse. From this evidence—published here for the first time—it became clear that most of the hype surrounding

Fahrenheit 9/11 was simply untrue. Moore's film was, in fact, a bust in the heartland.

What I learned about *Fahrenheit 9/11* cast doubt on other efforts by the new activists, as well. If Moore's movie—which was, after all, the most successful documentary in history—did not reach far beyond a hard-core blue audience, what chance did other films, and radio, and even Internet appeals, have of touching voters who could make the difference in the 2004 presidential race? The leaders of MoveOn, along with John Podesta, Robert Greenwald, and others, placed great emphasis on using un-wonky techniques, like comedy and films, to reach audiences who had not been politically active in the past. It was an appealing idea, and it attracted a lot of attention, but it appears that, in 2004 at least, it just didn't work.

The fundamental problem, of course, was that the activists on the Left were not the real majority of Americans, no matter how often they told themselves that they were. Many of these activists could not recognize that reality because they relied on intensely personal experiences, rather than hard, empirical evidence, to shape their view of the world. For example, Joan Blades, one of the founders of MoveOn, told me that she and her husband, Wes Boyd, got the idea for their organization while eating in a Chinese restaurant not far from their home in deep-blue Berkeley, California. It was the time of the Clinton impeachment, and it seemed that everyone in the restaurant agreed with them that anti-Clinton Republicans in Washington were insane. Inspired by the majority in the restaurant, Blades and Boyd went home and started MoveOn.

That MoveOn was able to grow so quickly seemed to confirm the notion that Boyd and Blades were indeed the voice of a new majority. By the 2004 campaign, MoveOn had surpassed 2.5 million members, a truly impressive number. The members were active, and vocal, and generous with their small contributions, which seemed to promise real political power. The problem was that they all agreed with one another; what Boyd and Blades accomplished was to organize a large number of people who already couldn't stand George W. Bush.

Other activists on the Left fell victim to the same illusion. Soros, an extraordinarily powerful man who is accustomed to having people listen to him, expressed confidence that his view was shared by the majority of Americans. The cheerleaders for *Fahrenheit 9/11* bought into the claims that the film had revealed a broad swath of Americans fed up with George W. Bush. Even America Coming Together, for all its resources and its extensive (and successful) efforts to register voters across the country, was made up of like-minded people and the like-minded organizations that made up the core of the voter turnout effort: NARAL agreed with Planned Parenthood, which agreed with the Sierra Club, which agreed with the Service Employees International Union, and so on—all in an essentially closed conversation.

Of course, no one could see that clearly at the time. The people who ran MoveOn, or promoted *Fahrenheit 9/11*, or organized America Coming Together, truly believed that their efforts were turning the tide against President Bush. They shared the good news—*2.5 million members! Number-one movie in America! 500,000 newly registered voters!*—and didn't ask hard questions of themselves. In the end, all their money and all their furious activity did not produce enough actual growth in the Democratic voting base to achieve the goal they shared: electing a Democrat as the next president of the United States.

NEXT TIME, WE WIN?

Still, it was a start, and a very big one. By Election Day 2004, the Left had gone from being a series of basically unconnected organizations—Podesta called them "stovepipe institutions"—to being a connected, integrated, coordinated movement. "I feel like I'm part of a team," Franken told Podesta during a conference call I listened to a few days before the election. "We're building an infrastructure incredibly quickly."

Indeed, it would be a mistake to look at any of the new groups as independent activist organizations. They were, rather, part of a single coordinated effort: Soros was connected to America Coming Together, which was connected to MoveOn, which was connected to the Center for American Progress, which was connected to Air America, and on and on. They worked *together*. And together—the billionaires, the Internet advocacy groups, the movies, the 527s, the think tanks, the radio network—they formed a political effort of striking size and scope.

What to call it? When liberals used the phrase "Vast Right Wing Conspiracy," first coined by Hillary Rodham Clinton to describe her husband's adversaries during the Monica Lewinsky scandal, they (usually) meant not a criminal conspiracy but a well-oiled right-wing machine that could get its message out—and launch attacks on liberal politicians—with impressive speed and efficiency. They sometimes called it an attack machine, or a noise machine, and they no doubt exaggerated its effectiveness. But in any event, they admired it.

By the time George W. Bush came to office, they wanted their own well-oiled machine. The name was easy; back in

2001, the liberal online magazine *Slate* published an article entitled "Wanted: A Vast Left Wing Conspiracy." Now the phrase has become increasingly common. "This is going to be the vast left-wing conspiracy," one Democrat told the *New Republic* magazine in 2003, referring to the array of new liberal institutions being built. And by the time of the 2004 Democratic National Convention in Boston, a group of young activists staged an organizing event that they called, naturally, "Building the Vast Left Wing Conspiracy." They weren't using the word "conspiracy" in a legal sense; what they meant was that the Left was getting organized.

And by 2008, they will be even better organized—and far stronger.

In mid-September, about six weeks before the election, I attended a speech given by Robert Borosage, who heads the Campaign for America's Future, at the Capital Hilton hotel in Washington. He was optimistic, sort of, about the election outcome. But he was clearly confident about the future. "For progressives, no matter which candidate wins, we will end this election more emboldened," he said. "They have grown in this election to greater sophistication, greater capacity, and greater energy. Progressives drove the challenge to Bush in the Democratic primaries. They're now fielding the grassroots mobilization that is sustaining the fervor of the Democratic base—and could save Kerry despite himself."

Well, that was going a bit too far. But Borosage was right on the basic point. The presidential election of 2004 had seen the creation of something new in American politics, something that was organized and powerful and would dramatically change the future.

CHAPTER ONE

Going Viral

MoveOn, the Web, and the Peacenik Crusade

On the morning of September 11, 2001, a young man named David Pickering was at his parents' home in Brooklyn—he had graduated from the University of Chicago a few months earlier and was looking for a job—when he heard about the attacks on the World Trade Center. He went outside to see what was happening across the East River. Astonished by the sight, Pickering, an aspiring filmmaker, grabbed his video camera and hopped on the subway; unlike the thousands of people struggling to flee Manhattan, he was actually trying to make his way closer to Ground Zero. He got as far as an elevated train platform with a view of the burning towers. And there he stood as the buildings fell.

All day and night, Pickering shot interviews with people on the street, trying to get a sense of what they were feeling. They were stunned, horrified, angry, and confused. Of course, Pickering felt some of the same things himself, but as he reflected on what happened, an idea came to him: September 11 was an opportunity, perhaps a once-in-a-lifetime opportunity, for peace, if only the U.S. government could be persuaded not to defend itself militarily. "It was this incredible moment in which all doors were opened and the world was seeming to come together," he told me from Paris, where he was attending La Fémis, the French national film school. "I had this feeling that it would be a shame if that were spoiled by a spirit of vengeance."

The next day, Pickering put his thoughts into writing. He drafted a petition imploring President George W. Bush and other world leaders to show "moderation and restraint" in responding to the attacks. He asked Bush "to use, wherever possible, international judicial institutions and international human rights law to bring to justice those responsible for the attacks, rather than the instruments of war, violence or destruction."

That evening, September 12, Pickering sent the petition to about thirty friends, asking that they "sign" the document—electronically, of course—and send it on to others. By the next morning, he told me, there were between 3,000 and 4,000 signatures. Then a friend from the University of Chicago posted the petition on the school's student server. A couple of days later, there were nearly 30,000 signatures.

One of the people who saw the petition was a young liberal activist named Eli Pariser. A 2000 graduate of Simon's Rock College of Bard in Great Barrington, Massachusetts, Pariser was working for More Than Money, a left-leaning Cambridge-based nonprofit educational organization. He, too, opposed military retaliation for the terrorist attacks, and he had set up his own website on September 12—he called it 9-11peace.org—with a message similar to Pickering's. Looking for a way to attract attention, Pariser e-mailed Pickering to suggest they combine their efforts. Pickering quickly agreed.

That's when the project took off. Within a month, about 500,000 people, perhaps half of them in the United States and the rest around the world, had signed the petition. Nearly every day, Pariser came up with new statements, and new petitions, to send out, and each of them managed to attract thousands of signatures. A born political rabble-rouser—the child of Vietnam War protesters, he is said to have started his picketing-and-demonstrating career at the age of seven— Pariser aggressively promoted the cause in ways that hadn't occurred to the introspective Pickering.

Soon it paid off. Thousands of miles away, in Berkeley, California, Wes Boyd and Joan Blades, the husband-and-wife founders of the left-wing activist website MoveOn.org, were reading 9-11peace.org, and they were impressed by what they saw. A few years later, in September 2004, I asked Blades what it was that had caught her eye. She told me the whole phenomenon reminded her of some of MoveOn's own petitions, including one calling for restraint after the September 11 attacks. "It was similar in results to the one we had," Blades said. "It went viral on an international scale."

MoveOn got in touch with Pariser, offering advice and technical assistance. Pariser was happy to accept, and soon he and MoveOn started working together, not only on the petition but on other issues as well. Not long after, Boyd and Blades offered him a job. For Pariser, it was an opportunity to join the world of big-time Internet organizing. For Boyd and Blades, it was a chance to recruit someone with lots of enthusiasm about both politics and the Internet. And one more thing: Pariser brought with him the e-mail addresses of the thousands of people who had signed the antiwar petition. For MoveOn, the list provided a healthy infusion of new contacts—people who could be asked to send contributions and sign petitions—which are the lifeblood of Internet activism.

Meanwhile, the swirl of events passed David Pickering by. During the Christmas holiday in 2001, he told me, Pariser broke the news that he had decided to join Boyd and Blades. With that, 9-11peace.org was over. Pickering wasn't really upset; although he had strong political feelings, he wanted to make statements through films, not petitions. I asked whether he had any hard feelings about Pariser getting all the credit for their work. Not at all, Pickering told me. That kind of politics just wasn't for him: "MoveOn was always Democrat in a way that I wasn't necessarily interested in." Not long afterward, he headed to France.

That brief period—the last few months of 2001—was a critical time not just for Pickering and Pariser but also for MoveOn. In the months before September 11, MoveOn was an organization searching for a purpose. Boyd and Blades had been trying to stir opposition to the policies of the Bush administration—tax cuts, energy, education, just about everything else—but on the eve of the terrorist attacks, MoveOn had no urgent, overarching cause, as it had in 1998, when it opposed the impeachment of President Bill Clinton. The attacks, and the petition, changed that.

After September 11, MoveOn became, in effect, a peace organization—and a radical one at that. In doing so, it threw off the façade of left-leaning moderation that it had carefully maintained during the Clinton years, when a large number of Americans essentially agreed with its views on impeachment. Opposing military retaliation for the terrorist attacks—a position supported by only a tiny portion of the public—shifted MoveOn to the left fringe of American politics. Animated by a new cause, it pioneered new ways of raising money through the Internet, of organizing its members through nationwide meetings, and of attracting attention in the press. But even though MoveOn would recruit a group of dedicated followers and receive much admiring coverage, its pacifist core and strident anti-Bushism—its leaders were peace advocates who loved to produce smashmouth political ads—ensured that MoveOn would remain on the political margins. To this day, Boyd and Blades insist that they represent the views of the "real majority" of Americans. But events proved otherwise.

CENSURE AND MOVE ON

Joan Blades remembers the beginning well. It was September 1998, and she and her husband were having lunch at a Chinese restaurant in Albany, California, a little town just north of Berkeley. Far away in Washington, the Clinton impeachment battle was raging, and Boyd and Blades, both supporters of the president, simply could not believe the nation's lawmakers would be wasting time on what they saw as a distraction from the real issues facing America. As it turned out, others in the restaurant—which was, of course, located in one of the most liberal areas in America—felt the same way. "We were hearing another table where people were saying, 'How can we be doing this?'" Blades told me. "We were just hearing all around us, 'This is crazy.'"

At the time, Boyd and Blades were beginning a new phase in their lives. The year before, they had sold their software company, Berkeley Systems, which had become famous for creating the "flying toaster" screensaver, as well as a video game called "You Don't Know Jack." Boyd and Blades have never said how much they got for the company, but some reports have placed the figure at $25 million. With their new fortune, they had new freedom, and they were looking for something to do. They had their eye on developing some sort of educational software, but by the fall of 1998, the idea had not yet become sufficiently focused to turn into reality. It never did—Blades told me she still hopes to get around to it someday—because after that moment of insight in the Chinese restaurant, they became consumed with a new cause.

When they got home, Blades, a lawyer who once taught mediation—she specialized in divorce, writing a book, *Mediate Your Divorce,* in 1985—drafted a one-sentence petition on the Clinton situation. It said, simply, "The Congress must immediately censure President Clinton and Move On to pressing issues facing the country." Boyd and Blades e-mailed the petition to friends and family members—fewer than a hundred people in all—asking each recipient to forward the e-mail to others. The response was amazing. "Within a week, we had a hundred thousand people sign it," Blades told me. And not only did Boyd and Blades have a new list of 100,000 potential activists, they had a way to use those names. MoveOn had asked each signer to give his ZIP code, which allowed Boyd and Blades to sort supporters by congressional district. They could then quickly match each e-mail address to a member of Congress, which meant they could urge specific people to get in touch with specific lawmakers on specific issues. The campaign, which Boyd and Blades called Censure and Move On, provided the building blocks for a new political organization.

The response convinced them they were on to something big. And while it certainly must have seemed that way—*100,000 names on our petition!*—Boyd and Blades's excitement was perhaps more the product of political naiveté than anything else. Yes, a list of 100,000 e-mail addresses was useful. But in a country where well over 50 *million* people vote on each side in a presidential election, the response to MoveOn's petition did not, in itself, indicate the birth of a new political movement. Nevertheless, Boyd and Blades made extravagant claims for their new creation. "'Censure and Move On' is a 'flash campaign,' possible only through the organizing capabilities of the Internet," they wrote in their first public statement on September 22, 1998. "Using e-mail and the web, we can focus a broad and deep consensus in the American public into action."

Did they really believe they could halt impeachment proceedings in the House of Representatives? I asked John Hlinko, a graduate of Harvard's Kennedy School of Government who volunteered at MoveOn in the early days. "I didn't think that Henry Hyde and everyone would suddenly hold up their hands and say, 'Oh my God! E-mails! Run!'" Hlinko told me. "But I did think that if we could show enough momentum and enough support for stopping impeachment, at the fringes we could affect a few members who could go one way or the other." And if that didn't happen—if Congress ignored MoveOn's demand and opened an impeachment proceeding—Boyd and Blades said they would extend the "flash campaign" into a longer-term effort. "We will shift focus," they warned, "to highlighting this issue in the fall [1998] elections."

When the House indeed opened an impeachment inquiry, Boyd and Blades made good on their threat. According to Federal Election Commission records, they formed MoveOn PAC, their political action committee, on October 23, 1998. Filing the paperwork with the FEC, Boyd wrote "Censure and Move On" in the space provided for the organization's name. He then crossed that out and wrote, simply, "MoveOn.org." Boyd gave the organization $1,000 of his own money—the only funds MoveOn PAC had at that time—and announced a wide-ranging effort to defeat Republicans in the elections, which were then just one week away. Citing a "huge groundswell of public feeling," Boyd and Blades promised to direct their new followers—neatly sorted by ZIP code and electoral district—to oppose any member of Congress who voted for impeachment.

Of course, even to suggest that a $1,000, seven-day campaign might have a noticeable effect on nationwide elections was just short of delusional. And on Election Day, Republicans kept control of the House. But the GOP lost five seats, hanging on to power by the barest majority. And then, a few days after the voting, House Speaker Newt Gingrich was forced to step down. To Boyd and Blades, it felt like victory. "When the election happened, we went, 'Whew, we did it,'" Blades told me.

But they hadn't done it; on December 19, 1998, the House voted to impeach Clinton. Boyd and Blades responded by launching a "We Will Remember" campaign to defeat impeachment leaders in the 2000 elections. But MoveOn PAC still had no money; it had not received any contributions since Boyd's original $1,000 stake. So on December 30, 1998, Boyd gave another $4,000, while Blades gave $5,000, and Boyd's family gave $2,000. That brought the PAC's entire take to $12,000. Boyd and Blades also loaned the organization $5,229 to cover operating expenses. It was a very small start.

Then MoveOn took off. In early 1999, Boyd and Blades sent

out a stream of calls to action—and requests for contributions—as the impeachment trial ran its course in the Senate.
Thousands of people responded; in 1999 and 2000, the "We
Will Remember" campaign brought in a total of $2.29 million
for MoveOn PAC. Nearly all of that, $2.13 million, came in the
form of what are known as "conduit receipts," meaning contributions that were sent to MoveOn for the purpose of being
passed on to specific House and Senate candidates. By the time
the 2000 elections came around, MoveOn had targeted thirty
House and Senate races across the country, earmarking 100
percent of its contributions for Democratic candidates. (Although Boyd and Blades called MoveOn a "nonpartisan" organization with a "nonpartisan agenda," that nonpartisanship
did not include supporting any Republicans.)

The effort failed. In November 2000, Democrats again fell
short of winning control of either house of Congress, and overall, the results were less satisfying than in 1998, when MoveOn
believed it had won a moral victory. To make matters worse,
most of the hated impeachment managers kept their seats. And
of course, in 2000, the big political story was not the House or
the Senate but the presidential election. In that, MoveOn simply was not a player—it appears to have made no direct contributions to any presidential candidates, having chosen instead
to stay focused on the impeachment revenge campaign.

But by the end of 2000, with the Florida recount raging, the
"We Will Remember" effort seemed increasingly an artifact of
an earlier era. Having failed to achieve its original goal,
MoveOn seemed out of ideas. Membership dropped. Energy
waned. I asked Blades what she and Boyd intended to do when
the anti-impeachment campaign had played itself out. "We

thought we were going away," she told me. "We had no plan on going past 2000." Boyd and Blades had ridden Democratic anger over the impeachment for as long as they could, and then a bit longer. And then they realized that they, too, had to move on.

But to what? In the months after the election, MoveOn fell into a sort of generalized opposition to George W. Bush and his policies. Boyd and Blades jumped on the campaign finance reform bandwagon, changing MoveOn's mission statement to say the group was committed "to broadening participation to counter the influence of monied interests and partisan extremes." But McCain-Feingold, while popular with MoveOn's members, simply did not stir the passions that impeachment had. MoveOn needed an issue.

They got one on September 11.

RADICAL DIGITAL CHIC

Joan Blades's reaction to the terrorist attacks was much the same as that of David Pickering and Eli Pariser: She was dismayed to think that the United States might take up arms in its defense. And like Pickering and Pariser, Blades wrote a petition to express her feelings about what should be done. Entitled "Justice, Not Terror," it read, in full, "Our leaders are under tremendous pressure to act in the aftermath of the terrible events of Sept. 11th. We the undersigned support justice, not escalating violence, which would only play into the terrorists' hands."

It was, to say the least, a minority opinion. A Gallup poll taken in the weeks after the terrorist attacks found that 82 percent of those surveyed favored direct U.S. military action against Afghanistan, while just 13 percent opposed (5 percent had no opinion). The 82 percent figure, Gallup found, included a significant number of Americans who had opposed other U.S. military actions in the past. Even people who had opposed the Vietnam War or the first Gulf War were in favor of war in Afghanistan. There was, in short, a national consensus—and MoveOn was not part of it.

Contributions to the political action committee slumped. In the 2001–2002 election cycle, MoveOn PAC took in $1.25 million, compared with $2.29 million in the 1999–2000 cycle. In the 2001–2002 period, the group gave $795,000 to candidates and committees, compared with $2.13 million in the 1999–2000 period. (MoveOn's 527 group, the MoveOn.org Voter Fund, would not be formed until 2003.) All contributions went to Democrats.

With their influence waning, Boyd and Blades began to use more aggressive, almost '60s-style rhetoric in their fund-raising appeals. Just days before the 2002 midterm elections, they sent out an e-mail saying, "Imagine that Bush, Cheney and the far right consolidate their power through their use of a permanent state of war, supported politically by corporate dollars. . . . Right-wing domination is America's worst nightmare." Boyd and Blades claimed to be working closely with a number of Democratic Senate campaigns—they boasted, "We talk to these campaigns every day, so they can adjust their last-minute spending"—but in spite of their efforts, Republicans again kept control of the House and Senate. For the third time in a row, MoveOn had set its sights on wresting control of Congress from the GOP, and for the third time it failed.

In response, MoveOn stepped up its antiwar work. Not

long after the 2002 elections, Eli Pariser joined the Reverend Bob Edgar, head of the National Council of Churches, NAACP chairman Julian Bond, and other left-wing leaders at a press conference to announce the creation of Win Without War, a new coalition of groups opposed to the prospect of war in Iraq. The relationship with the National Council of Churches and the NAACP put MoveOn in the first tier of antiwar organizations. And not incidentally, it brought more petition signatures and e-mail addresses to MoveOn.

In January 2003, I called Pariser, then twenty-two years old and MoveOn's "International Campaigns Director," to learn how the project worked. He was very, very optimistic. "People get an e-mail from a friend saying, 'I signed this petition at MoveOn, would you like to do that, too?'" Pariser told me. "They go on and fill out the petition [and] sign on to being kept in the loop for future actions. It's a word-of-mouth phenomenon, and at times like this it's incredibly powerful." The day before we spoke, Pariser and MoveOn had been featured in a *New York Times* article, "Protest Groups Using Updated Tactics to Spread Antiwar Message." As a result, Pariser told me, more than 20,000 people had joined MoveOn in the preceding twenty-four hours. After years of frustration, and three lost elections, MoveOn seemed to be back in the game.

Being back in the game meant getting lots more money. Blades boasted to a Bay Area newspaper that when MoveOn put out a call for money to buy an antiwar ad in the *Times*, "We wanted to raise $30,000 or $40,000—instead we raised $400,000." In mid-January, MoveOn generated even more attention for its antiwar efforts when it updated perhaps the most infamous political advertisement in American history: the anti–Barry Goldwater "Daisy" ad from 1964. Like its predecessor, the MoveOn ad showed a little girl picking petals from a daisy as a missile launch countdown could be heard; when the countdown reached the end, the screen filled with the image of a nuclear mushroom cloud. To make sure that no one missed the message about the dangers of going to war in Iraq, the ad continued with this warning: "War with Iraq. Maybe it will end quickly. Maybe not. Maybe it will spread. Maybe extremists will take over countries with nuclear weapons. Maybe the unthinkable." Pariser did not back down from that desperate message when he spoke to the press: The United States would be "playing with matches in a tinderbox" by going into Iraq, he said. "We wanted to run an ad that would highlight that very real possibility and help encourage a national discussion about the consequences of war."

At about the same time, MoveOn made a move in the direction of in-your-face politics that would set the tone for its campaigning in the future. Boyd and Blades had gotten an e-mail message from a man named Zack Exley, a thirty-two-year-old former labor organizer and computer programmer who was looking for a job. Exley wasn't a friend, but Boyd and Blades knew a few things about him. They knew, for example, that in the 2000 presidential campaign Exley had created a website called GWBush.com, which featured a doctored photo of George W. Bush with what appeared to be cocaine on his upper lip and nose. The site, which Exley called a "parody," sold bumper stickers with sayings like "GW Bush, Not a Crackhead Anymore" and "Born with a Silver Spoon Up His Nose." It also featured a cartoon of Bush dancing with a bottle in his hand as kegs of beer bounced around the screen and "Louie Louie" played in the background.

It was the kind of thing a certain type of Democrat loved.

But Exley and GWBush.com attracted relatively little attention until the real George W. Bush heard about the site and told reporters, with obvious disgust, "There's a lot of garbage in politics, and obviously [Exley] is a garbageman." It was a gift from God for Exley; Bush's statement, of course, sent the press looking for what had made the candidate so angry. And then the Bush campaign gave Exley even more publicity when it filed a complaint against GWBush.com with the Federal Election Commission, asking that the site be subject to campaign finance laws. Once that was over (Bush lost), the news coverage faded, and GWBush.com disappeared from view.

But Exley did not disappear—not entirely, anyway. He made a little money selling Bush-bashing merchandise—one popular item was a bumper sticker that read, "Some people are just too stupid to be president." He took part in anti-Bush protests during the Florida recount and during the inauguration, helping organize demonstrations through a website he created called CounterCoup.org. He planned to start an Internet magazine. And he had high hopes that Democrats might make a comeback in the 2002 elections.

When that didn't happen, a furious Exley created another new website—he did that a lot—which he named Angry-Dems.com, for the purpose of venting about what he saw as the party's lack of nerve. "Don't blame the media," Exley wrote. "Don't blame the Republicans. Don't blame Paul's plane"—a reference to the plane crash that killed Minnesota Senator Paul Wellstone. "Don't blame 9-11. Don't blame the Greens. And sure as hell don't blame the American people! BLAME THE DEMOCRATIC PARTY LEADERSHIP. [Party chairman] Terry McAuliffe is an idiot. [Senate Minority Leader Tom] Daschle is a complete wuss. [Senator Joe] Biden might as well not exist. It's time for us all to admit it." Exley also wrote what he called the "world's shortest petition," addressed to the head of the Democratic National Committee. It read, in its entirety, "Terry, you're fired!"

It was about that time that Exley got in touch with Boyd and Blades. In addition to his obvious flair for attracting attention on the Internet, Exley had the sort of political background that might prove useful to MoveOn. He had spent much of the 1990s as a union organizer, trying to unionize low-paid workers in a variety of businesses and even, occasionally, working undercover. He was also angry as hell—at MoveOn, they liked to call it "passion"—and convinced the system needed shaking up. And besides, Boyd and Blades liked all those jokes about George W. Bush. "He was the funniest one among us," Blades told me.

Exley would also prove to be MoveOn's link to the candidates who were at the time beginning their campaigns for the Democratic presidential nomination. The most Web-savvy of them was former Vermont governor Howard Dean, whose campaign manager, Joe Trippi, admired MoveOn's Internet organizing record and asked Boyd and Blades for help. MoveOn said yes, but, not wanting to appear to be playing favorites, it offered the same assistance to all the candidates. Dean's was the only campaign to take MoveOn up on the offer.

MoveOn dispatched Exley to Dean's Vermont headquarters for a couple of weeks. Exley helped Trippi and his team with little things, like the best time to send out mass e-mails (it was the middle of the night on Monday, because Tuesday response was always the best of the week). And he helped them improve the big things, like a system that was known inside the Dean campaign as Get Local. The system allowed supporters to organize events and let others on the Web know about them quickly and reliably. Exley also put Trippi and his crew in touch with a Chicago-area company called We Also Walk Dogs—the name was taken from the science fiction writer Robert Heinlein's 1941 short story of the same name, about a full-service company of the future that, in the words of one reviewer, did "everything from walk your pet to outfit the next expedition to Pluto." The people at We Also Walk Dogs—the Chicago version—created a new way for Dean supporters to set up and publicize their gatherings, a method that ultimately became one of the main organizing tools of the 2004 election.

Dean's team was happy for the help, but at the same time it didn't really know much about MoveOn's politics. For example, long after the Dean campaign had collapsed, I asked Trippi if he knew that MoveOn had opposed the war in Afghanistan (a war Dean himself had supported). "No," Trippi told me. "If you said that to me right now, it would be the first time I knew it." Did he know anything else about MoveOn? Not a lot. "My only memory of it was that it was an organization that was big in the Clinton impeachment," Trippi said, "and then I didn't really pay any attention."

Another indication of MoveOn's fringe politics came when Exley and the team staged what they called a "virtual primary," in which MoveOn members were asked to express their preferences among the Democratic field. As was widely predicted, Dean, the most prominent antiwar candidate, was the winner, with 44 percent of the vote. Ohio Representative Dennis Kucinich, the candidate who favored an immediate troop pullout from Iraq and the creation of a federal "Department of Peace," came in second, with 24 percent. Senator John Kerry came in third, with 16 percent, and the rest of the candidates were far back. All told, 68 percent of MoveOn supporters who took part in the primary voted for either Dean or Kucinich, the candidates farthest to the left on most issues. It was not exactly the reflection of a mainstream movement.

In addition, the actual number of votes cast was relatively small. In all, 317,639 people voted, of whom 139,360 chose Dean—about the size of the crowd at a large NASCAR race. But despite the results—a small number of people voting for what turned out to be unelectable candidates—MoveOn received rapturous praise for its efforts. "In the long run, MoveOn could be our Rush Limbaugh," the Democratic pollster Celinda Lake told me in July 2003. The *New York Times* published an editorial, entitled "Happy Days Are Virtually Here Again," in which it hailed MoveOn as a "glimpse into politics of the future." And several Democratic candidates, who had at one time failed to appreciate MoveOn's ability to attract donations and favorable press coverage, started listening.

Others were listening, too. Former vice president Al Gore was so impressed with MoveOn that he teamed up with Boyd and Blades to make a series of progressively more radical speeches that energized antiwar activists but left some others wondering whether Gore had lost his mind. In the first such speech, a relatively low-key affair in August 2003 at New York University, Gore accused Bush of "fuzz[ing] up facts" and engaging in "a systematic effort to manipulate facts in service to a totalistic ideology." A few months later, at Washington's DAR Constitution Hall, Gore warned that the Bush administration had "taken us much farther down the road toward an intrusive, 'Big Brother'–style government—toward the dangers prophesied by George Orwell in his book *1984*—than anyone ever thought would be possible in the United States of America." In the spring of 2004, Gore accused Bush of creating "an American gulag" in Iraq and yelled—literally yelled, his face twisted in a sort of vein-popping fury—"How dare the incompetent and willful members of this Bush-Cheney administration humiliate our nation and our people in the eyes of the world and in the conscience of our own people." By summer, he was calling members of the conservative press "digital brownshirts."

The speeches had two effects. First, they marginalized Gore to the degree that the national press began looking in the other direction when word came that he was about to give another "major address." And second, they kept MoveOn's name in the news as a sponsor of high-level, outrageous attacks on the Bush administration. That new attention led to more contributions, and it brought MoveOn an enormous payday in the form of a gift from the billionaire financier George Soros.

Soros had been watching MoveOn just as intently as Gore had, and in the fall of 2003, he invited Boyd to visit his home in Southampton, the exclusive enclave on the eastern end of Long Island. "A number of people suggested that it would be a good thing for Wes and George to meet," Michael Vachon, Soros's political advisor, told me. "Wes came in with no particular agenda. It was kind of a meet-and-greet thing." (Blades did not attend.) As it turned out, calling the session a meet-and-greet was a considerable understatement. At the end of the meeting, Soros proposed a deal: he would give MoveOn one dollar for every two dollars it raised itself. And Soros's close friend and partner in politics, Peter Lewis, chairman of Progressive Insurance, would do the same thing. Each man pledged to contribute up to $2.5 million.

According to records compiled by the nonpartisan Center for Public Integrity, Soros gave $500,000 on November 1, 2003, $955,715 on December 30, and $1,044,285 on March 8, 2004, bringing his total contribution to exactly $2.5 million. Lewis made contributions in precisely the same amounts. And Soros's contributions had a kind of pump-priming effect; other large contributors kicked in soon thereafter. In December 2003, the Hollywood mogul Stephen Bing gave $971,427. In 2004, the twenty-nine-year-old Colorado-based Internet entrepreneur Jared Polis gave $200,000. New York businessman and philanthropist Lewis Cullman kicked in $100,000, as did Hollywood music executive Richard Foos.

Over the years, Boyd and Blades had prided themselves on MoveOn's ability to attract thousands of small donations. That, they argued, was proof that MoveOn was in touch with the grass roots and not beholden to big-money interests. But now they were taking in some very big money. The contributions of Soros et al. were made to a new organization called the MoveOn.org Voter Fund, a 527 group that Boyd and Blades formed in September 2003 for the purpose of accepting unlimited contributions. All told, contributions from donors who gave $10,000 or more constituted more than half the $12,517,365 raised by the Voter Fund in the 2003–2004 cycle. Boyd and Blades once vowed to "counter the influence of monied interests and partisan extremes." Now they were in bed with them.

REALLY CREATIVE HITLER ADS

In January 2004, with Howard Dean, its favored candidate, having gone down in perhaps the most spectacular flameout in American political history, and with John Kerry not yet having cemented his hold on the Democratic nomination, MoveOn concentrated its energies on George W. Bush. Boyd and Blades came up with something they called the "Bush in 30 Seconds" contest, in which MoveOn supporters were invited to create their own anti-Bush ads, with the winner to be shown—at least MoveOn hoped—during the Super Bowl broadcast on February 1. Boyd and Blades asked contestants to come up with "really creative ads" that would help viewers "understand the truth about George Bush." "There are some legal limits on what you can do," they warned entrants, "and we're not going to post anything that would be inappropriate for television, but other than that what you put in your ads is up to you."

The contest, which began as another way to bring attention to the anti-Bush cause, ended up noisily identifying MoveOn with the Bush-hating Left. Among the ads submitted were two that starkly portrayed George W. Bush as a Nazi. One featured photos of a Nazi parade with an on-screen narrative that began, "A nation warped by lies. Lies fuel fear. Fear fuels aggression. Invasion. Occupation." Cutting from a photo of Adolf Hitler to a photo of Bush, the ad concluded, "What were war crimes in 1945 is foreign policy in 2003." The other ad showed Hitler in full rant, then cut to Bush, and asked the question, "Sound familiar?"

Republicans cried foul—and saw an opening. Not only did

Republican National Committee chairman Ed Gillespie demand that MoveOn apologize, he also wrote that every Democrat who received MoveOn's help should condemn the ads. To make matters worse, the Simon Wiesenthal Center, which, unlike Gillespie, had no partisan ax to grind, also complained.

MoveOn's response was at once apologetic and defiant. "We agree that the two ads in question were in poor taste and deeply regret that they slipped through our screening process," Boyd said in a statement. But he suggested that the real story was GOP misconduct—the statement was headlined "GOP Plays Dirty Politics in Attempt to Smear MoveOn.org Voter Fund"—and pointed out that while more than 1,500 ads had been entered in the contest, only two compared Bush to Hitler.

Nevertheless, it was undeniable that the Bush-Hitler comparison was, if not a common belief, at least part of the worldview in some circles at MoveOn. For example, the makers of one of the fifteen finalists in the "Bush in 30 Seconds" contest also made a Web video entitled "Bush Is Not a Nazi, So Stop Saying That." The video, featured on a far-left fringe website called TakeBackTheMedia.com, began with ominous music and the warning "The media will not tell you of the Bush family Nazi association." It went on to accuse the Bushes of financing the Third Reich and featured a series of intercut statements comparing George W. Bush to Hitler. "Both leaders had catastrophes occur allowing them to remove many civil rights," the movie said, showing side-by-side pictures of the Reichstag fire and the World Trade Center attacks.

Nearly lost in the Hitler controversy was what the *winning* ads actually said—and what their content suggested about MoveOn's political strategy as 2004 began. Selected by a MoveOn panel of judges that included the anti-Bush filmmaker Michael Moore, the anti-Bush comedian Al Franken, the anti-Bush comedienne Janeane Garofalo, anti-Bush musicians Moby and Michael Stipe, and the anti-Bush rapper Chuck D, the finalists issued an unending stream of ominous messages about the United States under a Republican administration. One, entitled "In My Country," featured an olive-skinned, vaguely Middle Eastern–looking man declaring earnestly, in a heavy accent: "In my country, a group of religious extremists are reshaping the government to promote their own agenda and morality." Mournful music played underneath. "Our citizens are seized and held in prison without being charged of a crime." And then the kicker: "Why should you care about what is happening in my country? Because my country is the United States of America."

Another "Bush in 30 Seconds" finalist told viewers to "imagine a world where corporations start wars to increase demands for their products." Yet another finalist featured children delivering political speeches. One promised, "If elected, I'll lie about weapons of mass destruction as a pretext to invade another country." Another said, "Our allies will go from respecting to hating us, and I don't care." And a third said, "I promise to keep you in a state of fear and anxiety, so you never question what we're doing."

The winning ad, called "Child's Pay," featured children working in factory jobs, as housecleaners, and as garbagemen, with the question "Guess who's going to pay off President Bush's $1 trillion deficit?" It was perhaps the mildest of the lot, yet when MoveOn tried to air it during the Super Bowl broadcast—the newly rich Voter Fund was willing to pay the $1.6 million cost—CBS said no, claiming that airing the spot would violate its policy against running advocacy ads. Boyd and Blades lobbied the network to change its position. "We tried to exert pressure in the right places, without going public," Blades told me. "MoveOn does have friends who know people." But CBS did not budge, and the ad did not air. Still, the episode allowed MoveOn to accuse the network of censorship, start a petition drive against CBS, and, of course, ask for more contributions.

THE APPEARANCE OF A MAJORITY

MoveOn did not use its newfound power on the Web just to help itself. As the campaign progressed, the group teamed up with other anti-Bush leaders in a number of joint efforts. The most prominent of those came in June, when MoveOn joined the promotional campaign for Michael Moore's new movie, *Fahrenheit 9/11*. The week before the film premiered, Pariser asked members to sign a pledge to see it during its first weekend. The point, he explained, was not simply to show support for Moore's picture. The point was to create the impression in the press that *Fahrenheit 9/11* was the leading edge of a wave of anti-Bush anger sweeping the country. "We launched this campaign around *Fahrenheit 9/11* because to the media, the pundits, and the politicians in power, the movie's success will be seen as a cultural referendum on the Bush administration and the Iraq war," Pariser told MoveOn members. "Together, we have an opportunity to knock this ball out of the park."

A few days later, on June 28, MoveOn organized "virtual house parties," featuring a live Internet link with Moore, in homes, coffee shops, and theaters around the country. Before wildly enthusiastic crowds—I attended one such gathering, filled with true believers, at a movie theater in Washington's Dupont Circle neighborhood—Pariser extolled the success of the new movie. "Due in part to your efforts, *Fahrenheit 9/11* was the number-one movie in the nation this weekend," Pariser told his "virtual" audience. "Now we're going to talk about how to turn that enormous momentum into action to beat Bush." Moore then delivered what was pretty much a monologue—the technology of supporters posing questions via the Web didn't seem to work all that well—and the evening ended with a please-register-to-vote appeal. "None of us want this just to be a movie where people just eat popcorn and go home," Moore said.

When *Fahrenheit 9/11* came under scrutiny from critics, MoveOn rushed to Moore's defense. Pariser encouraged members to write their local newspapers to praise the movie. And they didn't even have to write—all they had to do was click on MoveOn's "easy-to-use letter to the editor tool," enter a ZIP code, choose from a list of local papers, and then select a "pre-written" letter. "I am shocked that many critics have denounced Michael Moore's new movie, *Fahrenheit 9/11,* as unpatriotic and anti-soldier," said one such letter. "I find it interesting that the most fervent critics of the movie *Fahrenheit 9/11* seem more obsessed with attacking Michael Moore than in taking on the points he makes in his film," said another. "Moore's movie raises extremely difficult questions that deserve our attention as we move towards the November elections," said a third.

The strategy worked. Scores of newspapers around the country printed the letters as if they had been written by the people who sent them. The "I am shocked" letter, for example, found its way into the *Boston Globe,* the *Chicago Sun-Times,* the *Arizona Republic,* the *Fresno Bee,* and about a dozen other papers. Much the same was true for the other letters. As they had during the movie's premiere weekend, Pariser and MoveOn had taken another step forward in the effort to create the image of an energized majority.

As the campaign dragged on, MoveOn spent most of its money and energy on television ads, which had brought it so much publicity in the "Daisy" and "Bush in 30 Seconds" campaigns. The group released a commercial titled "He Knew," which—shades of 1998—called on Congress to censure the president for misleading the country on Iraq. Another ad suggested that Bush had deserted—"simply left"—his post with the Texas Air National Guard in the early 1970s. And "Quagmire" showed an American soldier sinking in quicksand in Iraq, his rifle raised above his head in a signal of surrender.

Each attracted some attention—the goal was always to have them played for free on news broadcasts—but there's no evidence that the ads had any actual effect on the campaign. And some Democrats wondered whether the spots were really intended to help the party in the first place. "I don't feel it's been effective impacting the race at all," one respected Democratic strategist—a former Howard Dean advisor—told me a few weeks before the November election. "I feel like it's been effective in getting attention and generating hits for their website and generating contributions to MoveOn." While that was not necessarily a bad thing, the strategist told me, it also was not terribly useful in a tough election. "The campaigns are trying to talk to swing voters," he said, "who are far more rational and less emotional than the histrionics of MoveOn's advertising would suggest."

But the ads—and the money that paid for them—were moving MoveOn back into the center of Democratic activism. And perhaps the surest sign that MoveOn's fringe politics had merged with the Democratic mainstream came in April 2004, when Zack Exley left MoveOn to join the Kerry campaign as its director of Internet organizing. "As a master of online organizing, he'll equip the most important presidential campaign in decades with an understanding of the powerful new techniques we've helped to pioneer," Boyd and Blades said in a statement. Republicans protested that Exley's move represented illegal "coordination" between MoveOn and the Kerry camp—the law forbade campaigns from working with outside groups like MoveOn. But the charge went nowhere, mostly because Exley really didn't need to coordinate with his old colleagues. They were all doing pretty much the same thing, and he simply switched from one part of the team to another.

That is not to say the people at MoveOn took the anticoordination laws all that seriously. In June 2004, the entire MoveOn crew appeared at a Washington hotel to accept an award given by Campaign for America's Future. It was a big dinner—George Soros was there, along with lots of movers and shakers in the Democratic 527 world, all mingling with one another. When Pariser—wearing a black T-shirt that said simply NOVEMBER 2—spoke, he praised the recently departed Exley as someone who was "not on stage with us but who deserves some of the credit. Because of the campaign finance laws, we're not in touch with Zack personally, so I wanted to use this opportunity to give him a very important message. So Zack, we're very proud of you, and the important message is: Please win."

The audience applauded, and the camera for the big-screen TV at the front of the stage zoomed in on none other than . . . Zack Exley. Sitting in the audience, hanging out with the people he was not supposed to be coordinating with, Exley seemed to be having a fine time. When his image went up on the screen, a person sitting nearby playfully put up his hand to shield Exley's face from the camera in a gesture that said, "We know he's not really supposed to be here." Everyone had a laugh.

As the campaign ran its course, MoveOn's last, biggest project was the Vote for Change Tour, a series of concerts featuring Bruce Springsteen, Dave Matthews, REM, the Dixie Chicks, James Taylor, and other musicians. Held to benefit the voter turnout group America Coming Together, the tour was advertised as "20 Artists. 28 Cities. 9 Battleground States." As that suggested, the purpose was not just to raise money; surely that could have been done in New York, Los Angeles, Boston, or San Francisco. But those cities were in safely Democratic states. For that matter, a lot of money could have been raised in Houston and Atlanta, but they were in safely Republican states. Rather, the point was to raise money while attracting lots of local news coverage in places like Wilkes-Barre, Pennsylvania; Clearwater, Florida; and Columbus, Ohio. That way, it was hoped, the stars' message would reach the maximum number of undecided voters.

The final concert of the tour was held on October 11 at the MCI Center in Washington, D.C. As it usually did with big events, MoveOn asked its members to mark the occasion with a nationwide series of house parties. The concert would air live on the Sundance Channel, and MoveOn members were to gather in homes to watch it unfold.

I attended a party in a modest home in the Virginia suburbs

of Washington. The group, about twenty in all, was all white and mostly middle-aged; the boomer-friendly roster of performers seemed perfectly designed to appeal to them. One man wore an Air America Radio T-shirt, another a shirt that advertised the ticket of "Bush-Satan '04," and yet another a shirt that said "Send Bush to Mars." They were there to do more than just listen to music; their job, as assigned by Eli Pariser, was to write five letters each to undecided voters in Ohio.

They undertook the task with great earnestness. Yes, there were the occasional cracks—no one in the group could really understand how anyone could be undecided at that point, and one man said he wanted to begin his letter with "Dear idiots who can't decide"—but overall, the partygoers tried their best to finish Pariser's assignment. Some of the letters relied on clichés, mentioning, for example, how the 2004 election was "the most important of our lifetime." One woman tried out a line on the group, saying, "How about, 'It is time to turn this country in the right direction'?" That was a bit much; someone called out, "That's a little trite, Elaine."

By the time the concert was over, the letters were finished and duly sent off to MoveOn, and then on to Ohio. Did they persuade any undecided voters? Certainly not enough to put John Kerry over the top. In the end, the project seemed to resemble nothing so much as the campaign by a British newspaper, the *Guardian*, to encourage its leftist readers to write letters to voters in Clark County, Ohio, urging them to vote against George W. Bush. People in Clark County didn't at all welcome such advice from outside. Their reaction to the letters from MoveOn in Washington, D.C., might well have been the same.

LOOKING FOR A LANDSLIDE

As Election Day approached, the MoveOn team was opti-mistic that Kerry would pull out a victory. Of course, they had felt that way all along. Back in June, I listened to Blades speak to a group of liberal activists at a Washington hotel, and she gave what could only be called an unabashedly rosy assessment of the presidential race. Actually, "rosy" would be a bit of an understatement—Blades was almost giddy with the prospect of victory.

She described a talk she had given a few weeks before, which she had titled "We Can Win." Now, Blades said, that idea was "a little behind the time," because she had come to believe that Democrats could do much more than just win. Even though the polls at the time showed Bush and Kerry in a dead heat, Blades explained that there was an "odd disconnect" between the numbers and what she viewed as the plain fact that a majority of voters wanted to be rid of George W. Bush. Blades said a woman had asked her recently, "Why aren't we talking about a landslide in November?" and the question had stuck in Blades's mind. "I decided okay, well, maybe I should say it out loud," she told the audience at the Omni Shoreham. "And everybody—yeah, and now, finally, everybody's saying, 'Yeah, we're going to win by a landslide.' It's time, I guess. I'm excited about this."

While a statement like that might seem reckless to a political realist, it was not at all unusual in the world of MoveOn. In fact, if one listened to anybody from MoveOn speak for very long, one would hear glowing descriptions of a great majority of like-minded strangers across the nation who never knew they agreed with one another—on Bush, on campaign finance reform, on whatever—until they were brought together by MoveOn. And once they came together, they were very, very powerful. "The beauty of the Internet was yes, we come together online, and then we come together in our communities," Blades told me. "People got to know other people who were engaged."

But what if they were in fact just a bunch of people who already agreed with one another? When I asked Blades if MoveOn might just be preaching to the choir, she resisted. "Have you seen the Errol Morris ads?" she asked me, referring to a series of commercials shot for MoveOn by the well-known documentary filmmaker. In each, a starkly lit subject explained that he or she had been a Republican but had chosen to switch to the Democratic Party. "We decided that the most powerful thing to do was to focus on the folks who switched," Blades said, "and a huge number of people called."

As it happened, a huge number did call. And a huge number joined MoveOn. But what is a huge number? Winning a national election in the United States involves *really* huge numbers. When Americans finally went to the polls in 2004, about 62 million people voted for Bush and more than 59 million voted for Kerry. On each side, some number—probably about 25 or 30 percent—could be called the hard-core ideological base. In absolute terms, that worked out to vast numbers of people. A few weeks before the election I asked the director of the nonpartisan Pew Research Center, Andrew Kohut, for his assessment of the situation. "My guess is you have 15 million people on the Republican side who are really dug in, and probably the same number on the Democratic side," he responded.

What Kohut was saying was that one could have an enormous audience, one that numbers in the millions, and still not reach beyond a single party's base. "MoveOn and Rush Limbaugh, and whatever the equivalents are Left and Right, are basically speaking to people who are highly politicized and have a point of view," Kohut explained. "I think it's good for the parties to have these outlets and these resources, but they don't much speak to ordinary voters."

As it became more successful and better known, MoveOn's list of members grew to about 2.5 million people. It was an impressive number, but not *that* impressive compared with the votes one needed to be elected president. The people at MoveOn, however—headquartered in the blue bastion of Berkeley, California, where in the 2000 election nearly twelve times as many people voted for Al Gore or Ralph Nader as voted for Bush—saw their followers as living proof of a far-reaching, fast-growing movement. And from that they concluded that what most people would view as a radical antiwar, anti-Bush agenda was actually the voice of a true national majority. They simply did not accept the idea that they might have managed to find 2.5 million truly devoted members of the entrenched Democratic base. In the end, Boyd and Blades and Pariser and Exley, who thought they were creating a new way of practicing politics, were in fact just talking to themselves.

~~~~~>

CHAPTER TWO

Vanity Crusade

The Bubble of George Soros's Politics

In June 2004, George Soros traveled to Washington, D.C., to address an audience of anti-Bush activists at the Take Back America conference sponsored by the Campaign for America's Future. Soros was, to say the least, in friendly territory. Introduced by Senator Hillary Rodham Clinton, who called him "fearless and willing to step up when it counts," Soros, the legendary businessman with a $7 billion net worth who had committed millions to defeating George W. Bush, received a standing ovation simply for walking onstage.

But then Soros began to talk, and something unexpected happened. The man who had so much to say about why Bush should not be reelected suddenly had a difficult time saying anything—so difficult that his remarks were punctuated by uncomfortably long pauses. "Uh, this [election] is a referendum on, um, the Bush administration's policies, the Bush doctrine and its application—uh, its first application, which was the invasion of Iraq," Soros said in an unsure and halting voice.

And then he stopped. Five seconds went by. Then ten. Then fifteen. Stammering, Soros tried to resume. "Uh, um, this, uh, um, this—"

Soros stood uneasily behind the lectern as nearly twenty seconds elapsed. Finally, he began to speak again. "The, the Bush doctrine, um, people don't actually talk about it very much as a, as a doctrine, but it really is quite an atrocious proposition." And then Soros stopped yet again, as if it were an accomplishment simply to finish a sentence. Sitting near the front of the room, I turned around to see how people were reacting. They applauded with a kind of uneasy enthusiasm, with some people appearing to be clapping as much in support of Soros—relieved that he had completed his thought— as in approval of what he had said.

As the speech continued, Soros offered a dry and rambling recitation of the ideas of his guru, the philosopher Karl Popper. He explained what he called the "bubble of American supremacy." And he applied his "boom-bust" theory of financial markets to the war in Iraq. His precise point was difficult to decipher, but Soros seemed to be comparing the United States to a hot company with a rising stock price that then overreached by invading Iraq, causing its stock to plunge— first boom, then bust. "This is, in fact, uh, what, uh, applies to, to the Bush administration's, uh, uh, performance because, uh, you have a reality, an underlying reality, and that, and that is the United States is the most powerful nation on earth," Soros said. "But then you had this ideology of, uh, this crude Social Darwinism applied to it, which is, which is, uh, which is a false idea, and it was the terrorist attacks of September 11 that moved you from, uh, let's see, what you might call near-equilibrium to far-from-equilibrium conditions, because it was the War on Terror and, and, uh, uh, the attack on Iraq that, uh, took us into this very, very, very dangerous, uh, area that you are, that we are in now."

It seemed doubtful that anyone in the room was completely clear on Soros's point, except that he opposed U.S. intervention in Iraq. Still, the audience paid rapt attention. The scene was reminiscent of a profile of Soros in the *New Republic* from a decade earlier, when the writer Michael Lewis accompanied Soros during a tour of Eastern Europe and spent a fair amount of time trying to understand precisely how the boom-bust theory applied to world history. By the end of the article, Lewis had given up in defeat. "I confess that after a half-dozen readings and an awkward attempt to get him to explain it to me I find his theory no more satisfying than when I first encountered it," Lewis wrote. "Even as a metaphor it is more than a little weird."

But why was such weirdness taken so seriously? There were seven billion reasons. As one of the world's richest and most powerful philanthropists, Soros spent a good deal of his time, perhaps most of his time, with people who either worked for him or wanted him to give them money. The Campaign for America's Future fit into the second category; Soros had, a few months earlier, given the group $300,000, making it unlikely that its leaders would have suggested that anything was odd about his ideas. It's a phenomenon that Soros understands and enjoys. In the *New Republic,* Lewis had asked Soros whether "his view of the world might be a tad distorted by the fact that everyone around him is always seeking to please him." Soros responded, "But that in itself is very pleasant. I mean, it's much more pleasant than if people want to annoy you."

At the Take Back America conference, no one wanted to

annoy him. So Soros talked on, turning, in a stammering voice, to the Abu Ghraib prison scandal. There was a sort of rough equivalence, Soros suggested, between what American troops had done to Iraqi detainees at Abu Ghraib and what Islamic extremists had done to Americans on September 11, 2001. "I, I think that, I think that those, those pictures [of Abu Ghraib] hit us the same way as the, as the terrorist attack itself," Soros said, "not quite with the same force, because in the terrorist attack, we were the victims. In the pictures, we were the perpetrators, we, uh, others were the victims. But there is, I'm afraid, a direct connection between those two events, because the, the way that we, uh, uh, President Bush, conducted the War on, on, on Terror, uh, uh, converted us from victims into perpetrators."

The audience broke into loud applause, this time in what appeared to be wholehearted approval of what Soros had said. If anyone was troubled by Soros's words—after all, he had come to Washington, one of the cities hit by the terrorist attacks, and downplayed the horror of those attacks by comparing them to a case in which prisoners were treated badly but not murdered by the thousands—no one said anything.

And who would? The activists in the room saw Soros as something close to the savior of the Democratic Party. At the time, he had pledged to give about $15 million to anti-Bush causes (the figure would later nearly double). Without that money, Democrats would have been in a far less advantageous position to fight the well-prepared and well-funded Bush re-election team. With the money, they were in the ballpark. So they were extremely unlikely to criticize anything Soros said.

In his anti-Bush book *The Bubble of American Supremacy,* Soros used the word "bubble" in the sense of the boom-bust cycle that characterizes financial markets. But in another sense, Soros walked through the Take Back America conference—and indeed the entire campaign of 2004—in a bubble of his own. It was a bubble filled with admirers who needed his money and were quick to applaud his theories. He had done amazing things in his life: made gazillions of dollars, roiled the currencies of entire countries, and spoken on a virtually equal basis with world leaders. So why would he *not* think he could take down the president of the United States?

By the end of the 2004 campaign, the sheer quantity of Soros's giving, highlighted by the $20 million he gave to the voter mobilization group America Coming Together, changed Democratic politics. Soros could legitimize an organization simply by contributing to it. He could embolden it simply by saying a word or two. And he had, by the force of his ideas and the size of his wallet, taken a great measure of power away from the Democratic Party and given it to outside groups that then became beholden to him. More than any other person, Soros remade politics in 2004; without him, the Vast Left Wing Conspiracy would not have been vast at all.

THE PURLOINED POWERPOINT

Soros was not always a high-profile partisan in American politics. Over the years, he supported Democrats, but not in a megadonor sort of way; before the 2004 election, the biggest single contribution he had ever made was $100,000 to the Democratic Congressional Campaign Committee in 2000. But Soros changed his approach to politics when George W. Bush moved into the White House. At first, the president's policy decisions—declining to go along with international initiatives like the Kyoto global warming treaty and the International Criminal Court—simply distressed Soros. But then, after September 11, when the president decided to invade Iraq, Soros concluded that Bush was leading the United States, and possibly the world, to catastrophe.

In June 2003, Soros announced he was pulling back from the pro-democracy work that his main foundation, the Open Society Institute, did in Eastern Europe and the former Soviet Union so that he could focus his attention on the United States. The change was necessary, Soros told reporters in Moscow, because the political scene in America had become "quite dangerous." In the Bush administration, Soros explained, "the executive branch has come under the influence of a group of ideologues who have forgotten the first principle of an open society: that they don't have a monopoly on truth."

"What really got him energized was the foreign policy of this administration," Soros's chief of staff and political advisor, Michael Vachon, told me. "He was motivated by his conviction that the Bush administration's foreign policy was leading the U.S. in a disastrous direction." So Soros decided that Bush had to go. Of course, Soros, a Hungarian-born naturalized U.S. citizen, had just one vote. But he had a lot of money. Still, even a man of Soros's wealth and reach didn't know quite how one went about toppling a president. So he called in the experts, or, more accurately, he had his expert—Vachon—call in the experts. Vachon told me he got in touch with two Democratic political consulting firms, TSD Communications, based in Washington, D.C., and M&R Strategic Services, with major offices in D.C. and in Portland, Oregon, and asked them to come up with suggestions for a Soros-funded anti-Bush campaign.

I asked Mark Steitz, the "S" in TSD Communications, what Soros wanted. "He said, 'I am concerned about the direction our country is going under this guy [Bush],'" Steitz, a former communications director for the Democratic National Committee and top advisor to Jesse Jackson, told me. "'I want to know what are the strategies that could be used to change this. Are there investments that could be made that could make a difference? How would you do this?' He approached it in a way that, I might imagine, he approaches investments."

Steitz and his colleagues, along with a separate team from M&R, studied the issue. Should Soros pour a lot of cash into anti-Bush television advertising? Should he pour it into Democratic efforts to win back Congress? Would the new McCain-Feingold campaign finance law, which Soros had vigorously supported, be a significant handicap in the effort?

Both groups of consultants came to the same conclusion. Rejecting an old-style, big-money TV campaign, Steitz and his colleagues argued that Soros could have the most impact by concentrating his donations in what is called the "voter contact" area. Much more than the old idea of getting out the vote, "voter contact" means an intensive effort to identify and profile potential voters in every voting district in critical swing states, getting in touch with them long before the election, and then keeping up with them, nurturing them, and making sure they get to the polls on Election Day. In July 2003, the consultants' team combined their research to make a presentation to Soros at his home in Southampton, the same Long Island estate where, a few months later, the billionaire would receive a fund-raising appeal from MoveOn's Wes Boyd.

Steitz was a true believer in the new approach, which was a radical departure from older mass-audience appeals of television ads and direct mail. As I talked with Steitz about how he and the consultant team had prepared the presentation for Soros, I learned that the plan had been heavily influenced by two factors. One—no surprise—was the success that Democratic-supporting labor unions had had in their get-out-the-vote efforts. But the other, perhaps more powerful, influence on Steitz's thinking—big surprise—was a secret, cutting-edge political strategy document prepared by Karl Rove, the president's top political advisor. The document, a PowerPoint presentation that outlined GOP strategy in the 2002 midterm elections and laid the groundwork for a similar strategy in 2004, had been made "unintentionally available" to Democrats in the first months of 2003, Steitz told me. It was not clear just how that happened—was it stolen? lost? leaked?—but once the document fell into Democratic hands, it was shared, e-mail to e-mail, among a number of top party strategists in Washington. One of them was Steitz, who read it eagerly and was deeply impressed. "A big influence on all this [the Soros plan] was the Rove PowerPoint presentation," Steitz told me. "It's a remarkable document." Armed with that knowledge, the strategists made their presentation, and during that presentation, they actually showed Soros portions of the Republicans' secret plan. "The purpose [of presenting the GOP document] was to show the importance of voter contact," Vachon told me. Soros might as well have been briefed by Karl Rove himself.

When Steitz told me the story, I immediately thought of a minor sensation in Washington political circles in June 2002, when a Democratic Senate aide found a CD-ROM lying on the ground in Lafayette Park, just across Pennsylvania Avenue from the White House. The aide had no idea what was on the unmarked disk, but soon found that it was the full text of two

PowerPoint presentations. One was a slide show to accompany a speech by Rove, and the other was meant to accompany a presentation by Rove's top aide, Ken Mehlman, who at the time was White House political director and who would later become the manager of the president's reelection campaign. The subject of both presentations was the then-upcoming 2002 House and Senate midterm elections. There were a few embarrassing news stories about the lost disk—the presentations contained some less-than-optimistic assessments of Republican chances in a couple of Senate contests at a time when the GOP was publicly saying chances looked good. But the story soon faded.

The PowerPoint presentation that Steitz and other Democrats had was a completely different document—much more detailed and sophisticated. It was apparently acquired by Democrats sometime in the late spring of 2003. I asked Steitz if he would show it to me, and he agreed. What I saw was a remarkable work. It's no wonder it had a profound effect on the Soros group.

The presentation, titled the "72 Hour Task Force," contained the results of a "top to bottom review," ordered by Rove, of GOP turnout efforts in the 2000 race. What was perhaps most remarkable about it was that it was a harrowingly self-critical assessment of the Bush campaign's performance. The essential question it asked was, Why did we come so close to losing? To find an answer, Rove began by taking a sober look at the difference between preelection state polls, which often showed Bush leading by significant margins, and the actual results of the election, in which Bush sometimes squeaked by. "In Arizona, the polling said we would win by ten, but we won by just six," the presentation said. "In Florida, the polling said we would win by two—we won by just a *chad*." That trend, Rove concluded, held true in nearly every other state Bush won.

As Rove looked ahead to 2004, he saw no particular reason for optimism. "Perhaps the president's leadership will lead to a realignment of the electorate, but we would be foolish to plan on it," the presentation said. Therefore, victory would probably go to whichever side was most successful in getting its voters to the polls. And the answer to that problem was deceptively simple: Rove's prescription was to "Get People Back into Campaigns." That did not mean simply asking GOP activists to try harder. Instead, the document said, it meant fundamentally rethinking the way the party motivated its voters and producing a blueprint for winning the next "turnout war." The "72 Hour Task Force" was that blueprint.

Rove was particularly impressed with Hillary Rodham Clinton's turnout plan in the 2000 New York Senate race. "Arguably the prototype for an exhaustive grassroots campaign," the Clinton plan was a six-month timeline, organized "down to the block level," with impressive big-labor support. The result simply blew away anything the GOP was doing at the time. "Unfortunately, too many of our campaigns make the mistake of believing that we can simply pay to send mail and phone calls that will achieve the same result," Rove said. Instead, he advocated using the labor union principle—to "get people to take responsibility for as small a number of voters as possible"—in a Republican context, that is, without labor unions. Rove wrote that the campaign should rely on highly motivated volunteers and make each responsible for reaching a relatively small number of people. If a campaign made a volunteer responsible for shepherding the votes of too many people—say, 4,000—then "you might as well give them 40,000." In other words, no one could keep up, or make personal contact, with so many voters. But if a worker was given responsibility for, say, 85 voters, then that worker could keep tabs on each one. Voters, Rove noted, are inundated with political ads and e-mails and phone calls, and "person-to-person contact cuts through the clutter." The presentation went on to describe extensive tests the Rove team conducted in off-year elections. Picking two similar state or local races, Rove's strategists poured money for old-fashioned politicking into one, and money for heavy voter contact into the other. The voter contact model won each time.

The copy of the PowerPoint that became "unintentionally available" to Democrats was rich in the details of Rove's testing models and conclusions. It contained not only the graphic slides to be presented to private GOP audiences, but also the script that the presenter used to describe the project. For Democrats, it was a gold mine of information. "It's really nice," Steitz told me. "The script is attached. I've been a student of it."

After the election, I asked Rove himself whether he knew at the time that Democrats had obtained a copy of the Power-Point. I asked the questions in the middle of a wide-ranging discussion of election strategy in which Rove was quite voluble, but when I got to the PowerPoint, his answers became very brief.

"Yes, I knew that at the time."

"Did you know how it got into Democratic hands?"

"No."

"Were you surprised that it did?"

"Yes."

"How did you react?"

"Problematic." That was Rove-speak for saying he viewed something as a potentially difficult situation.

But what was bad news for Rove and the Bush campaign was good news for George Soros. And on that summer day in Southampton, as he viewed Rove's secret PowerPoint, Soros was clearly fascinated with the nuts and bolts of political organizing. "He was sort of leaning forward and saying, 'So they go door-to-door to the same place?'" Steitz recalled. It was not long before Soros was sold.

But how would the voter contact idea be put into action? To address that part of things, the consultant team had invited two of the most important and successful organizers in Democratic politics: Ellen Malcolm, founder of the pro-choice political network EMILY's List, the largest political action committee in the country, and Steve Rosenthal, recently of the AFL-CIO, one of the best ground-level organizers in all of politics. Malcolm and Rosenthal were already planning to emphasize voter contact in the 2004 race, working through their new group, America Coming Together, or ACT, a 527 organization that would be allowed to accept unlimited contributions.

In a sense, Soros and his giving partner, Peter Lewis, were ahead of the activists. When I asked Malcolm what the group talked about after the consultants had made their presentation, she said that the talk quickly got deep into the details. "We had a lot of conversation about how it was all going to operate," she told me. "How did the coalition work? Who was going to make decisions? I remember Peter Lewis saying, 'If I'm mad about something that's happening in Ohio, who do I call on the phone and say, *Who's responsible, it's all screwed up?*'

And we hadn't really started. I mean, we had the concept, we knew what we wanted to build in terms of the canvassing and the voter contact, but we had a lot of things to work out."

After the presentation, Soros said he wanted to think about it overnight. But he didn't take long to decide. "By the end of the weekend, it was clear that he was in," Steitz said. And in in a big way: Malcolm told me that she and Rosenthal walked away with commitments for a total of $23 million from Soros, Lewis, and a few others at the meeting. Within weeks, Soros began writing checks to ACT. First came $1 million on August 19. Then $2 million on September 12. Then another $2 million on December 23. And then $4.55 million to the Joint Victory Fund, an umbrella organization that then distributed the money to ACT, on April 15, 2004. In the beginning, Soros had pledged $10 million to ACT and other Democratic 527s. Then the number became $15 million. Then $20 million. Then $25 million. And then more. The 527s had never seen that amount of money come in from one person at one time. Soros would become the biggest donor in history.

It is impossible to overstate the importance of Soros's money for Democrats. And not just the money, but the message the money sent. "Go back to what the political culture was like at that time," Malcolm told me. "Democrats were pretty damned depressed. Bush was running roughshod, there was a lot of dissatisfaction, why weren't we fighting back more? . . . One of the important pieces of [Soros's] contribution, I think, was to signal to potential donors that he had looked at what was going on and that this was pretty exciting, and that he was going to stand behind it, and it was the real deal." And indeed, once Soros began giving, and word spread that he was giving, other contributions began streaming in. Soros, ACT, and the Democratic Party—with an enormous and wholly unintentional assist from Karl Rove—were in business.

MY MONEY AGAINST YOUR PRESIDENT

By any historical standard, Soros's contributions were simply stunning. By way of contrast, the millionaire insurance executive W. Clement Stone gave $2 million to President Richard Nixon's reelection campaign in 1972. Stone's contribution, the biggest of its time, so horrified good-government campaign finance reformers that they cited it to argue, successfully, for what became the landmark Federal Election Campaign Act Amendments of 1974. Adjusted for inflation, Stone's gift would have been about $8.7 million in 2003 dollars. Of course that was a lot of money, but it was less than one-third of what Soros contributed to the anti-Bush effort. As a donor, Soros had moved into uncharted territory.

The irony of it all was that, until recently, Soros had been one of the nation's most important advocates of campaign finance reform. The annual reports of the Open Society Institute contain a long list of grants to reform groups in the years before the McCain-Feingold law passed in 2002. There was $625,000 to Common Cause; $2.5 million to the Brennan Center for Justice at New York University School of Law; $1.2 million to Public Campaign; $125,000 to Democracy 21; $1.7 million to the Center for Public Integrity; $75,000 to the Center for Responsive Politics; $650,000 to the Alliance for Better Campaigns. Although each organization approached the reform issue in a slightly different way, all intended, in the words of Public

Campaign's mission statement, "to dramatically reduce the role of big special interest money in American politics."

How could Soros support the cause so generously and then turn around and give sums of money that left W. Clement Stone in the dust? I asked Michael Vachon what had changed in Soros's thinking. He told me that nothing had changed, that Soros was simply following the law, which prohibited unlimited contributions to candidates, parties, and political action committees but allowed them to 527 groups. But hadn't Soros wanted to rein in that kind of unlimited contribution, too? "There's a difference between playing by the rules as they exist, and agitating for a change in the rules," Vachon told me. "Soros is playing by the rules." Vachon stressed repeatedly that what Soros was doing was legal, saying that the Soros team held monthly "compliance meetings" to make sure Soros's contributions were in line with campaign finance laws. "Because George realizes that he is a target—and having made these contributions, he has opened himself up to a lot of public scrutiny—he has done everything by the book," Vachon said.

But why, I asked Vachon, was Soros giving such huge sums? It seemed out of character for a man who had previously never made a contribution above $100,000. Vachon said Soros was simply trying to ensure a fair competition in the presidential race, to level the playing field between the rich Republican Party and the poor Democratic Party. "Look at the playing field," he told me. "There is so much money on the other side. This is what was available."

Vachon suggested I reread an article Soros had written for the *Washington Post* op-ed page in December 2003. In it, Soros wrote that much of Bush's campaign war chest came from corporations who were "buying the same level of access and influence for their corporate interests that they previously obtained" before campaign finance reform. Soros maintained that his contributions were different. "I don't seek such influence," he said. "My contributions are made in what I believe to be the common interest."

That still didn't quite answer the question. After we talked—this was just a few weeks before the election—I e-mailed Vachon a few follow-up questions on the campaign finance issue. "With Democrats raising record sums of money this election cycle, it seems that the playing field is now pretty much level (in part due to Mr. Soros's efforts)," I wrote. "So why is Mr. Soros still giving?" I also asked whether Soros's contention that he gave in the "common interest" was "a subjective argument which can be boiled down to: They're bad because I say they're bad, while I am good because I say I am good." And I asked whether "it would be fair to say that [Soros] would support efforts that would outlaw future contributors from doing what he and others have done in this election cycle?"

The queries seemed to strain Vachon's patience. "Byron, from your questions, and your publication [I write for *National Review*], it seems likely that you are planning yet another tiresome right-wing attack on Soros," Vachon wrote. "Doesn't your crew grow weary of the mudracking [*sic*]? Don't you have anything better to do? Why not investigate the motives of Richard Mellon Scaife?"—a reference to the Pittsburgh-based billionaire who has funded many conservative organizations over the years.

Vachon wrote that Soros's contributions had indeed made the playing field more level, but that pro-Bush forces still had more money than anti-Bush forces (an assertion that turned out, in the final accounting, to be incorrect). But beyond that, Vachon said, Soros had decided to give millions more to America Coming Together, over and above his original commitment, "to ensure the success of the project." That is, whatever shape the playing field was in, Soros wanted to beat Bush, and if it took more money than he originally contemplated, then he would spend more money.

Vachon also rejected the idea that Soros was subjectively asserting that his motives were more pure than those of others who contributed to the political process. "What Soros is saying is true," Vachon wrote, "i.e., he is not seeking any personal benefit in return for his contributions." And on the question of outlawing future big contributions, Vachon wrote, "Soros has said on many occasions that he supports continued campaign finance reform. . . . He supports additional public financing of elections and possible free airtime for candidates. So, no, it would not be fair to say that he 'would support efforts that would outlaw future contributors from doing what he and others have done in this election cycle.' That is what you would say if you were looking to say something unpleasant."

Questions about Soros's contributions, however unpleasant they might have seemed to his aides, were not just the province of curious journalists. They were also causing an enormous sense of cognitive dissonance among Soros's former allies in the campaign finance reform movement. Those reformers had relied on his money for years, and now he had betrayed them. Should they continue to accept his donations? I called two longtime leaders of the campaign finance reform world, Charles Lewis of the Center for Public Integrity and Fred Wertheimer of Democracy 21, and got very different answers.

More than a year after Soros first announced his campaign

against Bush, Lewis still seemed dumbfounded by the numbers involved. "They're jaw-dropping," he told me. "We've never seen numbers like this from an individual donor, not counting self-financed candidates like [Ross] Perot or [Steve] Forbes or [Jon] Corzine." Soros's contention that he, Soros, was giving for the common good, while others gave from selfish interests, also troubled Lewis. "Whether or not they believe it from the heart, there's still undue influence and inordinate influence [created] by one person writing that big check," he said.

Lewis told me that in January 2004, the board of directors of the Center for Public Integrity felt that it had to take some action on the Soros question. After a serious discussion, the board voted unanimously to forgo money from the Open Society Institute. "The fact is, we cannot be a nonpartisan group and continue to request and accept money in new grants from someone who has gone so publicly *mano a mano* against a sitting president from one party," Lewis told me. "It doesn't seem appropriate." At the same time, the Center was not eager to take a public stand against Soros—it was not in the business of needlessly alienating donors—and did not make any sort of public announcement of the decision (indeed, it was never reported in the press). I had been told about it not long after it happened by a source who insisted that I not use the information unless I could confirm it on the record. "It's a somewhat sensitive subject around here," the source said. "It's the rebuke that dare not speak its name."

Democracy 21 also faced the Soros issue, but decided that it could keep accepting the billionaire's money. I asked Wertheimer, a longtime crusader against big money in politics, whether he had any problem accepting Soros's money. "No," he said, "because we've done everything we can to stop these activities." I asked whether Wertheimer would accept another Soros grant, if offered, and Wertheimer did not rule it out. "We'll look at that," he told me.

When I asked Wertheimer whether Soros, formerly a good guy in the campaign finance reform world, had become a bad guy, he chose his words carefully, as if to make any criticism appear to be a sort of arm's-length transaction. "I've been quoted as saying that he's gone from being part of the solution to being part of the problem," he said. And indeed, Wertheimer had told *USA Today* in June 2004 that Soros "started out as part of the solution, and he's ended up as part of the problem." So I asked Wertheimer why he would only say to me that he'd "been quoted" criticizing Soros; why didn't he just say Soros was part of the problem? Wertheimer still demurred. He e-mailed me some clips of his criticisms, but he never spoke them directly to me.

By the end of the campaign, it was safe to say that Soros had made a number of new best friends in the 527 world and left a number of old friends in the campaign finance reform world shaking their heads. "Frankly, this has placed a lot of organizations in a very, very difficult spot," Charles Lewis told me a week before the election. "If Bush wins, then this very angry, $20 million–plus contributor who is a billionaire will continue to be angry and continue to feel very strongly about George W. Bush. . . . It does create an awkward situation."

SEPTEMBER 11: WHY ALL THE FUSS?

No one who listened to Soros for more than a minute or two had any trouble figuring out that he utterly loathed Bush (although Vachon was quick to point out that Soros had never actually met the president). But despite all that had been written about the two men, it was not always clear precisely *why* Soros felt so strongly. To be sure, Soros believed Bush had made a disastrous mistake in Iraq, but did that alone account for his decision to launch a personal crusade—and part with tens of millions of dollars—to get rid of the president?

No, there was more to it than that, and it had to do with the profoundly different ways in which Soros and Bush viewed the terrorist attacks of September 11. Simply put, Soros did not see the attacks as being as devastating to the United States as the president (and most Americans) did, and therefore he viewed Bush's response as an irresponsible overreaction. From that single difference of opinion flowed much, if not all, of Soros's anti-Bush activism.

It was an article of faith among Bush supporters that, in the popular phrase, "September 11 changed everything." But in his book *The Bubble of American Supremacy*—which remains the best and most revealing statement of Soros's thinking on the role of September 11 in American life—Soros openly wondered why Americans got quite so upset about the destruction of the World Trade Center, the carnage at the Pentagon, and the crash of Flight 93 in Pennsylvania. "How could a single event, even if it involved three thousand civilian casualties, have such a far-reaching effect?" Soros asked. "Admittedly, the terrorist attack was a historic event in its own right. Hijacking fully loaded airplanes and using them as suicide bombs was an audacious idea, and the execution could not have been more spectacular." But why had September 11 become such a big deal? "The answer," Soros wrote, "lies not so much in the event itself but in the way the United States, under the leadership of President George W. Bush, responded to it."

Although Soros later said that he believed the invasion of Afghanistan was justified, some of his public statements in the days after 9/11 suggested an ambivalence about what the United States should do. "We have suffered a big blow, and it's hard to take it without the instinct of hitting back, but I think we really have to restrain ourselves because the dangers are enormous," Soros told a group of foreign correspondents in Hong Kong about a week after the attacks. Fearing a negative reaction from Islamic countries, Soros advised caution. Beyond that, he simply hoped the attacks had taught the president a lesson. "If there is a positive fallout from this horrific event, it is that the Bush administration must realize we have to be concerned about the reactions of others," he said.

Soros took up that theme again a few weeks later, when he was asked, during an interview on CNBC, whether September 11 had darkened his view of the world. The answer was no. "I think that this is an opportunity, as well as a, as a terrible tragedy, because it, it shakes preconceived ideas, makes us more receptive to rethink things, and that, out of that comes progress," Soros answered. "So I saw the collapse of the Soviet system as a, as an opportunity. And in, in, in a, in a similar way, but not, of course, not, not, not to the same extent, I think this is a, it is an opportunity to rethink and to reshape the way we run our lives." September 11, Soros was saying, had given the president of the United States a chance to think more like George Soros. (I asked Michael Vachon what September 11 had been like for Soros, since he had been with his boss on that day—they were in Beijing. Vachon replied that Soros was "deeply affected by the tragedy." But that was all he would say.)

What should a newly educated George W. Bush have done in response to terrorism? A truly effective antiterrorism policy,

Soros said, would involve massive foreign aid, the enactment of more equitable trade laws, and in general, the United States being a more cooperative member of the world community. It was as if Soros, had he been active in the 1940s, wanted to go straight to the Marshall Plan without first winning the war. Soros, in fact, rejected the entire concept of war because he believed the terrorist attacks were primarily criminal matters. "Crime requires police work, not military action," he wrote. Indeed, the problem with Bush was that when he used the phrase "War on Terror," he actually meant it. "Declaring war on terrorism was understandable, perhaps even appropriate, as a figure of speech," Soros said in May 2004 speech at Columbia University. "But the president meant it literally, and that is when things started going seriously wrong."

Therefore, when Bush framed the war in Iraq as part of a continuing strategy to reduce the terrorist threat to the United States, Soros reacted with horror. Why was Bush thinking that way, when Soros's way was so obviously superior? Soros's answer was familiar to any reader of far-left magazines and websites: The war in Iraq happened because Bush came under the influence of a small group of "neoconservatives" who were promoting an ideology of American supremacy. In particular, Soros believed, Bush was influenced by the Project for the New American Century, a Washington think tank that the anti-Bush Left saw as the nerve center of the neoconservative conspiracy. In *The Bubble of American Supremacy*, Soros seemed nearly obsessed with the Project; the brief volume included the Project's mission statement in its entirety, plus a description of each founder—a group of conservative villains that included Dick Cheney, Paul Wolfowitz, Elliott Abrams, Norman Podhoretz, and William Bennett.

According to Soros's theory, the neocons at the Project had a long-standing plan to impose America's will on the world. The first step of that plan was war in Iraq. But the scheme faced two obstacles. First, the neocons' chosen president, Bush, came to office after the 2000 election without a clear mandate to lead the nation in a new direction. Second, the United States "did not have a clearly defined enemy that would have justified a dramatic increase in military spending." Then came September 11. As if by magic, Soros wrote, the terrorist attacks "removed both obstacles in one stroke."

Bush was then free to exploit September 11 for his own— and the neocons'—purposes. First he silenced dissent by fostering fear of further attacks. Then he began to implement the Project's supremacist ideology. And Soros's hope that a newly enlightened Bush might use September 11 as grounds to begin a more Soros-like foreign policy went up in smoke. At that point, the only hope for the United States, Soros believed, was to get rid of Bush and adopt the "Soros Doctrine," which was a "doctrine of preventive action of a constructive nature," like "fostering the development of open societies."

So Soros asked Michael Vachon to find out what he might do to drive Bush from office. And when the Democratic strategists came to the Hamptons with plans for a new organization, America Coming Together, already on the drawing board, Soros was ready to go. Yes, it meant spending a lot of money. Yes, it meant turning his attention from his other philanthropic work. And yes, it meant abandoning his devotion to campaign finance reform. But Soros was ready to save the world from George W. Bush.

"WAKE UP, AMERICA!"

As the campaign went on, and Bush held a steady lead in the polls, Soros appeared to become more and more frustrated. He gave more money to America Coming Together. He gave smaller amounts to smaller organizations. And he decided to become publicly involved by going on a speaking tour of battleground states. He traveled to Washington, D.C., in late September to announce the tour, which would wind through Ohio, Florida, Iowa, Pennsylvania, and Minnesota. "I have an important message to deliver to the American public before the elections," he told reporters at the National Press Club. He printed up a pamphlet—*A Personal Message from George Soros*—which he said he would mail to at least two million people in the swing states. (The pamphlet was part warning and part sales pitch for *The Bubble of American Supremacy*.) Soros also took out a two-page ad in the *Wall Street Journal* and planned to buy ads in the local papers where he would be speaking. In all, he said, he planned to spend between $2 million and $3 million on his tour.

When Soros met reporters in Washington, a new Gallup poll showed Bush leading Kerry by eight percentage points among likely voters. How could that be? After Soros had spent so much money? After America Coming Together had knocked on so many doors? Soros seemed almost beside himself. "I want to shout from the rooftops, 'Wake up, America!'" he told reporters. "'You must realize that we are being misled!'"

But Americans did not seem to think they were being misled. That failure to accept Soros's view of the situation appeared to be a serious shock to his system. Soros was used to getting results; when he talked, people listened. During that trip across Eastern Europe in 1994, after having met with the president of

Moldova in the morning and the president of Bulgaria in the evening, Soros turned to Michael Lewis and said, "You see, I have one president for breakfast and another for dinner." Later, Soros suggested that Lewis should "write that the former Soviet Empire is now called the Soros Empire." That was real power. And now some undecided voter in Ohio, or Wisconsin, or Pennsylvania, didn't seem to be listening when the emperor himself told him to wake up.

As he searched for an explanation, Soros blamed his enemies, or perhaps his imagined enemies. On October 14, 2004, he appeared on Al Franken's radio show on the liberal network Air America. Franken listed some of the attacks on Soros that had come from voices like Fox News's Bill O'Reilly and the right-wing website NewsMax.com. Soros interrupted Franken.

"NewsMax is financed by a sinister, shady billionaire by the name of Richard Mellon Scaife," Soros said. "I think he has been behind most of the campaign—"

"Against you?" Franken asked

"Yes," Soros answered. "And I find it rather amusing that I'm being accused of being a hypocrite by giving this money and being in favor of campaign finance reform at the same time, [by people] financed by this genuinely shady billionaire who stops at nothing and spends substantially larger amounts."

Franken asked, "You resent being compared to Scaife?"

"That's right," Soros said.

Soros's words—and Michael Vachon's earlier suggestion that I "investigate the motives of Richard Mellon Scaife"— indicated that Soros believed at least some of his image problem, such as it was, could be traced to a rival billionaire. Scaife, who, like Soros, gave most of his money to indisputably good causes, became notorious in the Clinton years for providing

$2.4 million to the conservative monthly the *American Specta- tor* for the Arkansas Project, which tried to dig up scandals about the president.* Scaife also helped fund a number of causes on the Right, especially think tanks like the Heritage Foundation, the American Enterprise Institute, the Hoover Institution, and the Center for Strategic and International Studies. While that giving certainly qualified as supporting conservative causes, it was hardly the sort of direct electoral financing that Soros undertook in his drive to defeat Bush. So it was not entirely clear what Soros meant when he said that Scaife spent "substantially larger amounts" on sinister or shady activities than Soros did on politics.

But Soros seemed to believe strongly that some enemy, out there somewhere, was responsible for his inability to command America's attention. How else could one explain public indif- ference to, or even criticism of, a man who so clearly acted in the "common interest" and who wanted only to warn Ameri- cans of the disastrous future they faced if they reelected George W. Bush? Sure, it seemed audacious for a single man, a private citizen who had never faced the voters himself, to believe he could bring down a president. Perhaps that offended people. But as he looked around, at his entourage of aides and grant- seekers, who was there to tell Soros he couldn't do it?

*I worked at the *Spectator* during part of that time, with no involvement in the project, and later wrote a long, critical account of the whole affair in the *Atlantic Monthly*.

CHAPTER THREE

Shell Game

America Coming Together and the World of 527s

In July 2004, in a conference room on the second floor of the luxurious Four Seasons Hotel near Boston Common, Steve Rosenthal was explaining what might be called the Palm Pilot theory of voter contact. A former political chief of the AFL-CIO, Rosenthal had come to the Democratic National Convention in his role as chief executive officer of America Coming Together, or ACT, the biggest of the "independent" 527 groups working to defeat George W. Bush. ACT did the hard, street-level job of political organizing; other groups like MoveOn might spend time producing Internet attack ads or holding virtual bake sales, but ACT was actually getting in touch with voters, one-by-one and face-to-face, trying to convince them to vote for John Kerry. The work, as Rosenthal explained it, was part shoe leather and part personal digital assistant.

"The system that we're developing is old as time, but with a modern twist," Rosenthal told a small group of reporters. ACT had thousands of canvassers spread across the swing states, he explained, and each canvasser was equipped with a Palm Pilot loaded with a software program developed by a pro-Democratic firm called VAN, which stood for Voter Activation Network. When the canvasser turned on the Palm, up popped a list of voters whom ACT wanted him to visit, a map showing him how to get to their homes, and a script of what he was to say once he arrived.

Rosenthal sketched out an example of how the system worked. A canvasser knocks on a door and asks a voter which issue concerns him most. The voter says the economy. The canvasser asks what it is about the economy that the voter finds most worrisome. The voter says low wages. The canvasser enters all this into the Palm, which already has a full file of commercial and demographic information about the voter. If the voter is a Democrat, the canvasser asks if he'll help the cause by volunteering to knock on some doors, or at least agree to read some "information" from ACT. If the voter says yes, he then begins to receive a stream of customized mailings and e-mails from ACT, focusing on the key problem facing America today, which is, of course, low wages.

The canvasser also shows the voter a brief video, which, like everything else, is programmed into the Palm. ACT pre-produced videos on a variety of topics, and the canvasser shows the voter the one closest to his concerns. The video is exactly sixteen seconds long. "We found that people will watch about sixteen seconds," Rosenthal explained, describing the painstaking research that went into the project. "Not more and not less. The first three or four seconds they look at the Palm Pilot kind of wondering what it is. It's a great way to break the ice and get voters involved in a discussion." And after that ice is broken,

Rosenthal said, the canvasser's job is to give the voter "good, solid information" that will "help them cast a vote."

Rosenthal appeared with the two other leaders of his group. One was Ellen Malcolm, who had built the pro-choice organization EMILY's List into the largest political action committee in the country; Malcolm had taken a leave from her job to serve as president of ACT. The other was Harold Ickes, the former Clinton White House aide and veteran of hardball New York politics who headed ACT's sister organization, the Media Fund, a group that produced and aired anti-Bush ads for television, radio, print, and the Internet. Their presentation was designed to convey the message that America Coming Together was the biggest, best, and most advanced political effort in the history of the world. But Palm Pilots aside, they found themselves with lots of questions to answer.

For example, how could they do what they were doing and not run afoul of the campaign finance laws? ACT was a 527, which meant that it could accept unlimited contributions from anyone. That much was well known; by the time of the Democratic convention, ACT had become famous as the beneficiary of millions of dollars in contributions from George Soros. But being a 527 also meant that ACT could not "coordinate"—that is, act in concert—with either the Kerry campaign or the Democratic Party. ACT was also specifically forbidden from urging people to vote against George W. Bush or for John Kerry. During convention week, ACT's leaders found themselves insisting, under mounting skepticism, that they were scrupulously following the rules.

First they had to explain why they were at the Four Seasons. During convention week, the hotel served as the headquarters of the Democratic National Committee's finance operation. Party fund-raisers were gathered on the second floor, which happened to be where America Coming Together had set up shop. And just to put a fine point on it, Ickes was a member of the DNC's executive committee. Everyone was walking around together, falling into conversations in the halls, going to meetings. Didn't that at least create the appearance that ACT and the Kerry Democrats were all working together?

Not at all, Malcolm said. In fact, she wondered why anyone would even ask such a thing. "It's important in our democracy that there are ways that people can come together with common interests to participate in the political process," she explained. ACT had looked carefully at the law and had determined that everything it did was perfectly appropriate, including staying at the Four Seasons. "There's absolutely no question that people can participate in politics," Malcolm continued. "EMILY's List is here, and ACT is here supporting Democratic candidates. All kinds of organizations are here."

But what about the question of ACT specifically advocating the defeat of President Bush? At that very moment, Malcolm was sending out a fund-raising appeal that said, "Here's what America Coming Together is all about. It's about people like you and me making a personal commitment to defeating George W. Bush." That seemed to be a pretty specific message. And ACT had on many other occasions made it quite clear that it was working to elect a Democratic president. Didn't that violate the rules governing 527s?

Rosenthal fielded that question. "We cannot expressly advocate on behalf of Kerry, or against Bush, so we will never use the words 'Vote for' or 'Vote against,'" he said. Instead, he continued, ACT could provide voters with "information" about issues. You think Bush has messed up the economy? Let us send you some information about how bad it is. You think Bush is destroying our civil liberties? Let us send you some information on that. ACT stuck closely to issues, Rosenthal said, and never made an overt campaign pitch. He did not address the issue of those letters calling for Americans to make "a personal commitment to defeating George W. Bush."

That question alone made ACT's compliance with the rules appear iffy at best. But what few, if any, of the reporters in the room that day knew was that questions about ACT's compliance with federal campaign finance laws went far deeper than worries about hotels or direct-mail appeals. At that moment, ACT was engaged in an elaborate financial sleight-of-hand designed to allow it to spend millions of dollars on the anti-Bush effort in ways that violated established standards governing such organizations. In filings before the Federal Election Commission, ACT claimed that it could spend the seven-figure contributions it received from donors like Soros on virtually anything it wanted—a tactic that one campaign finance reformer referred to as "a shell game." It was a serious matter that might have serious consequences for the organization. But any reckoning would be months in the future—long after the election—and ACT faced few questions about its accounting as the campaign rushed ahead.

Beyond the issue of money, the other major question Rosenthal, Malcolm, and Ickes faced was, Why were they so confident that they would win? Their answer had little to do with issues, or even the candidates, and everything to do with size: ACT would be victorious, Malcolm said, because it was really, really big. "There has never been anything of this magnitude in terms of voter contact in the history of this country," she explained. "It is an extraordinary undertaking, and the outpouring of support for what we're doing, both in terms of financial support and volunteer support, is exciting and overwhelming and really convinces me we are going to win this election for Democrats up and down the tickets in battleground states." ACT, she continued, had originally set a goal of raising $95 million, but having already raised more than $80 million of that, it had decided to make the goal $125 million.

Rosenthal filled in the details: ACT had 1,500 canvassers out every night in the swing states, talking to voters in their homes. There were 320 full-time ACT organizers on the ground in those states; many had been there all year. Another 220 full-time workers came from the Service Employees International Union, under what is called an "in-kind" contribution to ACT. (The supposedly nonpartisan union sent the workers to ACT under its "Heroes" program, in which workers had temporarily given up their jobs to campaign full-time for ACT.) And then there were thousands of volunteers who filled out the force.

Just in Ohio, Rosenthal said, ACT had 77 paid staffers, plus 42 from the union, plus volunteers working at 16 offices statewide—and that was still more than four months before the election (the totals would become far, far larger by November 2). "Our goal is to become the largest employer in Ohio," Rosenthal said. He was joking—sort of. By Election Day, ACT would indeed be among the top employers in the state, if only for a moment.

Given all those impressive numbers, there was a lot of confidence in the room that day in Boston. As their fellow Democratic organizers milled about in the Four Seasons atrium, Rosenthal, Malcolm, and Ickes happily cited statistic after statistic to show that ACT would simply overwhelm the Bush campaign come November. They didn't quite say it that way, but their argument boiled down to this: ACT was simply too big to fail. And its leaders would do whatever was necessary to win.

STOPPING THE ROVE JUGGERNAUT

The America Coming Together team wasn't always so confident. In fact, the group's founding owed more to feelings of fear and desperation than anything else. It started shortly after the Democrats' defeat in the 2002 midterm elections, when a group of veterans of Democratic politics—Malcolm, Rosenthal, Ickes, the Sierra Club's Carl Pope, and Andrew Stern and Gina Glantz of the Service Employees union—had dinner at BeDuCi, a Mediterranean restaurant in Washington's Dupont Circle neighborhood. It was a gloomy occasion. Democrats had just lost the House and the Senate for the fifth straight time, and the prospects for 2004 looked positively dismal.

It was a high-powered group. Before founding EMILY's List in 1985, Malcolm had worked at the advocacy group Common Cause in the 1970s, then in women's groups, and on the White House staff during the Carter years. Her creation, EMILY's List, was the embodiment of the idea that money is the most important commodity in politics—its name was an acronym for "Early Money Is Like Yeast," meaning that it "makes the dough rise." By 2002, EMILY's List had become the largest political action committee in the country. It handed out tens of millions of dollars to Democrats—always Democrats—on the condition that they support the right to abortion, even late-term abortion. EMILY's List backed women whenever possible, but supporters of abortion above all.

Rosenthal was widely recognized as a master of political organizing. Beginning with the Communications Workers of America, he worked at the Democratic National Committee and the Clinton administration Labor Department before becoming political director of the AFL-CIO in the mid-1990s. His specialty there was turnout, wringing more and more votes from the shrinking number of union households; under Rosenthal's guidance, the percentage of labor votes in the overall electorate actually rose, even as organized labor continued its long decline. In early 2003, Rosenthal got into the 527 game, heading a new organization called the Partnership for America's Families, which was created and funded by the Service Employees International Union, the AFL-CIO, the Laborers' International Union of North America, and other powerful labor groups.

The third member of the ACT leadership group was Ickes. The son of Franklin Delano Roosevelt's secretary of the interior, Ickes had become active in Democratic politics early, starting in the 1960s. A man who might be called an aggressive competitor—he once bit an adversary on the leg—Ickes served as deputy chief of staff in the Clinton White House, playing a key role in riding herd on the myriad scandal investigations that plagued the administration. He assumed a particularly important role in defending the White House during the fund-raising scandal, involving contributions from wealthy foreigners, that broke just before the 1996 elections.

Around the table at BeDuCi, the group surveyed a future that seemed almost unbearably bleak. "We thought that Karl Rove had a strategy to beat us on the money so badly that [Republicans] would go up on television in March, they would define the [Democratic] nominee, the nominee would be broke from the primaries, they'd get the whole thing over with by the summer, and then they'd take literally hundreds of millions of dollars and try to move into other races and basically create decades of a Republican majority in Congress," Malcolm told me when I visited her a few weeks before the election at the EMILY's List office in downtown Washington. It was truly a nightmare scenario for Democrats.

Making matters worse was the expected impact of the McCain-Feingold campaign finance reform law. The dirty little secret of campaign financing was that Democrats, who rhetorically claimed to be the party of the working man, were in fact beholden to millionaires in a way that Republicans weren't. At the time America Coming Together was getting started, the nonpartisan Center for Responsive Politics was finishing a study on political giving in the 2001–2002 election cycle that found that people who contributed less than $200 to politicians or parties gave 64 percent of their money to Republicans; just 35 percent of their contributions went to Democrats. On the other hand, people who gave $1 million or more to politicians or parties gave 92 percent to Democrats—and just 8 percent to Republicans.

McCain-Feingold meant that all those Democrats who wrote seven-figure checks—like Hollywood producer Haim Saban, of *Teenage Mutant Ninja Turtles* fame, who gave $7 million in 2002—would no longer be able to contribute vast sums to the Democratic Party. Meanwhile, all those Republicans who gave $200 or less to their party could keep giving. That would give the GOP an enormous fund-raising advantage. The group meeting at BeDuCi knew quite well that their party would have to find another way to make ends meet.

The other factor motivating Malcolm, Rosenthal, Ickes,

and the rest was the growing realization that they simply weren't as organized as they thought they were. After the 2000 election, EMILY's List had commissioned Democratic pollster Geoff Garin to study duplication of political effort by the Left. Garin selected four congressional districts and paid families to keep a diary of what political information they received in the last three weeks of the campaign. They would then tell researchers what affected their decisions on Election Day. What Garin found was a lot of overlapping campaigning. A pro-choice voter, for example, might receive three pieces of mail, one from Planned Parenthood, one from NARAL, and the other from a state Democratic Party, all on the same day, and all on the same subject. "It was very inefficient," Malcolm told me. "Nobody was working anything out." Rosenthal did a similar study in 2002, with similar results.

At the dinner, and in subsequent talks, the strategists came up with a three-part solution, or, more accurately, a three-group solution. The first was ACT, headed by Malcolm and Rosenthal, which would be created specifically to handle voter contact. The second was the Media Fund, headed by Ickes, which would handle mass-media advertising. And the third was an umbrella organization, America Votes, which would help coordinate the activities of a long list of allied Democratic base groups—NARAL; the Sierra Club; the NAACP National Voter Fund; the Association of Trial Lawyers of America; the American Federation of Teachers; AFL-CIO; the American Federation of State, County, and Municipal Employees; People for the American Way; the Human Rights Campaign; and more. Together they represented the entire Democratic coalition, only—if the plan worked—better organized and better coordinated.

America Votes had its first formal meeting on May 1, 2003, at the offices of EMILY's List. After that, the political directors of the groups got together every two weeks. "The purpose was to share polling research, share targeting information, share a lot of data on microtargeting and new ideas," America Votes president Cecile Richards, a former staffer for House Democratic leader Nancy Pelosi (and the daughter of former Texas governor Ann Richards), told me. "MoveOn had particular states they were interested in. Labor had its interest. Through these conversations, for the first time, people carved up what needed to happen. Your piece of the effort, my piece of the effort."

All of that was perfectly legal. Although the law clearly forbade "coordination" between the Kerry campaign and ACT, or America Votes, or any of the other 527s, there was nothing to keep the 527s from coordinating with one another all they wanted, and they did so from the very beginning.

As they started, Malcolm and Rosenthal had no idea how large ACT might become. They knew they wanted to focus on the swing states in the upcoming election, and they knew they wanted to make close and repeated contact with individual voters, but they didn't know how much money they would have to do it. They soon found out the answer when, out of the blue, they were contacted by a group of political consultants who had been hired by George Soros to come up with the most effective strategy for beating President Bush. In no time, Malcolm and Rosenthal were on a plane to the Hamptons. This was for the critical July 2003 strategy meeting at which Soros's consultants showed him portions of the secret Karl Rove strategy document that had been made "unintentionally available" to Democrats.

The meeting was, to say the least, a smashing success;

having Soros on board meant big, big money. "We came out of that with a big commitment from George and [Progressive Insurance chairman] Peter Lewis and some of the other participants," Malcolm told me. "So all of a sudden this little idea"—Malcolm paused—"we could do more." Soros told them that ACT should dramatically expand its plans. "He's very good at pushing out the limit," Malcolm told me. "At one point, we thought we could only do seven or nine states. And George would come in and say"—she imitated Soros's deep Hungarian accent—"'No, you can do this.' He helped us put together some other ways to raise money and pushed us into doing all the states. And he was right."

It is not an exaggeration to say that Soros was personally responsible for the breadth and depth of America Coming Together's efforts. The July 2003 meeting in Southampton was a critical moment, not just for ACT, but for the entire 2004 presidential campaign, and perhaps even for the history of American politics. By embracing campaign finance reform, and then embracing 527s, Democrats had shifted much of the money—the engine that drives all campaigns—out of the hands of the political parties and into the hands of "nonpartisan" organizing and advocacy groups. They had, in short, created what amounted to a new political party. No matter how the 2004 election turned out, the Left had fashioned a new way to run campaigns and thus for Americans to select their leaders. And all of this happened at the impetus not of the Democratic establishment but rather of outside forces, like Soros, that until that point had been relatively insignificant in the political world.

After Soros signed on, contributions started pouring in. According to Federal Election Commission records, ACT took in $12.5 million in 2003—and the organization had started fund-raising only in the late summer of that year. During the same time, the Media Fund took in $3 million. When 2003 turned into 2004 and the presidential race began in earnest, the sums became staggering. In all, ACT and the Media Fund took in about $200 million. Soros alone had given $20 million. There had never been anything like it.

And the list of contributors grew longer and longer. Beyond Soros and Peter Lewis, there was Hollywood producer Stephen Bing, who gave $12 million. There was Hyatt hotel heiress Linda Pritzker, whose family gave $5 million. And the Service Employees International Union, which gave $3 million. And Massachusetts technology entrepreneur Terry Ragon, who gave $3 million. And Texas technology executives Jonathan McHale and Christine Mattson, who together gave $3 million. And the American Federation of State, County, and Municipal Employees, which gave $2.1 million. And New York philanthropist Lewis Cullman, who gave $2 million. And Rockefeller heir Alida Messinger, who gave $1.5 million. And Agnes Varis, head of AgVar Chemicals, who gave $1.5 million. And Illinois broadcasting magnate Fred Eychaner, who gave $1.5 million. And Seattle tech entrepreneur Robert Glaser, who gave $1.2 million. And the Teamsters Union, which gave $1 million. And Colorado entrepreneur Tim Gill, who gave $1 million. And television producer Marcy Carsey, who gave $1 million. And Pennsylvania financier Theodore Aronson, who gave $1 million. And Oregon publisher Win McCormack, who gave $1 million. And heiress Anne Getty Earhart, who gave $1 million. And Texas technology entrepreneur James H. Clark, who gave $1 million. And the American Federation of Teachers, which gave $1 million. And Florida millionaire Dan Lewis, who gave $1 million. And Ohio philanthropist Richard Rosenthal, who gave $1 million. And clothing entrepreneur Susie Tompkins Buell, who gave $1 million. And those were just the ones who contributed $1 million or more, according to information compiled by the nonpartisan Center for Public Integrity.

Why did so many give so much? I asked Terry Ragon, the Massachusetts businessman who contributed $3 million. He told me he had been unhappy with George W. Bush's performance in office even before September 11, and then, afterward, felt the president mishandled the War on Terror. Ragon was appalled by the "Axis of Evil" speech, and the invasion of Iraq, and what he saw as America's deteriorating relations with some old allies. He felt he had to do something. Although he had never been a big political contributor in the past, he gave the maximum $2,000 personal contribution to the Kerry campaign and the maximum $25,000 contribution to the Democratic Party. But he felt there had to be something else he could do.

Since Ragon was based in Boston, he made a quick trip to visit Democratic officials during the party's convention in June. "I found about [ACT] through the Democratic National Convention," he told me. "I know that there's not supposed to be a connection between the two, and I don't think there's a very close one, but I wanted to give more money, and I asked them how to do that, and they told me about 527s and gave me a list of organizations." In no time, Ragon was at the Four Seasons, meeting with Malcolm and Rosenthal. "I liked what Ellen and Steve had to say," he told me.

ACT's lawyers would no doubt argue that there was no coordination between the party and the 527 in arranging for Ragon's contribution. Perhaps in some legal sense there wasn't. But in any commonsense view of the situation, the Democratic Party and ACT were working together in Boston, something

Ragon's experience seems to confirm. Whatever the case, Ragon became convinced that ACT could help get rid of Bush. But he had not settled on how much he would donate to the cause until he took a trip to the local movie theater.

"What really set me off—I had already decided to contribute to ACT, but I hadn't decided how much—was I went to see *Fahrenheit 9/11*," Ragon told me. "And I came out of that movie—the film clips were just priceless—and I just said to myself, What am I doing? I have to do more than just write a check for $25,000." Ragon had initially thought about giving $1 million to ACT. After *Fahrenheit 9/11*, that became $2 million.

He was happy to be supporting ACT in part because it seemed to be doing a better job than the Democratic candidate. "I was pretty disgusted with the way John Kerry was running his campaign at that point," Ragon told me. But things got better, in Ragon's view, in September, when Kerry came out more forcefully against the war in Iraq. About that time, Ragon attended an ACT fund-raiser for big donors held at Soros's apartment overlooking Central Park in Manhattan. He gave another $1 million, bringing his total contribution to $3 million.

Speaking with him a month after the election, I asked Ragon if it had been worth it. "I know that if I hadn't done anything, I'd be sitting here kicking myself saying I should have done something," he replied. "My view is that I could not afford to let a chance slip by."

THE 98 PERCENT SOLUTION

As ACT's bank account grew and grew, experts in campaign finance noticed something curious going on in the group's accounting. It had to do with the way ACT spent its money and the explanation it made for those expenditures in filings with the Federal Election Commission. At issue were complex rules covering the arcana of campaign finance and the precise legal meanings of terms like "hard money," "soft money," "federal accounts," "nonfederal accounts," and "allocation." The issues were difficult to understand—that's why they went mostly unreported in the press—but the evidence suggested that ACT had simply decided to ignore the rules that were supposed to govern its activities.

Although ACT is commonly referred to as a 527, it is in fact a two-part organization. One part is an old-fashioned political action committee, or PAC, which is covered by federal election laws and overseen by the Federal Election Commission. The other part is the 527, which is not covered by those laws. The PAC accepts what are called hard-money contributions—that is, those intended for the specific purpose of influencing fed-eral elections, meaning races for president, vice president, the House, and the Senate. Federal law places a $5,000 limit on those contributions; the money went into ACT's "federal account." But ACT's other side, the 527, is allowed to accept unlimited contributions—soft money—for what are called nonfederal purposes, which means things like voter registra-tion, fund-raising, get-out-the-vote activities, and state and local campaigns. That money went into ACT's "nonfederal account." Because it can accept unlimited contributions, ACT is not allowed to use nonfederal, or soft, money to advocate the election or defeat of any particular federal candidate.

Two-part organizations like ACT must keep careful records of their federal and nonfederal accounts and report them to the

FEC. They can by law spend soft money for get-out-the-vote and other nonfederal purposes only after raising a significant amount of hard money first. Most groups set a ratio of hard-money to soft-money spending of about 60 percent to 40 percent, or perhaps 70 percent to 30 percent; that means that for every two dollars in federal (hard) money that a group like ACT raised and spent, it could raise and spend a third dollar in non-federal (soft) money. The purpose of that practice was to make sure groups did not spend unlimited-contribution soft money to advocate the election or defeat of a specific federal candidate.

At least that's what the law said. But the leaders of ACT decided to virtually erase the distinction between the organization's two halves. Instead of following the typical ratios of federal to nonfederal spending, ACT simply declared that it would spend *98 percent* of its money for nonfederal purposes and just 2 percent for federal purposes. By making that claim, ACT was saying that 98 percent of its expenditures was going to nonfederal activities—that is, *not* advocating the defeat of George W. Bush or the election of John Kerry. *We're just helping to register voters, get out the vote, and support Democrats in local offices,* ACT was saying. *We're not really involved in that presidential thing.*

For anyone who knew anything about the campaign finance laws and who knew the role ACT was playing in the campaign, that position simply did not pass the laugh test. "ACT registered as a political committee [PAC] because I think they realized that they could completely game the FEC rules that applied to federal political committees," Donald Simon, counsel to the pro-reform group Democracy 21, told me. "They claimed the right to have this 98–2 split in their funding, even though it was clear to anybody that what they were about was influencing the presidential election."

In January 2004, Democracy 21 joined two other nonpartisan reform organizations, the Campaign Legal Center and the Center for Responsive Politics, to file a complaint with the Federal Election Commission. "The 'major purpose,' indeed the overriding purpose, of ACT's activities, including its purportedly 'nonfederal' account, is to promote the election of the Democratic nominee for president, and to defeat President Bush," the complaint said. "In fact, the soft money being given to the purportedly 'nonfederal' account is clearly being donated explicitly for the purpose of defeating President Bush, as George Soros and other donors have made clear."

The FEC, apparently unwilling to make a ruling in the middle of a presidential campaign, took no action on the reformers' complaint. In March 2004, the reformers tried again, sending a letter to the commission saying that the whole system of regulations that allowed organizations to allocate their money between federal and nonfederal accounts "leads to indefensible and absurd results." "Under the Commission's existing . . . rules, America Coming Together is claiming a right to spend *98 percent soft money* [emphasis in the original] on its voter mobilization activities, even though ACT and its donors have made publicly clear their overriding purpose is to mobilize voters to defeat President Bush in the 2004 elections."*

---

*The reformers also complained about the Leadership Forum, a 527 often described as being "loosely tied" to the House Republican leadership. But the Leadership Forum could not even approach the fund-raising prowess of the Democratic groups; according to federal records at the time the complaint was filed, the group had raised $1 million in 2002 and just $225,000 in 2003, a small fraction of what the Democratic groups had raised. Later, a few Republican 527s did begin to catch up with their Democratic counterparts. In the end, however, Democratic-supporting 527s spent more than $230 million on the presidential race— nearly two and a half times as much as Republican-supporting 527s.

Still, the FEC took no action. In June, the reformers filed yet another complaint, this one making the case that ACT was in fact created *for the specific purpose* of influencing a federal election—that is, the presidential race. The complaint cited millions of direct-mail fund-raising appeals, sent out by ACT, which arrived in voters' mailboxes in envelopes on which the following was printed:

17 States
25,000 Organizers
200,000 Volunteers
10 Million Doors Knocked On
. . . and a one-way ticket back to Crawford, Texas

That last phrase was one made famous by Howard Dean during his Democratic primary campaign. And other ACT fund-raising letters were even more overt. One accused George W. Bush and the Republican Party of "work[ing] hard to undermine a woman's right to choose," of displaying "reckless disregard for the environment," and of "making a shambles of our economy." The letter continued, "But wishing won't make Bush, Cheney, Ashcroft, DeLay and their extremist agenda go away. Wishing won't elect John Kerry. People-to-people organizing will—and organizing is what ACT is all about." Another fund-raising letter pledged that ACT would fill in "where the Kerry campaign and the Democratic Party simply don't have the resources to operate." And yet another appeal said that "when Election Day is over, we will have helped John Kerry defeat George W. Bush and elected progressive candidates across the nation."

Still ACT claimed, in its filings to the government, that it was largely uninvolved in partisan presidential politics. And the Media Fund, which operated solely on large soft-money contributions, was crossing the line just as often. The Fund, which was required by law to stay away from advocating the election or defeat of federal candidates, claimed that it was "supporting a progressive message and defending Democrats from attack ads funded by the deep pockets of the right wing." But it was on the offense from the beginning. In its first ad, which aired in the seventeen battleground states in early March, an announcer began, "President Bush, remember the American Dream?" Over video of flags and children and workers and farms, the announcer continued, "It's about hope, not fear. It's about more jobs at home, not tax breaks for shipping jobs overseas. . . . George Bush's priorities are eroding the American Dream. It's time to take our country back from corporate greed and make America work for every American."

Months later, the Fund's last ad was an attack based on themes developed in *Fahrenheit 9/11*. Over video of the Saudi royal family, accompanied by the kind of generic ominous music characteristic of attack ads, the announcer began, "The Saudi royal family. Wealthy. Powerful. Corrupt. And close Bush family friends." The narrator said that "rich Saudis bailed out George W. when his oil company went bust" and that fifteen of the nineteen September 11 hijackers were Saudi. "Kind of makes you wonder," the ad concluded. "Are Bush and the Saudis too close for comfort?"

Reformers believed the evidence would prove that ACT's and the Media Fund's contention that they had almost nothing to do with the federal election was in fact "indefensible and absurd." "There's no argument that meets the straight-faced test that these groups were not engaged in influencing a federal election,"

Donald Simon told me. And indeed, in mid-campaign, the FEC finally adopted new regulations requiring a 50–50 ratio in federal to nonfederal spending in some cases. The move might have significantly reined in ACT's programs—*if* it had applied to the 2004 campaign. But the regulation was written to take effect only after the election, so ACT and the Media Fund did not have to worry.

By the end of the election season, the leaders of ACT were no longer even claiming that they were not working to defeat Bush and elect Kerry; instead, they maintained that it was impossible to draw clear distinctions in the work they did. "I think that you can't separate easily what you do for a federal candidate versus what you do for a nonfederal candidate," Malcolm told me. And it was true that ACT often said it was working to elect Democrats "up and down the ticket." But did George Soros give all that money in order to elect Democrats up and down the ticket? If so, he never said so in dozens of public statements devoted to his desire to rid the White House of George W. Bush.

Ultimately, ACT's defiance of the rules would lead to new fights both in Congress and inside the FEC. And Malcolm, Rosenthal, and Ickes, all political veterans, no doubt knew that their practices would be challenged when the fight over campaign finance resumed after the election. I asked Malcolm whether she believed that what she and ACT had done in the 2004 election would lead to more campaign finance reform. "I think there will be more attempts to do that," she said. "And yes, I think there could be contribution limits on nonfederal contributions. But I think that it is a lot more complicated than the reformers would like to have you believe." At least, that is what ACT hoped.

SPENDING GEORGE'S MONEY

On October 30, just three days before the election, after knocking on millions of doors, ACT held its final "Action Day" of the campaign, in which staff and volunteers spread throughout the swing states in a last get-out-the-vote effort. By that time, the Palm Pilots were gone. No one was gathering any more information; the only goal was to get people to the polls to vote for Kerry. On that day, I traveled to Pennsylvania to get a final feel for what ACT, along with its companion organization America Votes, was doing in a state that was competitive but clearly leaning toward the Democrat.

With an ACT staffer, a young woman named Rebecca, I went to the staging area for the get-out-the-vote efforts in the suburbs of Philadelphia. Volunteers, perhaps one hundred of them, were gathering at the Bryn Mawr train station parking lot in Lower Merion. Most had come in from New York City, although some were from Washington, D.C.; for them, Pennsylvania was the perfect close-to-home swing state, offering a chance for activism without too much travel (it had much the same appeal for many New York– and Washington-based reporters). On this day, a few of the volunteers were people who had heard about ACT and just decided to sign up. But many more had been recruited by the National Abortion Rights Action League, which in the last few years has taken to calling itself NARAL Pro-Choice America. Others were brought in by the Service Employees International Union and a few other labor organizations.

A local Pennsylvania NARAL organizer named Shawn, whose short, spiky haircut revealed the Chinese characters tattooed on the back of her neck, divided the crowd into small groups. Everyone would have to be "trained," she announced, and there was a lot of standing around as the volunteers waited for a brief lecture on what they should say when they encountered a real, live voter.

I joined a group being trained by Lisa, another young woman from NARAL. She explained that the volunteers would be getting a map of the streets they were assigned to cover, plus a script with the get-out-the-vote pitch. The script was quite short. It simply reminded the voter that Election Day was November 2 (most of the volunteers were a bit sheepish about saying something so painfully obvious in a state that had been saturated with political advertising for months). If the voter said he or she was registered (at that point it was too late to register anyone who hadn't already done so), the canvasser was supposed to ask if he or she would like to volunteer to go door-to-door for ACT on Election Day. It seemed simple enough, but at that moment the complex laws governing 527s intruded on the proceedings when a volunteer asked, "What are the rules about talking about Kerry?"

"Well, actually, ACT is nonpartisan, so we're not allowed to be out there endorsing Kerry," Lisa told her. "We can talk about the issues, and talk about the facts of Bush's record and Kerry's record, but we cannot go out and say 'Vote for Kerry November 2' or 'Vote for Bush November 2.' Did everybody hear that?" Lisa also said that anyone wearing Kerry-Edwards buttons, hats, or anything else should remove them before hitting the neighborhoods.

Another woman asked, "If they say, 'I want to volunteer to get out the Democratic vote,' do you say you're supporting Democratic candidates?"

Before Lisa could answer, a person at the back of the group said, "I was told we were allowed to say we support Democratic candidates up and down the ticket, but you just can't mention them by name."

"That's what I've heard before," said another woman.

"Is there somebody here who actually knows the answer definitively?" still another asked.

"What if we're with NARAL?" asked the first woman.

"Actually, NARAL—we legally can't do it, either," Lisa answered.

"Well, if we're wearing a NARAL shirt, it's kind of obvious."

"Yeah, but it doesn't say 'Vote for Kerry,' 'Don't Vote for Bush,'" Lisa answered. "I was just told that we really have to be careful, there are a bunch of things that we can't say, and a bunch of things that we can say."

Finally, one of the women who had gone off looking for an answer returned. "We can say Democratic candidates up and down the ticket," she announced.

"Okay, there we go," Lisa said.

So off we went. With Rebecca as my ACT minder, I accompanied a group of three women, Carol, Shayne, and Laura, as they canvassed door-to-door. The three were friends, and all worked for the same company, a left-leaning public policy group, although they lived in different cities—one in Philadelphia, one in New York, and one in Portland, Oregon. We began canvassing in an affluent neighborhood of beautiful old stone houses in Lower Merion.

I walked with Carol and Shayne, who decided to go together, while Laura went off on her own. They knocked on their first door of the morning. Nobody was home.

Next was a house that had five signs in its front yard, supporting Kerry-Edwards, Democratic Representative Joe Hoeffel, who was running for Senate, and a few other Democrats. The canvassers decided there was no need to knock on that one.

On to the next house. Nobody home.

Two more houses had lots of Democratic signs. We skipped those.

Next house. Nobody home.

Next house. Nobody home.

Next house. A woman answered the door, but she had some physical difficulty speaking. She seemed to be saying that someone was upstairs, but Carol and Shayne couldn't make it out. "Did she say he was ten?" Carol asked. "No, she said his name was Ben," Shayne said. They decided to move on.

Next house. Nobody home.

Next house. A woman answered the door. "Hi, I'm Carol, and I'm with America Votes," Carol said.

"I'm not interested," the woman said, slamming the door.

Next house. Nobody home.

Next house. Nobody home.

I went across the street to join Laura, who seemed to be having better luck. She knocked on a door and a woman answered. The woman was quite friendly, and they had a nice conversation, but the upshot of it was that she was not an American citizen and could not vote.

Laura reported to Rebecca. "She was Irish. She said her congressman had been very helpful with visa issues."

"Was it Hoeffel?" Rebecca wanted to know.

"No, very *helpful*," Laura answered. "She said the congressman was Gerlach."

"He's a Republican," Rebecca said, somewhat dispiritedly, recognizing the name of Representative Jim Gerlach, who represented Pennsylvania's sixth congressional district.

"Well, she thought he was a Democrat," Laura said.

And on it went. With one exception, all the people the women encountered said they were registered to vote. No one volunteered to work on Election Day, but two people said they had already committed to do so. Most of the time, however, there was no one home when the volunteers knocked.

Later, Rebecca took me to ACT's main Pennsylvania get-out-the-vote headquarters, a large and cluttered rented space in a run-down neighborhood of West Philadelphia. I watched as staffers divided the city street-by-street, preparing maps for Election Day volunteers to use in the final get-out-the-vote effort. Looking back over the day's canvassing, in which we had reached a relatively small number of voters, I asked Rebecca whether she thought it was worth the effort. "I do," she told me. "I mean, it's one of those things like maybe you feel that how many, in terms of three canvassers, can you really affect an election, but when you have groups of two and three and six canvassers, hundreds of groups and thousands of canvassers doing the same thing, you do make a difference." She was very optimistic about a Kerry victory on Election Day.

THE BRILLIANT LOSING STRATEGY

When the election was over and the reality of having lost the presidential race set in, the leaders of ACT released a list of their accomplishments. They had held "conversations at 4.6 million doorsteps about the truth about the Iraq war, about the state of our healthcare system, about the economy." They had registered a half-million new voters. In the last days of the campaign they had made 23 million phone calls, sent out 16 million pieces of mail, and delivered 11 million flyers. And on top of it all, they had "launched the largest get-out-the-vote effort the Democratic Party has ever seen," turning out "unprecedented levels of voters in the battleground states."

And indeed, the efforts of ACT, the Media Fund, and a host of other Democratic-supporting 527s were unprecedented. In the end, ACT alone reported raising $141 million, with the Media Fund picking up another $60 million; no one at the dinner at BeDuCi ever envisioned coming up with that kind of cash. In addition, the leaders of ACT figured out how to circumvent the campaign finance reform laws—laws that many Democrats had championed—so they could spend all that money virtually as they pleased. In the process, the 527s—and their biggest donors—gained a measure of influence inside the Democratic Party that had never happened in previous campaigns. Suddenly outside activists became a critical part of the Democratic mainstream.

The only problem, of course, was that it didn't work. At least, it didn't elect John Kerry in 2004. In fact, when ACT listed its actual electoral accomplishments, they seemed almost pitifully small in relation to the overall effort. ACT had "helped ensure George W. Bush's defeat in several of the key states and made the race close in others." In addition, "We enabled Democrats to take back the Oregon state legislature for the first time in 10 years." Next, "In Missouri, Robin Carnahan handily defeated well-funded and well-known Speaker of the House Catherine Hanaway and won her election for Secretary of State." And last, "In New Hampshire, we saw wins for the presidential race and the governor's race, as well as a gain of four state senate seats." And that was it. George Soros had spent $20 million to elect a Democratic secretary of state in Missouri.

Nevertheless, ACT vowed to fight on. "While campaigns end, ACT does not," the message said. "Stay tuned." And indeed, the organization will no doubt keep going. Its sails will probably be trimmed a bit by Congress or the FEC—Malcolm as much as told me she expected that—but ACT will stay in business. Still, it seems safe to say that it will not have the same aura of being the hot new thing that it had in those untested months leading up to the 2004 election.

Malcolm, Rosenthal, and Ickes will undoubtedly learn from the beating they took from the Bush voter turnout organization. Unlike ACT, which emphasized paid workers and Palm Pilots, the Bush effort relied mostly on volunteers on the theory that voters were more likely to listen to political pitches from neighbors than a union organizer on leave from his job three states away. When I talked with Malcolm before the election, she seemed confident that her way was best. She had tried volunteers many times in the past, she told me, but this time ACT was trying to create a "paid infrastructure that you can depend on." She called the GOP plan an "Amway structure" and said her paid force would simply work better. "It's not dependent on volunteers, because you never know," she said. "I mean, people say they're going to come, they don't come, whatever."

But Republicans did come, in very large numbers. And to them, ACT's staffers appeared to be paid soldiers fighting a war for profit instead of passion. "It was mercenaries versus patriots," said one former GOP official who volunteered to go door-to-door asking Republicans to vote. But lest the contrast be taken too far, it should be said that the Bush effort also added a large paid staff to its army of volunteers. A few days before the election, Ken Mehlman, the president's campaign manager, told me that while the volunteers were the core of the effort, the campaign had dramatically beefed up its paid staff, too. "We had 22 paid staff in Florida in the 2000 election," Mehlman said. "We have 600 today." It was an impressive number, although still smaller than ACT's force. But as it turned out, in some ways smaller—and more dedicated—was better.

In the end, the real problem for ACT had little to do with the question of volunteers versus paid staff. Its problem was that despite its claims to be reaching more people than ever before, it really did not reach a lot of *new* people. America Coming Together was not, in fact, America coming together; it might more accurately have been named Traditional Democratic Party Constituencies Coordinating Like Never Before. My experience in the suburbs of Philadelphia wasn't unique. You could go to any office of ACT and find lots of people from NARAL, or the Service Employees International Union, or the Sierra Club, or Planned Parenthood. They were the same old groups.

Despite all the hype and all the press releases, the effort really wasn't about converting new voters to the Democratic Party. Rather, it was about squeezing just a little more juice out of a lemon that had been nearly squeezed dry in the past. Steve Rosenthal's well-regarded successes in previous elections had not involved attracting large numbers of new people to the cause. They involved getting union voters to turn out in ever-greater percentages, even as the total number of union households in the electorate shrank. The problem was, you could do that for only so long. At some point, every union member or union household member of voting age could turn out and it still wouldn't be enough to elect a Democratic candidate. For that, you had to expand your appeal, and that was something ACT failed to do. Malcolm, Rosenthal, and Ickes discovered that you could call it America Coming Together, but saying so didn't make it true.

CHAPTER FOUR

The Passion of Michael Moore

Preaching to the Choir with Fahrenheit 9/11

In early August 2004, Karl Rove, President Bush's top political advisor, was having lunch with a small group of journalists at the Oval Room, a restaurant across Lafayette Square from the White House. The talk—off the record, unless Rove agreed to be quoted—was about strategy in the presidential race. Was Kerry's emphasis on his Vietnam record a mistake? Was Bush going to offer a full-scale defense of the war in Iraq? Would he push issues like Social Security reform? After the discussion touched on a number of heavy topics, I asked Rove what he thought of Michael Moore's blastingly anti-Bush movie, *Fahrenheit 9/11*. Had it had an effect on the presidential race?

"It's an artful piece of propaganda," Rove said.

Was that all? Had he seen the picture?

"I plead guilty to violating the copyright laws of the United States by watching a bootleg DVD," Rove answered with a grin. "I refuse to enrich [Moore]," he added, giving the clear impression that he had a rather low opinion of the filmmaker.

With a little more prodding, Rove said he wasn't worried about the picture and did not see it playing a substantial role in the election. But he had watched it—at a time when some others on the White House staff were saying they would not see it. Rove was too careful a man, and his mind too wide-ranging, not to want to judge for himself.

Moore would undoubtedly have been delighted by the image of Karl Rove peering at a fuzzy bootleg of *Fahrenheit 9/11*. What publicity material that would have made! At the time, Moore was traveling around the country, promoting the movie as George W. Bush's worst nightmare, generating an enormous amount of free coverage in the process. The point—other than to make money for Michael Moore—was to create the impression that *Fahrenheit 9/11* had touched off an explosion of anti-Bush activism across the nation.

Democrats were happy to go along. When Moore held a Washington premiere on June 24 at the Uptown Theatre in Cleveland Park—a neighborhood that is home to many wealthy Democrats—he was embraced by the party's power structure. Senate Minority Leader Tom Daschle was there, along with Iowa Senator Tom Harkin, Montana Senator Max Baucus, South Carolina Senator Ernest Hollings, Michigan Senator Debbie Stabenow, Florida Senator Bill Nelson, New York Congressman Charles Rangel, and Washington State Congressman Jim McDermott. Democratic National Committee chairman Terry McAuliffe was there, along with party talking head Paul Begala, former Clinton/Gore attack man Chris Lehane (who was working for Moore), pollster Peter Fenn, People for the American Way chief Ralph Neas, and others. The event was organized by former Clinton White House social secretary Capricia Marshall, whom Miramax Pictures head Harvey Weinstein jokingly thanked for doing "an incredible job of, you know, bringing together such a bipartisan audience."

After the film, VIPs filed out to congratulate Moore. Richard Ben-Veniste, a Democratic member of the September 11 Commission, gave his regards. McDermott, who in September 2002 had traveled to Baghdad to issue a denunciation of George W. Bush, also stopped by.

"It was great," McDermott told Moore.

"You're the man," Moore answered.

"Great job."

McAuliffe reached across a gaggle of fans to shake Moore's hand. "Good job, Michael," he said. "It was great. Hope everybody sees it." McAuliffe said he found the movie "very powerful, much more powerful than I thought it would be."

A few moments later, I asked McAuliffe whether he believed one of the movie's main allegations, that the United States had gone to war in Afghanistan not to destroy al Qaeda but to benefit the Unocal Corporation, which wanted to build a natural gas pipeline across that country. "Uh, first I heard in the movie, but I believe it after seeing that," McAuliffe told me. "Check it out myself and look at it, but there are a lot of interesting facts that he brought out today that none of us knew about."

Standing nearby, Bill Schneider of CNN asked whether McAuliffe thought the picture was "essentially fair and factually based."

"I do," McAuliffe said. "I think anyone who goes to see this movie will come out *en masse* and vote for John Kerry."

That, of course, was the idea; McAuliffe had not come to the theater for a night at the movies. Indeed, in 2004, Democrats hoped that *Fahrenheit 9/11* would do substantial damage to the Bush campaign. Party officials, and the leaders of allied groups like MoveOn, believed that a movie, rather than, say, traditional political advertisements or stump speeches, might reach potential Kerry voters who would otherwise have remained detached from the political process.

At least for a while, the plan appeared to be working. *Fahrenheit 9/11* did an impressive business, earning far more than any other documentary in history. And many reporters and analysts, spurred on by Moore and his publicity team, interpreted the movie's success as evidence of a deeply felt and growing anti-Bush sentiment among the public, not just in the blue states, where the movie might have been expected to do well, but also in the red states won by George W. Bush in 2000.

But a little more than four months later, after Election Day, things looked much different. Not only had Moore's movie not propelled the Democratic candidate to victory, but some Democrats wondered privately whether *Fahrenheit 9/11* and all the attendant fuss might have done more harm than good. What went wrong?

The answer, although no one beyond a few Hollywood executives, and probably Moore himself, knew it at the time, was that *Fahrenheit 9/11* never had the sort of national appeal that its maker and its publicists claimed. The truth was just the opposite; deep inside the dense compilations of audience research figures that are used by movie studios to chart a film's performance was evidence that *Fahrenheit 9/11*'s appeal was narrowly limited to those areas that were already solidly anti-Bush. Moore's daily pronouncements about the movie's success in pro-Bush areas, and the growing anti-Bush movement it was supposedly engendering, were little more than wishful thinking.

In the end, Karl Rove was right. There was no need to worry.

SOLD OUT IN FAYETTEVILLE

On June 28, a couple of days after *Fahrenheit 9/11*'s premiere, Moore spoke to thousands of people via an Internet hookup at "Turn Up the Heat: A National Town Meeting on *Fahrenheit 9/11*," organized by MoveOn. "It was the number-one movie in every single red state in America," Moore said, as cheers went up in the room in which I was watching with about two hundred MoveOn supporters. "Every single state that Bush won in 2000, it was the number-one film in it." The news seemed ominous for the president; a real sense of excitement and hope filled the room. "I'm sure when the White House read that this morning, that was one of their worst nightmares come true," Moore said.

Press accounts added to the idea that *Fahrenheit 9/11* was winning over Bush supporters. The day before Moore spoke to MoveOn, the *Los Angeles Times* ran a story headlined "'Fahrenheit' Is Casting a Wide Net at Theaters: Anti-Bush Sentiment Runs High at Showings of the Documentary, Which Has Opened with a Strong Box-Office from 868 Screens." The story began with a woman, a supporter of the president, who had gotten into stinging political arguments with her anti-Bush college-student son. The son urged her to see *Fahrenheit 9/11,* and she emerged from the movie with tears in her eyes. "My emotions are just . . . ," she said, unable to continue. "I feel like we haven't seen the whole truth before." The *Times* wrote of another man, a well-to-do retired insurance agent, who described himself as a lifelong Republican but who, after seeing the movie, vowed to leave the GOP. "I won't be voting for a Republican presidential candidate this time," he told the *Times.*

On the same day, the *New York Times* cited a retired Republican stockbroker who said that after he watched *Fahrenheit 9/11* his vote for president was "going to take a lot of thought." The paper also described a young waitress who said she was a conservative Republican but added, "After watching [the movie], I do question my loyalty to the president. And that's scary for me."

Summing up the emerging conventional wisdom, *Time* magazine wrote, "You would have expected Moore's movie to play well in the liberal big cities, and it is doing so. But the film is also touching the heart of the heartland. In Bartlett, Tenn., a Memphis suburb, the rooms at Stage Road Cinema showing *Fahrenheit 9/11* have been packed with viewers who clap, boo, laugh and cry nearly on cue. Even the dissenters are impressed. When the lights came up after a showing last week, one gent rose from his seat and said grudgingly, 'It's bullshit, but I gotta admit it was done well.'" Calling *Fahrenheit 9/11* "a shaping force in the presidential campaign," *Time* wrote that the film was attracting "the curious, the hostile, the indifferent.... [Moore is] doing what he does best—pestering—to get them into theaters. And then to the polls."

As publicity for *Fahrenheit 9/11*, Moore himself could not have written better stories. And he did seem to write some of them. "It sold out in Fayetteville, North Carolina, home of Fort Bragg," he told the group at the MoveOn town meeting. "It sold out in Tulsa, Oklahoma. It got a standing ovation in Greensboro, North Carolina." In a matter of hours, those quotes found their way into news reports, feeding the impression that *Fahrenheit 9/11* was exciting audiences everywhere, made up of all kinds of viewers. And that impression was amplified by a separate campaign, coordinated by MoveOn, encouraging the group's members to pack early screenings and write pro-Moore letters to newspapers, all of which was designed to create the sense that the movie was a phenomenon sweeping the country.

But was that really true? Certainly the picture had a spectacular opening weekend for a documentary. But Moore always claimed a special status for the movie, that it was much more than a documentary. (He withdrew it from Academy Award consideration in the documentary category, opting instead to position it—unsuccessfully, as it turned out—for a Best Picture nomination.) And as a film phenomenon, *Fahrenheit 9/11*'s opening was not nearly as spectacular as Moore claimed.

To make a comparison: Which film had a better opening weekend, *Fahrenheit 9/11* or *Barbershop 2: Back in Business*? The correct answer is *Barbershop*. In terms of opening receipts, *Mean Girls* also beat *Fahrenheit 9/11*, as did *Starsky & Hutch, Anchorman: The Legend of Ron Burgundy, Scooby-Doo 2: Monsters Unleashed, Alien vs. Predator, 50 First Dates,* and several others. The year's big hits, like *Shrek 2, Harry Potter and the Prisoner of Azkaban,* and *Spiderman 2* all had openings between four and five times the size of *Fahrenheit 9/11*'s. In the end, *Fahrenheit 9/11* had the 32nd-best opening weekend of 2004, taking in $23,920,637 in its first days.

Moore's defenders would say that was because *Fahrenheit 9/11* opened in fewer theaters than movies that became blockbusters. To some extent, that is true. *Shrek 2,* for example, opened in 4,163 theaters, and *Harry Potter* opened in 3,855, while *Fahrenheit 9/11* opened in just 868. But the film's opening on a small number of screens reflected a carefully thought-out strategy. The idea was to come out of the gate strong in big cities where the picture was expected to do well. Those cities were also the places with the highest ticket prices, which would help ensure a large opening gross. Opening in places where the film might do poorly would add somewhat to the gross but would dilute the sense that the movie was doing gangbusters everywhere it played. After the initial rush of publicity created nationwide curiosity about the movie, its distributor, Lions Gate, expanded the number of theaters in which *Fahrenheit 9/11* played, ultimately reaching 2,011, which was probably the maximum number in which the film could have profitably played.

None of that addressed the issue of whether *Fahrenheit 9/11* was truly the nationwide phenomenon that Moore claimed. The reporters and commentators talking about the film could not have known the answer to that question at the time they were confidently asserting that the picture was indeed doing well in red states as well as blue. Sold out in Tulsa? A standing ovation in Greensboro? That sort of thing was anecdotal evidence at best. To learn how well the film really did would take weeks and would require a detailed look at its performance everywhere it played. The newspapers and magazines didn't have time for that.

But the movie studios did. Motion picture companies keep track of ticket sales data in excruciating detail. For any given movie, they know who bought tickets, where, and why. They do research not just on a national basis, or a market-by-market basis, or a city-by-city basis, but on a screen-by-screen basis. Did *Shrek 2* underperform at AMC's Crestwood Plaza 10 theaters outside St. Louis? They know the answer. Did *Mean Girls* overperform at Loews Foothills Cinemas 15 in Tucson? They know that, too.

But the public doesn't hear much about it. Studios routinely release box-office figures—the numbers are part of the horse-race reporting that goes on every opening weekend—but executives prefer to keep audience information confidential. That information is quite valuable to them for planning a movie's advertising campaign, as well as mapping out the releases of future pictures and comparing one picture's performance against another's. And releasing it would inevitably lead to more questions from exhibitors and the press. Why is this movie doing so badly in Orlando? Why is that picture a hit in Denver?

Looking for answers to similar questions about *Fahrenheit 9/11,* I came across a source in the movie business who had access to the details of the film's box-office business, and of other releases' performances, as well. He provided me with an Excel spreadsheet of numbers—compiled by Nielsen EDI, a division of the famed Nielsen media measurement firm—which revealed a picture of *Fahrenheit 9/11*'s performance that bore almost no resemblance to Michael Moore's hype.

First, a few words about how such figures are gathered. Movie studios divide the nation into about 250 different zones called designated market areas, or DMAs. Some, like New York and Boston, are dominated by one city. Others, like Albuquerque/Santa Fe and Grand Rapids/Kalamazoo, are geographical areas that include more than one town. The markets were originally designed by ACNielsen, which uses them to measure national and local television audiences.

Movie analysts use the same geographic areas, but they do not mark those areas exactly as TV analysts do. West Palm Beach/Fort Pierce, Florida, for example, is the forty-ninth-largest television market but the thirty-first-largest movie market, meaning that people there tend to watch a lot of films. New York is the biggest television market but the second-largest film market, behind Los Angeles. San Francisco is the fifth-largest TV market but the third-largest movie market.

Also, most motion-picture grosses are measured on a North American basis, meaning they include ticket sales in both the United States and Canada. Toronto, for example, is not included in American television ratings but is the fifth-largest DMA for moviegoing.

One key measure studios apply to a picture's performance is whether it does better or worse than might be expected in any given DMA. They do that by calculating each DMA's share of the total North American box office. Los Angeles, for example, accounts for 8.32 percent of the box office for all films, New York for 7.78 percent, and San Francisco for 3.40 percent. If the San Francisco box office for a film accounts for more than 3.40 percent of a film's total gross, the film is said to have overperformed in San Francisco. If the city accounted for, say, 5.10 percent of a picture's North American gross, then the film would be said to have overperformed by 50 percent. Studios use those measurements to compare films with one another, and entire film genres with one another. Do action pictures do better in Philadelphia? Romantic comedies in St. Louis? That sort of thing.

Overall, *Fahrenheit 9/11* did extremely well in North America's top eight markets, according to the numbers compiled by Nielsen EDI. The film actually underperformed slightly in the largest market, Los Angeles, down just under 4 percent from the market's normal DMA share. (That was probably due to the presence of conservative Orange County, which makes up a significant part of the Los Angeles DMA.) But it overperformed in the next seven largest markets. In New York it overperformed by nearly 43 percent; *Fahrenheit 9/11* took in 11.12 percent of its total box office in that city alone. It did even better in San Francisco, overperforming by 73 percent. It did a little above normal business in Chicago, with an overperformance of about 11 percent, but a huge business in Toronto, overperforming by 79 percent there. It did okay in Philadelphia, outpacing the norm by about 5 percent; well in Boston, overperforming by 49 percent; and very well in Washington, D.C., overperforming by 62 percent. Those eight cities alone accounted for about 44 percent of *Fahrenheit 9/11*'s entire gross receipts (the cities' normal share of North American grosses would be about 33 percent), which means the movie got off to a very strong start in big, blue-state markets.

Fahrenheit 9/11 did well in several other places. In Seattle-Tacoma, it overperformed by 27 percent. In Montreal, it overperformed by almost 50 percent. In Vancouver, British Columbia, by 96 percent; Portland, Oregon, by 37 percent; Calgary, Alberta, by 31 percent; Ottawa, Ontario, by 68 percent; Austin, Texas, the college town and state capital, by 29 percent; Victoria, British Columbia, by 82 percent; Halifax, Nova Scotia, by 23 percent; Monterey, California, by 68 percent; Burlington, Vermont–Plattsburgh, New York, by 146 percent; and Saskatoon, Saskatchewan, by 50 percent.

Two things stand out from those numbers. One is that the picture overperformed only in blue states, and even then only in the most urban parts of those blue states. And the second is that it did very well in Canada. *Fahrenheit 9/11* consistently overperformed in Canadian cities; without that boffo business, the film's gross would have been significantly smaller than it was.

TABLE ONE

PREACHING TO THE CHOIR—AND TO CANADIANS:
WHERE *FAHRENHEIT 9/11* OVERPERFORMED
(Top 100 North American Markets)

MARKET	PERCENTAGE IT DIFFERED FROM EXPECTATIONS
New York, NY	+42.90
San Francisco/Oakland, CA	+73.20
Chicago, IL	+10.70
Toronto/Hamilton (Canada)	+79.00
Philadelphia, PA	+ 4.60
Boston, MA/Manchester, NH	+48.90
Washington, D.C./Hagerstown, MD	+61.90
Seattle/Tacoma, WA	+26.90
Denver, CO	+ 6.70
Montreal (Canada)	+49.60
Cleveland, OH	+ 4.90
Vancouver (Canada)	+96.00
Portland, OR	+36.70
Hartford/New Haven, CT	+19.40
Calgary/Lethbridge (Canada)	+31.30
Edmonton (Canada)	+ 9.40
Ottawa/Hull (Canada)	+67.80
Providence, RI/New Bedford, MA	+ 8.90
Austin, TX	+29.10
Albuquerque/Santa Fe, NM	+ 7.80
Victoria (Canada)	+82.10
Quebec City (Canada)	+ 2.80
Albany/Schenectady, NY	+33.30
Winnipeg/Brandon (Canada)	+15.60

MARKET	PERCENTAGE IT DIFFERED FROM EXPECTATIONS
Halifax (Canada)	+23.30
Madison, WI	+23.30
Monterey/Salinas, CA	+67.90
Kitchener (Canada)	+65.20
Portland/Auburn, ME	+31.80
London (Canada)	+45.50
Syracuse, NY	+19.00
Sudbury/Timmins/North Bay (Canada)	+30.00
Windsor (Canada)	+30.00
Springfield/Holyoke, MA	+30.00

That's the upside of the story. The downside revealed by the Nielsen EDI numbers is that *Fahrenheit 9/11*, far from being the runaway nationwide hit that Moore claimed, underperformed in dozens of markets throughout red states and, most important—as far as the presidential election was concerned—swing states.

Dallas/Fort Worth, the ninth-largest movie market, accounts for 2.07 percent of North American box office but made up just 1.21 percent of *Fahrenheit 9/11* box office, for an underperformance of nearly 42 percent. In Phoenix, the tenth-largest market, *Fahrenheit 9/11* underperformed by 29 percent. In Houston, ranked twelfth for movies, it underperformed by 38 percent. In Orlando, it underperformed by 38 percent; Tampa–St. Petersburg, by 41 percent; Salt Lake City, by 61 percent.

The list goes on for quite a while, as Table 2 reveals. In Las Vegas, *Fahrenheit 9/11* underperformed by 28 percent; Raleigh-Durham, by 40 percent; San Antonio, by 46 percent;

Norfolk, by 45 percent; Charlotte, by 41 percent; Nashville, by 41 percent; Fresno-Visalia, California, by 53 percent; Memphis (where *Time* magazine was so impressed by a few anti-Bush crowds), by 53 percent; Jacksonville, by 51 percent; Oklahoma City, by 52 percent; Greenville-Spartanburg, South Carolina, by 65 percent; Mobile, by 60 percent; Birmingham, by 51 percent; Flint–Saginaw–Bay City, Michigan—Michael Moore's home turf—by 31 percent; and El Paso, by 55 percent.

In Greensboro, North Carolina, where Moore said the film had been enthusiastically received, it underperformed by nearly 27 percent. And in Fayetteville and Tulsa, where Moore boasted that his movie had sold out, *Fahrenheit 9/11* underperformed by 41 percent and 50 percent, respectively.

TABLE TWO

NOT A "RED-STATE MOVIE":
WHERE *FAHRENHEIT 9/11* UNDERPERFORMED
(Top 100 North American Markets)

MARKET	PERCENTAGE IT DIFFERED FROM EXPECTATIONS
Los Angeles, CA	− 3.80
Dallas/Fort Worth, TX	−41.50
Phoenix, AZ	−28.90
Detroit, MI	−15.60
Houston, TX	−38.40
Atlanta, GA	−20.90
Miami/Fort Lauderdale, FL	− 2.40
San Diego, CA	− 2.60
Sacramento/Stockton/Modesto, CA	−19.30

MARKET	PERCENTAGE IT DIFFERED FROM EXPECTATIONS
Minneapolis/St. Paul, MN	− 1.40
Orlando/Daytona Beach, FL	−38.40
Tampa/St. Petersburg, FL	−40.70
Baltimore, MD	− 4.20
Salt Lake City, UT	−61.10
Las Vegas, NV	−28.20
Kansas City, MO	−20.50
St. Louis, MO	− 2.60
West Palm Beach/Fort Pierce, FL	− 8.50
Raleigh/Durham, NC	−40.30
San Antonio, TX	−45.50
Pittsburgh, PA	− 6.10
Norfolk/Portsmouth/Newport News, VA	−44.60
Charlotte, NC	−40.60
Milwaukee, WI	− 9.70
Columbus, OH	−17.50
Nashville, TN	−41.10
Grand Rapids/Kalamazoo, MI	−25.50
Cincinnati, OH	−15.10
New Orleans, LA	−39.10
Fresno/Visalia, CA	−53.30
Memphis, TN	−53.30
Jacksonville, FL	−51.10
Indianapolis, IN	−39.50
Oklahoma City, OK	−52.40
Greenville/Spartanburg, SC	−65.00
Buffalo, NY	−41.70
Birmingham, AL	−51.40
Mobile, AL/Pensacola, FL	−60.00

MARKET	PERCENTAGE IT DIFFERED FROM EXPECTATIONS
Harlingen/Weslaco/Brownsville/McAllen, TX	−76.50
Fort Myers/Naples, FL	−35.30
Louisville, KY	−18.20
Richmond/Petersburg, VA	−30.30
Flint/Saginaw/Bay City, MI	−31.30
El Paso, TX	−54.80
Omaha, NE	−58.10
Greensboro/High Point, NC	−26.70
Harrisburg/Lancaster, PA	−33.30
Tulsa, OK	−50.00
Colorado Springs/Pueblo, CO	−65.50
Rochester, NY	−10.30
Wilkes-Barre/Scranton, PA	−33.30
Dayton, OH	−33.30
Knoxville, TN	−48.10
Honolulu, HI	−38.50
Spokane, WA	−16.00
Little Rock/Pine Bluff, AR	−58.30
Waco/Temple/Bryan, TX	−66.70
Toledo, OH	−25.00
Lansing, MI	−12.50
Reno, NV	−25.00
Boise, ID	−40.90
Charleston, SC	−72.70
Lexington, KY	−25.00
Green Bay/Appleton, WI	−35.00
Anchorage, AK	−15.80

Despite Moore's PR campaign, the data, which the public did not see at the time, showed that *Fahrenheit 9/11* had a very limited appeal. Moore's claim that his documentary was a "red-state movie" was simply untrue, and all the articles based on its alleged national appeal were, in the end, just hype.

THE CASE THAT WASN'T

Fahrenheit 9/11's underperformance in so many red-state and swing-state areas had political consequences—most important, that the many allegations in the film, which Moore said amounted to a damning indictment of George W. Bush, never reached audiences that had the power to defeat the president at the polls. Usually billed as an antiwar film, *Fahrenheit 9/11* was in fact a grab bag of anti-Bush accusations. The film attacked the president's service in the Texas Air National Guard; it attacked his sale of stock in Harken Energy; it attacked his conduct during the 2000 Florida recount; it attacked his vacation habits; it attacked his immediate reaction to the September 11 strikes—those minutes he spent listening as students read the story "The Pet Goat" in a Florida classroom; it attacked his long-term reaction to the September 11 strikes; and, of course, it attacked the war in Iraq.

Some of Moore's accusations could not be proved one way or the other. Did the president go on vacation too much? Who was to say? But a number of others, including the most serious charges, were substantially debunked by the time the movie arrived in theaters. There was, for example, the notion that the United States went to war in Afghanistan not as part of a wide-ranging response to the terrorist attacks of September 11, but for the financial benefit of Texas oil interests, specifically Vice President Dick Cheney and disgraced former Enron chief Kenneth Lay. In the movie's narrative track, Moore suggested that the Afghan conflict was not, in fact, about terrorism. "Was the war in Afghanistan really about something else?" he asked.

> Perhaps the answer was in Houston, Texas. In 1997, while George W. Bush was governor of Texas, a delegation of Taliban leaders from Afghanistan flew to Houston to meet with Unocal executives to discuss the building of a pipeline through Afghanistan, bringing natural gas from the Caspian Sea. And who got a Caspian Sea drilling contract the same day Unocal signed the pipeline deal? A company headed by a man named Dick Cheney. Halliburton. . . . And who else stood to benefit from the pipeline? Bush's number one campaign contributor, Kenneth Lay, and the good people of Enron.

Moore wasn't making a new claim. Before *Fahrenheit 9/11,* the Afghan-pipeline scenario had bounced around among conspiracy theorists of the fringe Left for quite a while. But Moore gave the allegation its first exposure to a mass audience. And as is often the case with such matters, it began with a kernel of truth. In the mid-1990s, the Unocal Corporation, with the enthusiastic support of the Clinton administration, was indeed involved in bidding for a pipeline across Afghanistan. But a few years later, the difficulties of dealing with the Taliban and the economics of the oil industry made the project much less attractive, and in 1998 Unocal dropped the project. At the time, the Associated Press reported, "Unocal Corp. withdrew from a consortium planning to build a pipeline across Afghanistan, saying low oil prices and turmoil in the Central Asian nation have made the project too risky." By the time the Bush administration entered office, the project was dead, as far as Unocal was concerned. Moore's contention—perhaps the most incendiary in the entire movie and the one that seemed so convincing to Terry McAuliffe—had no basis in fact.

In a book, *The Official* Fahrenheit 9/11 *Reader,* released shortly after the movie's premiere, Moore offered "supporting evidence" for his claims. But that evidence, rather than backing up his assertions, served more to illustrate the conspiratorial mindset with which he approached the subject. Take the quote above. It is true, as Moore said, that George W. Bush was governor of Texas in 1997. And it is true that in 1997 a group of Taliban officials flew to Texas to meet with Unocal executives. They did not, however, meet with George W. Bush or his representatives, and the pipeline project had nothing to do with the governor. Moore had placed them all together in the same sentence as if they were somehow related, when they were not.

In addition, Halliburton, which was indeed headed by Dick Cheney, did announce a contract for work in the Caspian Sea, but it, too, was not related to the Afghan pipeline project. And Enron was not involved, either; the Unocal press release announcing the Afghan pipeline deal listed ten companies that were taking part, and neither Enron nor Halliburton was among them. On the other hand, Moore was correct in saying that Kenneth Lay was the president's top campaign contributor in 2000.

Through a mixture of truths, falsehoods, and misdirection, Moore made what must have seemed, to many audiences, a compelling case that George W. Bush went to war in Afghanistan to benefit his rich Texas supporters. It was the kind of argument that could be found throughout *Fahrenheit 9/11*. To give another example, *Newsweek*'s Michael Isikoff and Mark Hosenball examined what they called Moore's "eye-popping claim that Saudi Arabian interests 'have given' $1.4 billion to firms connected to the family and friends" of George W. Bush. The money, Moore implied, ensured that the president would not strike back hard at the Saudis for their role in abetting terrorism. But Isikoff and Hosenball reported that nearly all of the cash—$1.18 billion—came from a single contract the Saudi government awarded in the 1990s to an American company called BDM. At the time, BDM was owned by the Carlyle Group, the investment firm that included former president George H. W. Bush on one of its advisory boards. The problem with Moore's assertion, Isikoff and Hosenball concluded, was that the elder Bush joined the Carlyle Group's advisory board *after* the contract was awarded—and, in fact, *after* the Carlyle Group had sold BDM to another company. Moore's connection turned out to be no connection at all.

And then there was Moore's suggestion that the Bush administration cleared the way for members of Osama bin Laden's family to leave the United States in a rush in the days after 9/11, when others were not allowed to fly. "In the days following September 11, all commercial and private airline traffic was grounded," Moore said in the movie. The picture then cut to a newscaster saying, "The FAA has taken action to close all of the airports in the United States . . . even grounding the president's father. . . . Thousands of travelers were stranded, among them, Ricky Martin, due to perform at tonight's Latin Grammy awards."

"Not even Ricky Martin could fly," Moore said, resuming

the narration. "But really, who wanted to fly? No one, except the bin Ladens." The movie then cut, in classic Moore fashion, to music—Eric Burdon and the Animals singing, "We gotta get out of this place / If it's the last thing we ever do . . ."

The clip—along with an interview with Democratic Senator Byron Dorgan saying, "We had some airplanes authorized at the highest levels of our government to fly to pick up Osama bin Laden's family members and others from Saudi Arabia and transport them out of this country"—suggested that the White House broke the no-fly rule to let the bin Ladens leave. As it turned out—and as reported by the September 11 Commission—that simply did not happen. The bin Ladens did not fly until the ban had been lifted.

There remained the question, however, of whether American authorities adequately investigated the family members before allowing them to leave, and on that issue Moore had at least the beginning of a point. The questioning of the bin Ladens appears to have been cursory at best, and a number of authorities I discussed the issue with believed it would have been better to keep the family members in the United States long enough for investigators to find out everything they knew about their terrorist relative. Moore would have had a good point if he had relied on solid information to raise that question. But instead he placed a legitimate issue alongside a number of baseless ones, in the process discrediting the whole thing.

The same was true of his treatment of the Iraq war. Moore spent a significant amount of time telling the poignant story of Lila Lipscomb, a Michigan woman whose son, Michael Pedersen, was an Army sergeant killed in Iraq. In addition, *Fahrenheit 9/11* had never-before-seen video footage of U.S. troops fighting in Iraq, as well as interviews with servicemen who had served in Iraq and turned against the war. Together, those elements might have served as the core of a serious antiwar documentary, had Moore been serious.

Instead, Moore's idea of treating the war was to play an interview with Howard Lipscomb Sr., the husband of Lila Lipscomb, discussing Michael Pedersen's death. "I really feel sorry for the other families that is losing their kids as we speak," Lipscomb said plaintively. "And for what? I don't— That's the, I guess, sickening part. For what?" At that point, Moore cut to a clip from a promotional film for Halliburton. That was what passed for analysis in *Fahrenheit 9/11*.

MASTERS OF DISASTER

Moore knew his film would be criticized, knew that there would be questions about its spectacular and mostly unsubstantiated allegations. To deal with those questions—and to make them, in effect, part of the movie's promotional campaign—Moore hired Chris Lehane, a veteran of the Clinton White House damage control team, where he was known as one of the "masters of disaster." (Lehane also served as Al Gore's spokesman in the 2000 presidential campaign.) For *Fahrenheit 9/11*, Lehane spent a lot of time fielding reporters' questions, insisting that everything in the film was accurate. Months later, when it was all over—and after John Kerry had lost—I asked him whether he felt the effort had been successful.

"Absolutely," he told me. "There was a perceptible change in Bush's poll numbers when the movie came out. It dominated the national discussion around the campaign for a period of three or four or five weeks. Look at the issues discussed during the campaign. 'The Pet Goat,' the Saudis, finding bin Laden—all of those were put into the debate by *Fahrenheit 9/11*."

I asked Lehane about the whispers I had heard from some liberals in the weeks after the election, whispers to the effect that *Fahrenheit 9/11* did not in fact help Kerry and might in the end have helped Bush by inciting the Republican base to anger against Michael Moore. Nonsense, Lehane said. "That's an idea that is being propagated by the Right, because they realize that Michael Moore is one of the very few effective communicators on the Left. He scares them."

Lehane's comments reflected the baldly political strategy that lay behind the *Fahrenheit 9/11* campaign. Did it succeed? Of course it did; Bush's poll numbers went down, didn't they? "The Pet Goat" became a political issue, didn't it? Perhaps the ultimate indicator of the degree to which Moore inspired the anti-Bush mind came just days before the election, when Osama bin Laden himself released a video statement that seemed to reference *Fahrenheit 9/11*. "It appeared to [Bush] that a little girl's talk about her goat and its butting was more important than the planes and their butting of the skyscrapers," bin Laden said. "That gave us three times the required time to carry out the operations, thank God."

Moore seemed delighted by bin Laden's attention. "Hey, did you get the feeling that he had a bootleg of my movie?" Moore wrote proudly on his website. "Are there DVD players in those caves in Afghanistan?"

MICHAEL VS. MEL

On June 28, 2004, the first Monday after the release of *Fahrenheit 9/11*, the *New York Times* wrote that attendance for Moore's film "resembled nothing so much as the other surprise movie event of this year, the fervor ignited by Mel Gibson's movie about the Crucifixion, 'The Passion of the Christ.'" Both films had made a lot of money, the *Times* said, and both had "sailed to blockbuster status on a wave of media controversy and debate."

The comparison rested on little more than those superficial similarities. In fact, the telling point about the audiences for *Fahrenheit 9/11* and *The Passion of the Christ* was not that they were similar but that they were dramatically different from each other—and those differences revealed something important about the 2004 political season.

The anonymous source who gave me market-by-market analysis of *Fahrenheit 9/11*'s box office provided the same type of numbers for *The Passion*. The contrast between the two had caught his eye early on, and he wanted me to have a look. The story the numbers told was striking.

Start with the top DMAs. Unlike *Fahrenheit 9/11,* which did well, and sometimes very well, in most of the biggest cities, *The Passion* generally underperformed. It came in slightly below average in Los Angeles—but only slightly, down by about 8 percent from what one would normally expect. It underperformed a bit more significantly in New York, down nearly 11 percent. It did not do well in San Francisco, down 33 percent. It did reasonably well in Chicago, overperforming by nearly 6 percent. It was unpopular in Toronto, underperforming by 29 percent. It was basically even in Philadelphia, but underperformed by 30 percent in Boston and was down slightly, 4 percent, in

Washington, D.C. Those eight DMAs—which made up nearly 44 percent of *Fahrenheit 9/11*'s grosses—accounted for a little less than 29 percent of *The Passion*'s.

When one ventured outside the top eight markets, however, *The Passion* began performing impressively. The movie over-performed by nearly 16 percent in Dallas, 20 percent in Houston, and 23 percent in Atlanta. It was up 21 percent in Raleigh, 32 percent in Pittsburgh, 36 percent in Charlotte, 38 percent in Nashville, 22 percent in Grand Rapids, and 32 percent in Cincinnati. It overperformed by 26 percent in New Orleans, 24 percent in Jacksonville, 33 percent in Indianapolis, 33 percent in Oklahoma City, 28 percent in Wichita, 35 percent in Green Bay, 32 percent in Bakersfield, 32 percent in Fort Myers, and 22 percent in Flint, which had turned in a well-below-average per-formance for hometown son Michael Moore.

The performances in other areas were even stronger. *The Passion* overperformed by 57 percent in Greensboro, 43 percent in Harrisburg, 52 percent in Dayton, 48 percent in Knoxville, 50 percent in Toledo, 65 percent in Greenville-Spartanburg, 79 percent in Little Rock, 80 percent in Birmingham, 71 percent in Chattanooga, 44 percent in Springfield, Missouri, 67 percent in Charleston, West Virginia, 50 percent in Sioux Falls, 85 percent in Jackson, Mississippi, and 63 percent in Beaumont, Texas.

The Passion did fail to perform up to normal expectations in some places outside the top eight markets. For instance, it underperformed by 22 percent in Seattle; 27 percent in the college town of Madison, Wisconsin; 39 percent in Honolulu; 32 percent in Portland, Maine; 21 percent in Eugene, Oregon; and 46 percent in Burlington, Vermont. And it underper-formed significantly in Canada—by 54 percent in Montreal, 34 percent in Vancouver, 27 percent in Calgary, 28 percent in

Edmonton, 46 percent in Ottawa, 67 percent in Quebec City, and 40 percent in Halifax.

Taken as a whole, it was precisely the opposite of *Fahrenheit 9/11*'s performance. But there was more to it than that. One could chart the films' performances on a map of the United States, coloring the areas where *The Passion* overperformed in, say, red, and where *Fahrenheit 9/11* overperformed in, say, blue, and come up with a map that looked strikingly similar to the red-blue breakdown in the 2004 presidential contest. In retrospect, the pictures turned out to be uncannily accurate indicators of how Americans voted for president.

TABLE THREE

A GUIDE TO RED AND BLUE AMERICA: HOW *THE PASSION OF THE CHRIST* AND *FAHRENHEIT 9/11* PERFORMED IN SELECT CITIES

	THE PASSION OF THE CHRIST	FAHRENHEIT 9/11
New York, NY	−10.90	+42.90
San Francisco/Oakland, CA	−32.90	+73.20
Toronto/Hamilton (Canada)	−29.40	+79.00
Boston, MA/Manchester, NH	−29.80	+48.90
Washington, D.C./Hagerstown, MD	− 4.00	+61.90
Seattle/Tacoma, WA	−21.60	+26.90
Denver, CO	−11.40	+ 6.70
Montreal (Canada)	−53.50	+49.60
Portland, OR	−11.10	+36.70
Hartford/New Haven, CT	− 9.00	+19.40

	THE PASSION OF THE CHRIST	FAHRENHEIT 9/11
Austin, TX	−16.40	+29.10
Albany/Schenectady, NY	−21.20	+33.30
Madison, WI	−26.70	+23.30
Monterey/Salinas, CA	−17.90	+67.90
Portland/Auburn, ME	−31.80	+31.80
Dallas/Fort Worth, TX	+15.50	−41.50
Houston, TX	+19.80	−38.40
Atlanta, GA	+23.30	−20.90
Tampa/St. Petersburg, FL	+13.60	−40.70
Raleigh/Durham, NC	+20.90	−40.30
San Antonio, TX	+16.70	−45.50
Norfolk/Portsmouth/		
Newport News, VA	+13.80	−44.60
Charlotte, NC	+35.90	−40.60
Nashville, TN	+37.50	−41.10
Cincinnati, OH	+32.10	−15.10
New Orleans, LA	+26.10	−39.10
Jacksonville, FL	+24.40	−51.10
Indianapolis, IN	+32.60	−39.50
Oklahoma City, OK	+33.30	−52.40
Greenville-Spartanburg, SC	+65.00	−65.00
Birmingham, AL	+80.00	−51.40
Flint/Saginaw/Bay City, MI	+21.90	−31.30
El Paso, TX	+22.60	−54.80
Greensboro/High Point, NC	+56.70	−26.70
Tulsa, OK	+23.30	−50.00

What does that mean? Certainly the numbers seem to support the idea that values, in some sense, did indeed play a significant role in the presidential election. But not necessarily religious values; the resentment many people feel toward Hollywood elites might also have played an important role. Audiences knew not only that *The Passion* was a religious film but also that it was, in effect, an anti-Hollywood film; Gibson had made it on his own, without studio support. The movie was not overtly political, but everyone knew it was a statement that the movie industry as a whole—the kind one sees on display on Oscar night—would not have made. On the other hand, *Fahrenheit 9/11,* while not a big-studio production—indeed, Moore had gotten a lot of publicity when Disney declined to distribute it—was embraced by Hollywood and Hollywood celebrities. It was as overtly political as one could possibly imagine, and especially when it won the seal of approval of the Democratic Party, along with the Palme d'Or, the highest award at France's Cannes Film Festival, it seemed to connect Democrats to the worst excesses of the movie industry and international elites.

Audiences voted with their ticket-buying dollars. As of December 31, 2004, *The Passion* grossed $370,274,604 and *Fahrenheit 9/11* grossed $119,194,771. How many people was that? Well, in 2004, the nationwide estimated average ticket price for a movie was $6.14. Most of Moore's audience came in higher-priced urban areas, while much of Gibson's came in somewhat lower-priced suburban areas. Still, if one figures using the average price, *The Passion* sold about 60.3 million tickets, while *Fahrenheit 9/11* sold about 19.4 million. (These figures do not take into account the number of people who saw the movies more than once, but they are useful in a comparative sense.)

The Nielsen EDI numbers suggest that Moore, like the Democratic Party, ceded the South and large portions of the West and Midwest before voting (or moviegoing) even began. And unfortunately for the Democratic Party, Canadians did not have a vote, as they did in *Fahrenheit 9/11*'s North American gross totals. Put it all together and Moore's appeal, like the Democrats', was just too narrow to win the contest, either at the box office or the polls.

A CALL TO ARMS

At the Washington premiere of *Fahrenheit 9/11* in June, Moore told the audience that he used to live in Cleveland Park—just a few blocks away from where the premiere was taking place—back when he was editing his first movie, *Roger & Me*. Moore said that he and his wife, Kathleen, would often walk to the Uptown to see movies. One night, the theater hosted the premiere of *Dick Tracy,* starring Warren Beatty, and Moore and Kathleen came by to join the crowd. "They had the big red carpet out, and there was Warren Beatty and Madonna and all the stars of the film, and we stood on the outer edge of the carpet, past the police line, watching it and thinking how cool it was that there was a Hollywood premiere at the Uptown Theatre, our little neighborhood theater," Moore recalled. "So to come here tonight, and be able to walk that red carpet and see the crowd that was out there cheering us on, on the other side of the police line, I was so moved by that."

The story had a classic Hollywood look-at-me-now quality. And there was no doubt that Moore was the star that June night, with the red carpet and fans and limousines and security men talking into their cuff links. But at that moment, speaking to the audience about to see his movie, Moore seemed to realize that his personal story of success, while genuinely impressive, didn't quite fit the bigger story he was trying to sell. So he made a midcourse correction.

"I was so moved by that," he said, "and just felt that, uh, it's not just Kathleen and myself coming down this carpet. All of America is coming down this carpet, and I think we'll see that in a few months, so thank you very much for being here tonight."

That was more like it. Indeed, every time he spoke, Moore turned his pitch for *Fahrenheit 9/11* into a political call to arms. "I'm encouraging everyone on my website to take one weekend in October and drive to a swing state," he said a couple of days later at "Turn Up the Heat: A National Town Meeting on *Fahrenheit 9/11.*" "I'm encouraging people to pack up the family, get in the car, take one weekend in October, and show up at the local headquarters to volunteer." In the last weeks of the campaign, he set off on a sixty-city "Slacker Uprising" tour of college campuses around the swing states, trying to build on the momentum—such as it was—of his movie.

With each speech, Moore seemed to imagine that he was raising an army of angry Americans to vote against George W. Bush. But all he had really done was make a successful film. That was certainly an accomplishment in his line of work, but he had wanted more. With his movie, Moore had wanted to change the direction of American politics. It was a big idea, and an audacious one. And in the end, he never came close.

CHAPTER FIVE

Unwatched

Robert Greenwald and the Guerrilla Documentary

During the first months of 2004, Ellen Brodsky never, ever missed an episode of *The FOX Report with Shepard Smith.* Monday through Friday, every day, every week, Brodsky was in front of the television set at her home in New Mexico, tuned to the Fox News Channel, studying every word that came out of Smith's mouth. She didn't watch because she liked the anchorman, or Fox, or even television news. Just the opposite. Brodsky, a librarian, writer, and fan of the liberal radio network Air America, kept a close eye on Smith, and Fox, to help prove that the news network was just as unfair and just as unbalanced as her fellow Democrats believed it was.

The idea of watching Fox News began in late 2003, when MoveOn—Brodsky is a member—started a group called Fox Watch and asked for volunteers to monitor the network. The plan was to chart the "alarming disintegration of journalistic standards" that Fox supposedly represented. Brodsky signed up, but for various reasons never got around to doing much work. The same could be said of the entire MoveOn campaign; Fox Watch got off to a noisy start, but never amounted to much.

Then came Robert Greenwald. A veteran Hollywood producer and director, Greenwald had finished a film called *Uncovered*, which billed itself as "the whole truth" about the war in Iraq, and was looking for another project. He wanted to do something on Fox—it would be titled *Outfoxed: Rupert Murdoch's War on Journalism*—in which he would expose the network as not simply a right-wing organization but also a megaphone for Republican Party talking points. Greenwald drew up what amounted to a bill of indictment against Fox and began looking for people to watch the network for examples that would prove the points he wanted to make. He went to MoveOn, which had helped fund *Uncovered;* MoveOn then got in touch with Brodsky and a few other people from the Fox Watch project.

"They said that a producer was looking for volunteers to do a documentary on Fox News," Brodsky told me. "That sounded right up my alley." She was assigned the Smith show and began taping the program every day. Months later, as she looked back, she told me she was amazed by what she saw. "Before I started, I thought Fox was going to be a conservative-leaning version of CNN," Brodsky said. "I had just no idea how biased it was. That just shocked me all the way through."

Brodsky didn't know any of her fellow Fox monitors—there were eight in all, scattered around the country, taping *The O'Reilly Factor* and *Hannity & Colmes* and other Fox programs. But as it turned out, the volunteers Greenwald recruited were a very compatible group, in large part because they were remarkably alike. All were women. All were white. All were between the ages of forty-five and sixty-three. All were liberals, and all were determined to help defeat George W. Bush in 2004. Several were single, and although they lived far apart from one another, a number had their roots in the bluest areas of the Northeast. And of course, all were appalled by Fox. If Greenwald was looking for a cross section of Americans to rise up against the network, he did not succeed; a less diverse group could hardly be imagined.

Greenwald gave the women a list of eight or nine categories of reporting in which he was interested. For example, he wanted them to watch for instances of what he saw as anti-Kerry bias, pro-Bush bias, fearmongering about terrorism, and for reports that featured good news about the war in Iraq—Greenwald called those Fox's "Happy Iraq" moments. By structuring the project in that way, he signaled to the team—and ultimately to the audience—that the resulting film would be not so much an examination of Fox's programming as an illustration of the points Greenwald wanted to make about Fox's programming. While there was nothing intrinsically wrong with that—many documentaries started with a strong point of view—Greenwald's approach tended to limit the appeal of his film to people who shared that point of view. And that, in turn, undermined his desire, which he often spoke about in public, to use the film to convert those who were undecided about Fox, and about the issue of media bias in general.

When it was finished, *Outfoxed* became the best-known of a new type of film, the so-called guerrilla documentary, that came to the fore in the 2004 presidential race. In an admiring *New York Times Magazine* profile, Greenwald was praised for coming up with a new weapon in the political wars, "creating timely political films on short schedules and small budgets and then promoting and selling them on DVD through partnerships with grass-roots political organizations like MoveOn.org." The idea—developed mainly by Greenwald, Wes Boyd of MoveOn, and John Podesta, who ran the new liberal think tank the Center for American Progress—was to use film, instead of dry policy tomes or wonkish seminars, to reach people who might be persuaded to vote against Bush but who could not be reached by the old methods.

The plan had its first test in the 2004 election. In retrospect, the measure of its failure is not that it didn't single-handedly elect John Kerry—nobody expected it to do that—but that, by any measure, "guerrilla" filmmaking reached a tiny, tiny audience. If *Fahrenheit 9/11,* which made more money than any other documentary in history—279 times the gross theatrical receipts of *Outfoxed*—could not extend its reach beyond the realm of true believers, that was doubly true, perhaps 279 times as true, of Greenwald's movies. In the end, the devotees of *Outfoxed* and of Greenwald's other pictures were no more diverse than the people who researched and produced them, ensuring that the films had little impact on politics as a whole.

UNCOVERED

Greenwald, fifty-nine, has been a Hollywood fixture, although never a leading light, for three decades. He directed such pictures as the 1978 television movie *Katie: Portrait of a Centerfold,* the 1979 theatrical release *Flatbed Annie & Sweetiepie: Lady Truckers* (featuring an appearance by then–First Brother Billy Carter), the 1984 TV movie *The Burning Bed,* and the 1995 TV miniseries *A Woman of Independent Means.* In all, he served as director, producer, or executive producer of more than sixty pictures, most of them for television.

Greenwald has long been a supporter of left-leaning political groups. In the 1980s, according to Federal Election Commission records, he contributed to an antinuclear organization called Freeze Voter '84, to the Hollywood Women's Political Committee, and to the Jesse Jackson for President campaign, among others. In the 1990s and after, he supported Vermont socialist congressman Bernie Sanders and Ohio's Dennis Kucinich, as well as groups like Progressive Majority.

Greenwald began the 2004 presidential race supporting former Vermont governor Howard Dean. He gave Dean the maximum allowable $2,000 contribution in June 2003, but in November of that year—before Dean's legendary meltdown—Greenwald gave $2,000 to retired general Wesley Clark. He did not seem to be a fan of John Kerry; only in late March 2004, after Kerry had secured the party nomination, did Greenwald give a less-than-maximum $1,000 contribution to Kerry for President. Greenwald's largest contribution, $5,000, went to PunkVoter, a 527 group organized by punk rock musicians dedicated to "taking an in-your-face attitude in order to rebel against the problems of our society" (according to the group's mission statement). In particular, Greenwald backed Fat Mike, the politically active singer of the group NOFX, which helped produce a series of Rock Against Bush CDs.

Greenwald's film work became political, too. Angered by the outcome of the 2000 Florida recount, in 2002 he produced *Unprecedented: The 2000 Presidential Election,* a short (fifty-minute) documentary billed as a "riveting story about . . . the undermining of democracy in America." It was not released in theaters, but it played in a number of film festivals and was given a Washington premiere by the liberal activist group People for the American Way Foundation. Later in 2002, Greenwald joined with his friend and fellow liberal activist Mike Farrell, the actor, to form the antiwar group Artists United to Win Without War. In December of that year, the two men appeared at the Hollywood celebrity hangout Les Deux Cafe to read a manifesto urging the disarming of Saddam Hussein "through legal diplomatic means." The statement was signed by a long list of entertainment figures, including Ed Asner, Kim Basinger, Ed Begley Jr., Jackson Browne, Jill Clayburgh, David Duchovny, Mia Farrow, Laurence Fishburne, Janeane Garofalo, Danny Glover, Elliott Gould, Ethan Hawke, Helen Hunt, Angelica Huston, Samuel L. Jackson, Jessica Lange, Téa Leoni, Bonnie Raitt, Carl Reiner, Tim Robbins, Susan Sarandon, Martin Sheen, Lily Tomlin, Alfre Woodard, and Peter Yarrow.

Greenwald's next film project, *Uncovered: The Whole Truth About the Iraq War,* grew out of his antiwar activism. (Later, he would make yet another movie on a related subject, the issue of the Patriot Act and civil rights, titled *Unconstitutional,* which he called the third part of his "Un- trilogy.") Produced in conjunction with MoveOn, the Nation Institute, the Center for American Progress, and the left-wing websites AlterNet and BuzzFlash, *Uncovered* featured a number of high-profile critics of the Bush administration accusing the president of lying about weapons of mass destruction during the run-up to the Iraq war.

During production, John Podesta, who was working on plans for his new think tank, heard about the project and offered to help. He thought a film like *Uncovered* might fit into his plan to diversify the ways in which the liberal message was sold to the public. "I always had a vision that a lot of people don't get their political information through traditional vehicles," Podesta told me just days before the election, "that working with cultural products like film, plays, cartoons, humor—I think we always had a sense that in order to deeply penetrate the public consciousness on policy stuff, you needed to experiment with different vehicles than the *Washington Post* and *New York Times* editorial pages." *Uncovered* might be such a vehicle.

Podesta gave Greenwald some money and research assistance. Greenwald supplied the anger. "Like most good, or many good, films, this started with pure unadulterated rage," the director said of his movie. But Greenwald said he tried hard to keep his "very strong, very passionate personal feelings" under control as he made the picture. And indeed, the finished *Uncovered* did not look like an angry film; its tone, especially when compared with that of *Fahrenheit 9/11,* was noticeably quiet. Nevertheless, its maker's fury came through in another way, not in its volume level but in its relentless exclusion of points of view that disagreed with Greenwald's. *Uncovered* treated debates over pre-war intelligence as if they were a conflict between one side telling an unadulterated lie and the other side telling the unadulterated truth. George W. Bush, of course, was the liar-in-chief.

For example, it is generally agreed that for years before the war there existed a bipartisan consensus that Iraq had weapons of mass destruction. Officials of the Clinton administration believed that, said so publicly, and took various actions based on that belief. The United Nations took actions based on that belief. The Bush administration took actions based on that belief. And yet one could search *Uncovered* in vain for any mention of the name "Clinton" or "Gore" or any substantive reference to the administration that preceded Bush's, or what its official position on Iraq was.

Even when Greenwald did engage an opposing view—for example, the idea that there were ties between Iraq and al Qaeda—he engaged it only enough to knock it down. "The ties with al Qaeda were just a scare tactic," former CIA analyst Ray McGovern said in the film. McGovern, who was so angry at Bush administration policies that he helped found a group called Veteran Intelligence Professionals for Sanity and wrote a long list of anti-Bush articles for the left-wing website CounterPunch, told Greenwald that the "scare tactic" of linking Iraq to al Qaeda was "a very successful and very deliberate and very unethical and immoral operation on the part of the PR people of this administration." Likewise, Richard Clarke, the former White House counterterrorism chief, told Greenwald's camera that his former bosses "wanted to believe that there was a connection, but the CIA was sitting there, the FBI was sitting there, I was sitting there, saying, 'We've looked at this issue for years, there's just no connection.'" Other former officials told Greenwald much the same thing.

Uncovered accepted their testimony unquestioningly. The problem with that was not that Greenwald's witnesses were entirely wrong; indeed, when they said there was no evidence that Saddam Hussein played a role in the September 11 attacks, they were correct. The problem was that Greenwald, in using their sound bites to present his point of view, ignored a significant body of evidence suggesting other, meaningful ties between Iraq and al Qaeda.

One source of that evidence was the September 11 Commission report, released in July 2004, after Greenwald finished an early version of the film but before he added new material to it for theatrical release. The report told how Osama bin Laden, who left Sudan for Afghanistan in 1996, was by the next year unsure that his new hosts, the Taliban, would be a reliable ally. Looking for an escape route, if that became necessary, bin Laden made overtures to Saddam Hussein. Hussein, who was at the time eager to improve relations with Saudi Arabia, rebuffed bin Laden. But in 1998, the Commission reported, the situation was reversed, and Saddam made overtures to bin Laden, going so far as to offer the terrorist leader safe haven in Iraq:

> In March 1998, after bin Laden's public *fatwa* against the United States, two al Qaeda members reportedly went to Iraq to meet with Iraqi intelligence. In July, an Iraqi delegation traveled to Afghanistan to meet first with the Taliban and then with bin Laden. Sources reported that one, or perhaps both, of these meetings was apparently arranged through bin Laden's Egyptian deputy, Zawahiri, who had ties of his own to the Iraqis. In 1998, Iraq was under intensifying U.S. pressure, which culminated in a series of large air attacks in December. . . . Similar meetings between Iraqi officials and bin Laden or his aides may have occurred in 1999 during a period of some reported strains with the Taliban. According to the reporting, Iraqi officials offered bin Laden a safe haven in Iraq. Bin Laden declined, apparently judging that his circumstances in Afghanistan remained more favorable than the Iraqi alternative. The reports describe friendly contacts and indicate some common themes in both sides' hatred of the United States.

There was more. The September 11 Commission also reported that one of Greenwald's star witnesses, Richard Clarke himself, had been quite concerned about the Iraq–al Qaeda connection back when he was in the White House. In February 1999, when the CIA proposed U-2 surveillance missions over Afghanistan, Clarke worried that the flights might spook bin Laden into leaving Afghanistan. "Clarke was nervous about such a mission," the report said,

> because he continued to fear that bin Laden might leave for someplace less accessible. He wrote Deputy National Security Advisor Donald Kerrick that one reliable source reported bin Laden's having met with Iraqi officials, who "may have offered him asylum." Other intelligence sources said that some Taliban leaders, though not Mullah Omar, had urged bin Laden to go to Iraq. If bin Laden actually moved to Iraq, wrote Clarke, his network would be at Saddam Hussein's service, and it would be "virtually impossible" to find him. Better to get bin Laden in Afghanistan, Clarke declared. [National Security Advisor Sandy] Berger suggested sending one U-2 flight, but Clarke opposed even this. It would require Pakistani approval, he wrote; and "Pak[istan's] intel[ligence service] is in bed with" bin Laden and would warn him that the United States was getting ready for a bombing campaign: "Armed with that knowledge [Clarke wrote], old wily Usama will likely boogie to Baghdad." Though told also by Bruce Riedel of the NSC staff that Saddam Hussein wanted bin Laden in Baghdad, Berger conditionally authorized a single U-2 flight.

That flight never occurred, and bin Laden was not tipped off. None of that is definitive proof of what the Commission called an "operational" relationship between Saddam and al Qaeda, but it did suggest that Greenwald's portrayal of the issue in *Uncovered* was so simplistic that it did not approach the "whole truth" about the subject. And while some of Greenwald's witnesses were legitimate critics of the war, he also relied on a sort of rogues' gallery of freelance Bush-bashers, including former ambassador Joseph Wilson, former UN weapons inspector Scott Ritter, and former Nixon White House counsel John Dean. They might have given the film some celebrity appeal and credibility in the MoveOn/BuzzFlash world, but the larger effect of their inclusion was to pigeonhole *Uncovered* as the work of one small faction of the anti-Bush Left.

That was the substance. But perhaps just as striking was the picture's style, which could only be described as sedate. That wasn't an accident. Greenwald and his team consciously saw themselves as doing serious research, quite apart from the rabble-rousing of Michael Moore. "When we started *Uncovered*, we were so conscious that everyone would try to rip the film to shreds, if anybody saw it," Jim Gilliam, a former dot-com executive who handled much of the research for *Uncovered*, told me. For that reason, Gilliam explained, Greenwald's team compiled mountains of research material. "Not to disparage Michael Moore, but I think he does something a little bit different," Gilliam continued. "He calls it the larger truth, but he's looking for something more entertaining. He is kind of throwing all these things up and saying, 'Hmmmm, doesn't it make you wonder?' We felt like we were documenting something. . . . Reviews have said that *Uncovered* is a legal brief. We approached it in that way. It wasn't sort of meant to entertain."

And it didn't. But the legal-brief approach substantially

undermined the notion that film was a popular and naturally accessible vehicle for political organizing. Put simply, boring people was not what John Podesta wanted to do. And yet that is what *Uncovered* had done, at least as far as a wide audience was concerned.

Nevertheless, Podesta's new group embraced the picture, which premiered in November 2003 at the opening party for the Center for American Progress. It was not an entirely smooth event. When the lights went down in the screening room, the video opening of *Uncovered* came on screen with no sound. Seconds, and then minutes, went by; still no sound. The crowd began to talk among themselves. Finally, out of the darkness, Al Franken's voice boomed. "I don't like it so far," he said, as the audience broke into laughter. As the delay stretched on, Podesta got up to make a joke about the glitch being the result of Bush White House interference. Franken had a different idea. "I actually think this is proof that the Center doesn't have its shit together," he said, to more laughter. After a bit more riffing, *Uncovered* was finally unveiled.

After the screening, Greenwald talked about using "an alternative distribution mechanism" to reach audiences, by which he meant MoveOn, AlterNet, BuzzFlash, and other venues. True to the plan, *Uncovered* got its biggest boost a month later, on December 7, when MoveOn held a nationwide series of 2,700 "house parties" to show the film. "Clearly, *Uncovered* is becoming the hot video product bolstering the growing 'regime change movement,'" reported AlterNet. "If there are 20 people at an average party, this means there will be more than 54,000 people watching *Uncovered* at the same time on 'opening night.' That's quite an accomplishment; but still, it's only the beginning; those who see the film may show it to their family and friends in a sophisticated, Internet-facilitated example of 'viral' marketing."

At least that was the plan. But who actually watched *Uncovered*? On the MoveOn website, house-party hosts described their gatherings for those who might want to attend. While some listings were just name-and-address notices, others went into some detail, and the events they described did not suggest much political or cultural diversity. "We will meet at 5pm to start mingling, drinking, shmokin', and enjoying vegan treats," read a notice for one house party in Oakland, California. "At 5:30 pm PST we'll join the huge cross-country conference call featuring director Robert Greenwald. . . . Afterwards, we'll hang, imbibe as we feel like it, and continue to discuss what a disaster W's policies are for the U.S. and the world and how we can best one-term him like his father."

"Why come to my house?" read another notice. "Because I'm a Kucinich fan and because we HAVE to get Bush out of the White House while we still have a country left." Yet another notice began, "Joyful gathering of Dean supporters." And one more read, "UNCOVERED screening and vegan dessert party. Non smoking household (no, not even on the front porch) with 3 friendly, trained, but furry indoor dogs. Guests must like and respect dogs."

It was, true to Greenwald's vision, an alternative distribution system. But Greenwald, of course, wanted more people to see the film. After the house parties, he added new material to the original version of *Uncovered*, making it long enough for theatrical release, and in August 2004, it went into a small number of theaters. In all, it did a minuscule $233,554 in box office, which, at the national average ticket price of $6.14, means that fewer than 39,000 people saw *Uncovered* in the traditional way.

A look at where the film played, using the same type of data described in the previous chapter's discussion of *Fahrenheit 9/11,* shows that *Uncovered* did well—a relative term—in ten big markets: Los Angeles; New York; San Francisco; San Diego; Washington, D.C.; Chicago; Boston; Detroit; Baltimore; and Minneapolis. Together, they accounted for 79 percent of the picture's gross receipts. Proportionately, it did best in San Francisco, exceeding the expected gross by 315 percent. It also did particularly well in Monterey, California, overperforming by 646 percent.

On the other side, *Uncovered* did poorly in Atlanta, where it underperformed by 76 percent. It underperformed by 67 percent in Cleveland, 82 percent in Dallas, 70 percent in Houston, 55 percent in Miami, and 54 percent in West Palm Beach. Given the size of *Uncovered*'s total business, those percentages translated into terribly small numbers. The film grossed $941 in Atlanta, $839 in Dallas, $776 in Cleveland, and $743 in West Palm Beach.

Uncovered sold about 100,000 copies on DVD; Greenwald priced it at a low $9.95 to allow the maximum number of people to see it (he also donated several thousand DVDs to Fat Mike, of NOFX, to hand out at anti-Bush concerts). Still, when one adds everything together—the screenings, the MoveOn parties, theaters, and DVD—it seems likely that the picture was seen by less than one million people. In some businesses, that would qualify as a big success—if one million people pay to see a low-budget documentary, or one million people buy a book, the creators make a good deal of money. But *Uncovered* was aiming to change the political climate and influence the presidential race in a land of 120 million voters. In that sense, speaking to a small fraction of one party's hardiest followers was not exactly a model of political outreach.

Nevertheless, Greenwald was hailed as the pioneer of a new type of political activism. After *Uncovered's* "grass-roots success," the *New York Times* reported, "some in the entertainment industry argue that the collaboration between Greenwald and his political partners promises a new paradigm." Flush with that "success," Greenwald quickly moved to his next guerrilla action.

OUTFOXED

After the Washington premiere of *Uncovered*, Podesta gave Greenwald a ride to Dulles Airport. The men began to talk about the media, and about the Fox News Channel in particular. "We were just comparing notes about, 'Okay, now what?'" Podesta told me, "and I think that's actually where *Outfoxed* got hatched." Greenwald said later that he and Podesta, and Wes Boyd of MoveOn, "all agreed that really the one to do was on the media, with the focus on Fox News. Unless you're able to change the media, you'll never be able to get the social changes you want in the country."

So the next film would be about Fox. But in what way? Greenwald knew ahead of time the conclusion he wanted his movie to reach: Fox was not only a conservative network but a Republican network, consistently advancing the Bush White House's agenda. What he needed was a vehicle to tell the story. He decided to set up a seven-day-a-week Fox-monitoring program to find clips to make his points. But who, at least who among those who shared Greenwald's view of Fox, would want to watch Fox all day, every day? That was when Green-wald turned to MoveOn's Fox Watch group.

The women who volunteered—Ellen in New Mexico, Christina in California, Deborah in Pennsylvania, Nancy in Maine, Judy in Michigan, Melanie in Colorado, Chris in Mis-souri, and Eleanor in Tennessee—were each assigned a pro-gram to watch every day. Greenwald gave them the list of categories of clips—anti-Kerry, pro-Bush, Happy Iraq—that he wanted them to find. When they came across something that might fit the bill, they were to write it down and e-mail it to Greenwald. "We look forward to making some waves and kicking some butt with this," he told them during an early conference call.

At his production facility in Los Angeles, Greenwald set up a system to record Fox on DVD twenty-four hours a day, seven days a week. When one of the monitors sent in an example of the kind of reporting that Greenwald wanted, the staff would then search for that specific clip on the hundreds of DVDs of recorded Fox programming. "I know that there's a clip here that's showing an example of fearmongering that happened on February 12 at 9:00 A.M.," an assistant editor explained as she searched for the right DVD. "So I have to come over here and find that disk among these many."

The women—they called themselves the Newshounds—found the watching tough going. "After five months of it, my anger level went through the roof," Christina said during one conference call with Greenwald. "I began to not be able to sleep. It made me very upset and nervous." Nancy was also angry. "I was absolutely appalled at the lies, the misinforma-tion that passes for knowledge because some talking head on television says it," she said. And Judy was amazed at the partisanship she detected. "The same themes kept coming up," she said. "All Republicans, or right-wing radical wackos, come off looking like accommodating, reasonable, positive people, and anyone who disagrees comes off looking negative."

After a few months, the Newshounds had given Greenwald hundreds of examples of what they believed was right-wing bias at Fox. They could have sent Greenwald other clips that suggested a more complex picture—for example, Brodsky told me that in her view Shepard Smith was "not a screamer" and that he "doesn't put in a lot of his opinions; it's hard to know what he really thinks"—but Greenwald had not asked for that. So Greenwald got what he wanted.

The film began with a still photo of Michael Corleone in *The Godfather: Part II.* A voice—that of Robert McChesney, a University of Illinois professor who has crusaded against media consolidation—described a scene from the movie in which the gangster Hyman Roth is meeting with Corleone and other crime figures, dividing up business in prerevolutionary Cuba. It is Roth's birthday, and he is cutting a cake with the outline of Cuba in the icing. "And while Hyman Roth is doing this he says, 'Isn't it great to be in a country with a government that respects private enterprise?'" McChesney recounted. "And that's how media policies have been done in the United States for the past fifty years, and it's increasing in the past twenty years. Extraordinarily powerful lobbyists duke it out behind closed doors for the biggest slice of the cake. The public knows nothing about it, it doesn't participate."

And with that, *Outfoxed* began on an inaccurate note. McChesney's memory was faulty; in the scene he described, Hyman Roth said nothing about private enterprise. Instead, Roth told the group that "this kind of government"—the

Cuban government of dictator Fulgencio Batista—"knows how to help business, to encourage it," without the interference of "the goddamn Justice Department and the FBI." Roth, for whom the word "business" referred to what others know as "crime," never mentioned private enterprise.

From there, *Outfoxed* cut to Rupert Murdoch, head of News Corporation, which owns Fox. Commentators ranging from McChesney to Jeff Cohen, founder of the left-wing group Fairness and Accuracy in Reporting, to David Brock, the former self-professed "right-wing hit man" turned left-wing media watchdog, to left-wing media critic Eric Alterman, to left-wing media critic James Wolcott, to Al Franken all commented on the one-sidedness of Fox.

The film also included a number of people who told firsthand stories of Fox's alleged bias. But many of these supposed insiders had only tenuous connections to Fox and contributed little to the argument Greenwald tried to make. For example, there was a former music supervisor for the network who had written the theme for the "Fox News Alert"; he complained that, in time, Fox came to use the alert graphic and music for less-than-urgent news. There were also two former employees of Fox's local station in Washington, D.C., WTTG-TV, who had never worked for the Fox News Channel and had no personal knowledge of how it operated.

Even some of those who had worked inside Fox News didn't have much to offer. There was a former Fox military consultant who said, alarmingly, "The Christian fundamentalist movement believes in, 'We're right, you're wrong, no matter what,' and I saw a lot of that at Fox," without mentioning that he had left the network quickly after the *New York Times* reported that he had embellished his military credentials. There was a producer who left Fox and later joined Rock Against Bush events. And there was a former employee whose indictment of Fox was, "If you don't go along with the mindset of the hierarchy in New York, if you challenge them on their attitudes about things, you're history"—as if that could not possibly be true at other news organizations.

All in all, it was not a terribly impressive lineup. More serious was a succession of quotations from internal Fox memos written by the network's top news executive, John Moody, that purported to show Moody directing his staff to tilt Fox's coverage to the right. For example, one memo concerned a speech John Kerry was scheduled to make on April 6, 2004. "Kerry's speech on the economy at Georgetown is likely to move onto the topic of Iraq," Moody wrote. "We should take the beginning of Kerry's speech, see if it contains new information (aside from a promise to create 10 million jobs) and see if other news at that time is more compelling. It is not required to take it start to finish."

Outfoxed played ominous music as a stern-voiced narrator gave Moody's memo a dramatic reading. The point, apparently, was to suggest that Fox, as a matter of policy, shortchanged coverage of the Kerry campaign. But just what did the memo mean, precisely? First of all, Moody did not write the memo just to shape Fox's Kerry coverage. The Kerry directive was just one paragraph in a longer morning memo outlining the highlights of the coming day's coverage (that day's memo also covered the war in Iraq, then–national security advisor Condoleezza Rice's upcoming testimony before Congress, the prescription drug case against conservative radio host Rush Limbaugh, and congressional hearings on the United

Nations oil-for-food scandal). More to the point, such directions are entirely routine in the television business, as producers look for guidance on when to air live events. (I spent a number of years as a producer for CNN and for NBC's local station in Washington.) Making such decisions is a basic function of news judgment, and Moody had simply said that it was not necessary to air every word of Kerry's speech. Producers make this kind of call every day.

Nor did *Outfoxed* mention other Moody memos that gave a more nuanced picture of Fox's campaign coverage. Greenwald obtained thirty-three memos in all (he never said how he got them), many of which touched on the campaign. Just a few were included in *Outfoxed*. Greenwald posted all the memos on his website but quickly took them down amid worries that Fox might take legal action against him. Once in the public domain, however, they remained available to anyone who was willing to search for them. In one memo, written a few days before the Kerry speech memo quoted in the film, Moody wrote, "We have competing speeches from the candidates for president. George Bush speaks on home ownership in New Mexico. John Kerry gives an economic policy address in Detroit. We'll take whichever one starts first, time how long we stay with it, then give the same time to the other. Try not to get caught in the ritual 'thank you's' that usually precede the meat of the speech." In another memo obtained by Greenwald but not included in *Outfoxed*, Moody wrote, "The President is on the stump, this time for women's rights. His remarks may be worth dipping into and then getting out." And in a third memo, Moody wrote, "John Kerry has positioned himself squarely on the fight over abortion. He attends a pro-choice rally in DC, then addresses newspaper editors. We'll take the latter live." None of the memos was particularly dramatic, which was perhaps the point; contrary to Greenwald's suggestion, the memos did not say much of anything about Fox's coverage, other than that it followed the routine conventions of television news.

Still another campaign-related memo obtained by Greenwald but not included in *Outfoxed* concerned the controversy that erupted when some of Kerry's fellow Vietnam veterans, led by former swift boat commander John O'Neill, accused the Democratic candidate of being "unfit for command." At the height of that political fight, Moody wrote, "Let's not overdo the appearances by Kerry's swiftboat mate John O'Neil [*sic*]. While his appearances so far have been OK, he represents one side of the 30 year recollections of what Kerry did, or didn't do, in uniform. Other people have different recollections." Including that memo in *Outfoxed* would have directly contradicted the film's premise of Fox's supposedly unbalanced coverage.

One memo that was included in *Outfoxed* concerned coverage of the war in Iraq. "Let's refer to the US Marines we see in the foreground as 'sharpshooters,' not snipers, which carries a negative connotation," Moody wrote in April 2004. *Outfoxed*, which gave the memo the same dramatic treatment it gave the note on Kerry's Georgetown speech, portrayed this as an effort by Fox to sugarcoat bad news from Iraq. I asked a well-connected source at Fox—who did not want to be named—what the memo meant and was told that Moody was trying to draw a distinction between the work of snipers who targeted civilians in places like Yugoslavia in the 1990s, and U.S. Marines in Iraq, who targeted Iraqi insurgents. The note was not, the source said, an attempt to prettify the news. That seemed at least a plausible way of reading the text. And by the way, the kicker to the story, not mentioned in *Outfoxed*, was that a number of Marines were unhappy with Fox's change of terms— they were quite proud to be known as snipers and didn't want to be called sharpshooters.

In yet another memo, from May 2003, Moody wrote, "Let's spend a good deal of time on the battle over judicial nominations, which the president will address this morning. Nominees who both sides admit are qualified are being held up because of their POSSIBLE, not demonstrated, views on one issue—abortion. This should be a trademark issue for FNC today and in days to come." Greenwald presented the quotation as evidence of slanted coverage, but Moody's statement was, in fact, accurate; abortion was indeed playing a large role in the fights over several Bush nominees, and saying so did not make Fox's coverage biased. Also, the source at Fox News told me that at the time, Moody tried to make the point that the battle over the confirmation of federal appeals court judges, which was intense and portended future battles over Supreme Court nominations, had not been covered sufficiently in the press. A reasonable case could be made that that, too, was accurate.

In all, the message of the memos appeared to be a bit more complicated than *Outfoxed* suggested. Greenwald had presented a selective portrait not only of the editorial process inside Fox but of the process inside the television news business as a whole. What might he have made, for example, of a memo by ABC News political director Mark Halperin, leaked during the campaign, which directed ABC News staffers to cast a more critical eye toward George W. Bush's "distortions" than toward John Kerry's, because Kerry's "distortions," unlike the president's, were "not central to his efforts to win"? At the very least, Halperin's note suggested that internal, point-of-view memos were not unique to Fox News. But that kind of detail did not find its way into *Outfoxed*.

Other parts of the film were simply off-key. For example, one of the most quoted sources in *Outfoxed* was a man named John Nichols, a writer for *The Nation* magazine and the *Capital Times* in Madison, Wisconsin, and also the author of a book about Vice President Cheney entitled *Dick: The Man Who Is President*. Unlike the former employees of Fox, or former newspeople, or even media watchers like Jeff Cohen and Eric Alterman, Nichols had no particular expertise to say anything about Fox. Yet in the movie, Greenwald gave him an extraordinary amount of time to make a wide variety of charges. Among them:

- "They [Fox] don't like to spend money doing serious stories. They like to do cheap, easy stories that will get a gut reaction."
- "Fox has made a decision to present the Iraq war as a success and as an ongoing success."
- "Fox portrays [George W. Bush's] every action as a heroic move. As, you know, something dramatic and significant. I imagine it's pretty hard for the Fox producers. Some days George Bush doesn't do anything interesting and yet, they've got to find something that makes him heroic that day."

Nichols's most dramatic complaint was his assertion that Fox helped decide the 2000 Florida recount in Bush's favor. "The first person who made the call to say that George W. Bush had been elected president of the United States was the person who was in charge of Fox News's election analysis division, the people that crunch the exit polling numbers," Nichols said in *Outfoxed.* "That person was a gentleman named John Ellis, and he is George W. Bush's first cousin. At around two in the morning, on election night, a new set of data had come in and it was complex data from precincts all over Florida. The proper answer in analyzing that data unquestionably was: you couldn't tell, it was too close to call, there was simply no clear winner. Instead, John Ellis called it as a clear win for George Bush. Fox News then interrupted its ongoing election coverage and announced that George Bush had been elected president of the United States.

"Now, what's significant about that," Nichols continued, "is not the intervention of the president's cousin to declare his relative the new president of the United States. It was the fact that within minutes, ABC, NBC, and CBS also fell right in line calling Bush as the winner. . . . I would suggest to you that that call on election night had more to do with making George Bush president than any recount or ballot design issue."

It was an extraordinary charge, suggesting that Bush owed his victory more to Fox than to the results of a series of recounts that showed him winning more votes than Al Gore, plus the Supreme Court decision that ended the recounting. And Nichols did not mention that earlier on that same election night, Fox— along with ABC, CBS, NBC, and CNN—had in fact called Florida for Gore. A lot went wrong in the reporting of election night 2000, but one call by one network did not turn the tide of history.

Greenwald promoted *Outfoxed* the same way he had promoted *Uncovered.* There were showings with Podesta in Washington. There were MoveOn house parties. There were DVD handouts (distributed by a group called the Disinformation Company). And there was a limited national release in theaters. Reaction was mixed. In the *New York Times Magazine*'s friendly profile of Greenwald, *Outfoxed* was described as "an unwavering argument against Fox News that combines the leftist partisan vigor of a Michael Moore film with the sober tone and delivery of a PBS special." But *The New Yorker*, which might have been expected to approach the picture sympathetically, criticized it for having "no interviews with current Fox employees, or with anyone else who might offer a defense of the network or challenge some of the movie's assertions. *Outfoxed* is not a work of reporting; it is a brief for the prosecution." In the end, Greenwald's method of determining the points he wanted to make, and then searching for examples to prove them, had simplified his rushed production process, but at the same time it had yielded a decidedly unenlightening result.

And a not terribly popular one, too. In theaters, *Outfoxed* did better than *Uncovered*, but not by much, earning $427,554. Even more than *Uncovered*'s, its revenues were concentrated in a small number of deep-blue cities. *Outfoxed*'s top five markets— New York; San Francisco; Los Angeles; Washington, D.C.; and Monterey—accounted for 70 percent of its gross theatrical receipts. It did well in all of those places, overperforming in New York by 225 percent, in San Francisco by 408 percent, in Los Angeles by 93 percent, in Washington by 217 percent, and in Monterey—a veritable hotbed of *Outfoxed* mania—by 1,436 percent.

Similarly, the picture did poorly in the expected places, underperforming by 30 percent in Atlanta, by 25 percent in Dallas, by 66 percent in Miami, by 52 percent in Tampa, and by 38 percent in Las Vegas. Add up all of the people who saw it—in theaters, special showings, at house parties, on DVD—and as with *Uncovered,* the number most likely came to less than one million.

SMALL CHANGE

I hoped to talk with Greenwald about his work. When I got in touch with him, asking if I might visit him at his office in Los Angeles, I received a quick reply. "No, I will not be doing this interview," he said, via e-mail. I sent him another note, asking that he reconsider. I told him I had already spoken with, among others, Jim Gilliam, John Podesta, Joan Blades of MoveOn, and others. A short time later, I received a note, not from Greenwald but from a man named Ira Arlook. I had never heard of him. As it turned out, Arlook was a top executive at Fenton Communications, an aggressive public relations agency that handled a number of "progressive" clients like MoveOn, George Soros, and Greenwald's own Artists United to Win Without War. Arlook's e-mail said, "I didn't think Joan Blades did it, but maybe she did. We've advised everyone against it." Apparently, Arlook mistakenly sent me a note intended for Greenwald. And the message seemed clear that no one associated with Greenwald (or Fenton) would be talking to me. I called Arlook but got no response. Later, Greenwald sent another quick note repeating his refusal.

Fortunately, Greenwald in effect interviewed himself for the behind-the-scenes features that accompanied his movies in their DVD versions, offering insights into his goals and methodology. I used those as a substitute for an interview of my own, and some of the quotes from Greenwald in this chapter were taken from them. A few of the quotes from the News-hounds and Greenwald's staff were also featured in the DVD extras, although Ellen Brodsky was kind enough to speak to me.

In the end, what seemed most notable about Greenwald's political work was its sheer smallness when compared with the rhetorical claims that he and his allies sometimes made for it. Perhaps at some point in the future it will become clear that Greenwald was, in fact, an agent of great change in the way Americans elect their leaders. But after the 2004 campaign, his films seemed to be, more than anything else, the cinematic version of an impassioned conversation among like-minded, true-blue, somewhat marginalized Democrats in San Francisco, Monterey, Los Angeles, and New York. Interesting—to them—yes. A new paradigm—no.

CHAPTER SIX

Ideologues and Businessmen
The Bipolar World of Liberal Radio

In a conference room in a stylishly refurbished bare-brick loft in Washington's Penn Quarter district, a man named Mark Walsh was standing at an easel, drawing a graph. A former America Online executive who also served as the Internet advisor for the Democratic National Committee and the Kerry campaign, Walsh had just finished a stint as head of Air America, the new liberal talk radio network. When I asked him what kind of listeners the network hoped to attract—this was the early summer of 2004, and Air America had been on the air just a few months—he walked to the easel and, using a red felt-tip pen, sketched a horizontal axis, which he marked KNOWLEDGE. Then he drew a vertical axis, which he labeled RAGE. Then he traced a line beginning at the lower left-hand corner and projecting out between the two axes at about 45 degrees. On that line, he told me—the middle ground—was the ideal Air America listener.

"We tried to avoid the two extremes," Walsh explained.

"Somebody who is very, very knowledgeable about all the things that are happening in America and is seemingly unconcerned—they're not going to like what we do. And somebody who just thinks that what's going on is horrible, stop it, whatever it takes, run through the streets with flaming torches, and doesn't really care to hear the details as to why they should be concerned—that is, zero knowledge, maximum rage—is not an appealing audience to us, as well."

Several months earlier, when Air America was still in the planning stages, I had asked Walsh the same question, and his answer—without the graph—was much the same. In that conversation, in November 2003, he emphasized that the network would strive for "centrist" programming. "I think that it's important to us that we not say the word 'liberal,'" Walsh told me then. "I think some of our hosts will be decidedly nonliberal and more centrist."

At least that was the plan. But the plan, it became clear when Air America debuted on March 31, 2004, did not become the reality. As it turned out, the network not only wasn't centrist, it veered well toward the RAGE axis on a fairly regular basis. There was the time, for example, on May 10, 2004, when one of Air America's stars, the former Florida radio talk show host Randi Rhodes, compared George W. Bush to Fredo Corleone, the weak son in the *Godfather* movies who was, on his brother Michael's orders, taken on a fishing trip during which he was murdered with a single gunshot to the head. "They *are* the Corleones," Rhodes said of the Bushes. "The Fredo of the family is the president of the United States, so why doesn't his father take him, or his brother, one of them, take him out for a little, uh, fishing? You know, let him say some Hail Marys, he loves God so much. Yeah, take him out, you know, 'Hail Mary, full of grace, God is with thee'—POW!" Rhodes paused briefly before adding, "Works for me."

Then there was the time, on October 1, 2004, when the network's biggest star, Al Franken, was discussing the previous night's debate between Bush and Senator John Kerry, and said he had written a few questions for Kerry to ask the president. One of the questions addressed Bush as "you moron." Another addressed him as "stupid schmuck." Yet another called him "idiot putz." It was all just a joke, Franken explained for those who might have been inclined to think he meant what he said; Franken actually intended for the salutations to be "silent."

And then there was the time, on April 5, 2004, after four American contractors were murdered and their bodies mutilated, burned, and strung from a bridge in Fallujah, Iraq, that Markos Moulitsas Zúniga, creator of the anti-Bush website Daily Kos, appeared on Air America host Janeane Garofalo's program. Moulitsas had created a sensation on the Web when he wrote, "I feel nothing over the death of the mercenaries. They aren't in Iraq because of orders, or because they are there trying to help the people make Iraq a better place. They are there to wage war for profit. Screw them." The statement was so far off the incivility scale that even the angrily partisan Moulitsas felt the need to apologize, telling Garofalo, "I overreacted" and "I came off as a jerk." But Garofalo, who regularly denounced those who disagreed with her as "fascists," "racists," "bigots," and "homophobes," would have none of it. "I don't think you need to apologize," she told Moulitsas. "I think that it is wrong to have made you feel that you needed to apologize. You were right on."

It seems fair to say that those examples, and dozens of others that could be cited, were not consistent with the center-left image that was originally planned for Air America. Instead, a much more militant point of view had taken over. What had changed? To put it simply, an idea met reality, and reality won. Air America executives learned that, on the Left as in some quarters of the Right, the hard stuff sells. They learned that, unlike political groups that sought to persuade undecided voters, talk radio could succeed, and possibly succeed handsomely, by ignoring the center and preaching to the angry liberal choir.

WHO'S OUR RUSH?

For years, media-minded liberals had been frustrated by the question: Why isn't there a liberal Rush Limbaugh, attracting Limbaugh-sized audiences on the Left? There were plenty of answers. Some were self-serving, like the idea that liberals tended to see complexity in issues and could not be hemmed in by the allegedly simplistic, black-and-white rhetorical demands of talk radio. That was at once flattering—*We're smarter than they are*—and pessimistic, since, if true, it meant that liberals might never succeed in a politically important entertainment medium. Other answers were simply defeatist, like the idea that Limbaugh was a uniquely talented performer whose success just couldn't be replicated—a notion that did not explain why other conservative hosts like Sean Hannity, Laura Ingraham, Neal Boortz, and others had achieved success that, if not at Limbaugh's level, was still beyond anything a liberal had achieved.

Whatever the answer, something was clearly wrong. Liberals cheered when Jim Hightower, the outspoken former Texas agriculture commissioner, got a shot at a national show. It didn't work. Then they cheered when Mario Cuomo, the former governor of New York whose oratory had thrilled the liberal wing of the Democratic Party, got *his* shot at a national show. That didn't work either. And then they resumed theorizing about why nothing worked.

Finally, around 2002, another idea began to take hold. Liberal radio had failed because the earlier efforts had tried to replicate Limbaugh by producing a *single show*—a Mario-versus-Rush showdown. But the talk radio day was so dominated by conservatives, the theory went, that a liberal show sandwiched between Rush and Sean and Laura simply could not attract many listeners. What was needed was an entire liberal radio *network*. That way, fans could listen to left-leaning talk all day and not have to search around the dial for a lonely liberal voice.

That was the state of thinking when a man named Sheldon Drobny entered the picture. A wealthy, Chicago-based venture capitalist who had been a big donor to Democratic causes, Drobny was angry about the results of the 2000 presidential election and believed the media were in large part responsible for Al Gore's defeat. With his wife and business partner, Anita, Drobny began to explore the possibility of a new liberal radio project. They talked to Gore about it, and the former vice president put them in touch with a number of rich and influential Democrats who might be interested in supporting the project.

The Drobnys formed a company, AnShell Media—Anita and Shelly—and hired a veteran radio executive named Jon Sinton, who had been involved with some of the failed liberal efforts of the past. Sinton tried to convince them to try something really new. "The Drobnys had an idea to do a show," Sinton told me. "I said, 'You can't do a show because one show is going to get lost in the shuffle. You have to do a network.' I had tried to syndicate Jim Hightower as a one-off. As a consultant, I worked with Mario Cuomo. You were never going to survive in this increasingly hostile landscape." Sinton's pitch was very convincing; the Drobnys were sold on the network idea.

But they needed money. They tried the usual suspects on the Left—Barbra Streisand, Norman Lear, Ed Asner, the whole Hollywood crowd—but got no takers. They talked to former Clinton administration figures John Podesta and Joe Lockhart in Washington. They talked to Bill Clinton himself. Gore connected them with some top broadcasters. At one point, they hoped to have a major infusion of cash from a labor union. None of it materialized, and beyond their own funds and some investments they were able to secure through their private financial firm, they made little progress raising money.

The project got a huge boost in late 2002, when a *New York Times* reporter heard about what was going on. Sensing the chance, as he later wrote in a memoir of the radio project, "to get AnShell millions of dollars worth of free publicity," Drobny worked with the reporter to shape the story. The result, a report headlined "Liberal Radio Is Planned by Rich Group of Democrats," appeared on the front of the paper's business section on February 17, 2003, and reported that the Drobnys had pledged up to $10 million of their own money to the new project.

The article called the effort "the most ambitious undertaking yet to come from liberal Democrats who believe they are overshadowed in the political propaganda wars by conservative radio and television personalities." The paper reported that AnShell was in talks with Franken, which gave the venture a measure of star power from the very beginning. And it said the group planned programming for throughout the day, rather than a single program.

As Drobny had anticipated, the *Times* piece created a wave

of publicity for AnShell. Other papers did stories. Television news did stories. And some liberal commentators rushed to praise the founders. "Mr. and Mrs. Drobny, I salute you, you're wonderful," *Newsweek*'s Anna Quindlen wrote (although she questioned whether liberals could ever master the technique of "disdain, derogation and dismissal" that she said was the hallmark of conservative radio). For a moment, Shelly and Anita were the toast of the liberal world.

And then . . . well, then, nothing much happened. Although the Drobnys had used the figure $10 million, it was never clear exactly how much they were actually prepared to put into the effort. In any event, an enterprise the size of what they proposed would probably cost quite a bit more than that. And the Drobnys still had trouble raising money, even after the *Times* article. They discovered that Democratic donors would rather put money in groups like America Coming Together that were openly dedicated to defeating George W. Bush, and liberal-minded business investors were simply wary, suspecting that the new enterprise wasn't entirely serious.

Weeks went by, and then months. The new network was little more than a PowerPoint presentation for potential investors. There was no contract with Franken or with any other on-air performers. In October 2003, I got in touch with Sheldon Drobny, wanting to know what was happening. "Everything is going very well," he told me, putting on a game face. "This is being run as a business, just like they're doing in the Rush Limbaugh side of the world." Drobny told me that the network would be on the air—in a "very big way"—in January 2004.

The enterprise looked more than a little shaky at that time, and during my research on the new network, I discovered questions about Drobny that went far beyond issues of money and investors. Doing a routine Internet search, I found a series of columns Drobny had written for a small website called MakeThemAccountable.com. In some of those writings, Drobny, the man at the helm of one of the flagship efforts of the new liberal activism, seemed to align himself with the farthest fringes of the Bush-hating Left.

In one column, for example, Drobny wrote that he saw similarities between President Bush's decision to go to war in Iraq and the pre–World War II policies of Adolf Hitler. "The corporate masters and their current spokesman, George W. Bush . . . use exactly the same excuses Hitler used to sell the public his maniacal desire to conquer Europe," Drobny wrote. Those corporate masters, Drobny said, included the unlikely trio of General Electric, Rupert Murdoch's News Corporation (owner of Fox News and the *New York Post,* among other companies), and the conservative philanthropist Richard Mellon Scaife. Together, Drobny wrote, they "essentially dictate what the government does" in a process he called "quasi-fascist."

In another column, Drobny wrote at some length about what he said were the Bush family's little-known—but extensive— links to the Nazis. "Very few Americans know that Prescott Bush, our president's grandfather, supplied Nazi Germany with [support for its rearmament]," Drobny wrote. "The information is documented, but is not known by most Americans because, as in any successful fascist regime, the press is prevented from publishing it."

I sent Drobny an e-mail saying that I had come upon his writings. I asked a few basic questions: "Do you believe there are some similarities between the current Bush administration and the Third Reich?" "Do you believe the Bush administration is a fascist regime?" "Do you believe the press has been reluctant to publicize what you suggest is the Bush family's Nazi-sympathizing past?" "Are these ideas that you would like to see discussed on a new talk radio network?" I received a quick response from Drobny saying his secretary would be setting up a time for us to talk. "However," he added, "you can go to GOOGLE and use the search words BUSH NAZI and you will get over 400,000 hits. I have copied a few for you. The Bush-Nazi connection is [*sic*] pretty well known during WW2."

Drobny had attached a copy of a chapter from a 1991 book entitled *George Bush: The Unauthorized Biography,* by Webster Griffin Tarpley and Anton Chaitkin. The authors argued that Prescott Bush got rich helping finance the Third Reich, and the money he made became the core of the Bush family's wealth. "For his part in the Hitler revolution, Prescott Bush was paid a fortune," Tarpley and Chaitkin wrote. "This is the legacy he left to his son, President George Bush." Since the book was written in 1991, it did not say that that legacy was then passed down to the second President Bush, but that seemed to be the point in Drobny's sending it now. (The charges were a gross distortion of the historical record. In fact, the elder Bush had a relatively minor business connection with a German industrialist who had once supported Hitler but who then turned on the German leader and was consequently imprisoned by the Nazis in the late 1930s. Looking at the record, the liberal journalist Joe Conason, who has criticized virtually everything George W. Bush has done, concluded, "Imputing Nazi sympathies to the president or his family ought to be beneath his adversaries.")

The chapter that Drobny had sent me, entitled "The Hitler Project," had been cited on popular left-wing websites like

BuzzFlash.com and BartCop.com. But Tarpley and Chaitkin were not the sort of authors one usually found in the anti-Bush library. Both men were longtime associates of the fringe political figure Lyndon LaRouche, and *George Bush: The Unauthorized Biography* was published by a LaRouche organization called Executive Intelligence Review. The same press also published titles like *George Bush and the 12333 Serial Murder Ring,* which attempted to link the former president and former British prime minister Margaret Thatcher to the 1986 murder of Swedish prime minister Olof Palme, and *Would a President Bob Dole Prosecute Drug Super-Kingpin George Bush?,* which was exactly what its title suggested.

On the telephone, I asked Drobny whether he believed all that. As it turned out, his views were significantly more nuanced, but he did, in fact, take the alleged Bush-Nazi connection very seriously. "If Prescott Bush built his family's wealth on the backs of slave labor and the Nazi regime, what responsibility does the Bush family have to own up to that?" he asked. "I don't suggest that I blame him for his grandfather's sins, but I do suggest that if a family has built wealth on the backs of slave labor, what is their responsibility?"

Drobny wanted to emphasize that his comparison of George W. Bush to Hitler was quite specific and limited. "I wasn't comparing Bush to Hitler on the racism side," he explained. "I don't believe George Bush is a racist or has or will ever have genocidal beliefs. What I'm talking about is fascism." Still, it was rather strong stuff, to say the least, and since Drobny would be the guiding force and the main financial backer of the new liberal talk radio network, I asked him whether those ideas would be a good subject for on-air discussion. "I'm not suggesting that at all," Drobny replied. "As a venture capitalist, I'm not the one who does the programming, nor would I interject my own opinion into programming. My business decisions are completely separate from my personal beliefs."

Nevertheless, Drobny's opinions seemed to raise questions about what kind of influence he might exert on the new network. They might, for example, influence his choices of on-air talent. So I asked him about a man who was his original choice to be a host on the network, a radio veteran named Mike Malloy. Malloy had done talk shows on WLS radio in Chicago and WSB in Atlanta—he'd been fired from both, which was not all that unusual in the radio business—and at the time I spoke to Drobny, Malloy was doing a program on something called the i.e. America Radio Network, which was a little-known liberal talk show network owned by the United Auto Workers. Not long before I spoke to Drobny, Malloy had been highly praised on the liberal website *Salon* in an article entitled "Where's the Liberal Rush Limbaugh?"

I listened to a few of Malloy's programs. Each was given a topic title. For example, there was a series of three shows called "Is It Time for the Bastard's Impeachment?" (The bastard was Bush.) Then there was "What's Your Life Worth to the Bush Crime Family?" And "The Scum Who Heads the Justice Department." (The scum was then–attorney general John Ashcroft.) And "The Bastards Continue to Lie." Was this the kind of material, I asked Drobny, that might make it on the new network? "I love Mike Malloy," Drobny told me. "I think he's a great entertainer. You'll love him or you'll hate him." But Drobny declined to say whether Malloy would be a part of the network, although he said that Malloy "tries to appeal in a very entertaining way to a very passionate audience."

I called Malloy to ask if he'd like to join the new network. Of course he would, he told me, but he didn't know what was going on. I asked whether his approach was perhaps a bit too rough-edged for the mass audience being contemplated by AnShell Media. "I don't think so," Malloy told me. "Just go back to the '90s, with the 'Clinton Chronicles,' Hillary is a lesbian, Bill and Hillary are drug dealers, Bill and Hillary left a trail of bodies. You have a talk radio that has been breast-fed on 'Hillary and Bill are murderers' and radicalized by a thug like Rush Limbaugh, with the crumbs swept up by a junior thug like Sean Hannity. And then somebody wants to ask me if I'm being a little bit strong in saying that John Ashcroft and the Patriot Act are totally, totally destroying constitutional government in this country?"

Malloy was an open and engaging man, but his responses raised questions about the whole idea of a liberal talk network. How could an enterprise featuring such rhetoric—a left-wing version of a caricature of conservative talk radio—financed by a man who liked to speculate about the "Bush-Nazi connection," be taken seriously? Such questions might become a real issue if Air America were to actually make it onto the air. But for the moment they were pushed aside, in large part because Sheldon Drobny's role in the project was about to undergo a sudden change.

BLOWTORCH

Whatever Drobny's political views, the real problem at AnShell in late 2003 was that the project was not moving forward. Even though Drobny had assured me that things were going very well, the fall of 2003 turned into winter, and AnShell did not seem to be building a network. And then, almost out of the blue, word came that the Drobnys had sold the venture to a new group of investors led by a financier named Evan Cohen. Sheldon and Anita remained involved—in a much-diminished capacity—and Cohen and his investment team, which was said to have between $20 million and $30 million to put into the project, brought in Mark Walsh as the CEO of what was renamed Air America. (Jon Sinton remained, the only executive to stay with the network through its various stages of life.)

With new ownership in place, the talk coming from Air America became more confident and detailed. And the word one heard a lot coming from top management was "centrist." When I called Walsh to learn what changes might be in store—of course, the network hadn't even gone on the air yet—he spoke at some length about his aversion to the term "liberal." "To label ourselves as liberal radio out of the box is a little regrettable, and something I'm trying to avoid," he told me.

Things moved ahead quickly with the new group in charge. Air America signed Franken, Janeane Garofalo, Randi Rhodes, and a number of other on-air personalities. The company also signed a group of writers, some of whom had solid credentials in television comedy. And executives began to sketch out what the network would actually look—or sound—like.

They did that after carefully studying conservative talk radio, in all its varieties. How did each show work? Why did most of them have a single host? Were there guests? Callers? And how did successful conservative hosts engage the ideas of the opposition? "The gut thinking was that absolute blowtorch right-wing radio hosts, Michael Savage through the others, have a core value of opposition," Walsh told me. "Unvarnished, aggressive, didactic, sometimes humiliating ripping of the opposition. And every now and then, a phone call from someone who supports [the host]. Sprinkled in, in a not-so-liberal way, would be the occasional idiot representative of the Left, whom the host would then shred, dance over the corpse, declare victory, and say, 'See? They are complete idiots.'" And that, the new executives believed, was conservative talk radio.

Of course, that kind of model—the "angry white man" idea—was not just a caricature of conservative talk radio; it was also precisely what Air America executives, including Walsh himself, had said they wanted to avoid. But things changed. "We concluded it's a very good model, 'cause it works," Walsh told me months later. "It gets good ratings, generates advertising revenue, is syndicated on a lot of stations." It no longer mattered greatly that most of the people associated with the project said they wanted the new network to occupy a higher moral ground than those angry conservatives. Air America was a business, not a Democratic 527. It was there to make money.

The network set a debut date of March 31, 2004. In the weeks leading up to the first show, Air America was the subject of a series of favorable articles in the nation's biggest newspapers. It got a big Style-section preview in the *Washington Post* a few days before the debut, and a front-page report after its first day. Franken was on the cover of the *New York Times Magazine* before the debut, and the paper fronted its Arts section with another preview on the network's opening day. The *Times* published yet another report the next day, which, while it offered a generally positive assessment of Air America's performance, fretted that the network's personalities might simply be too nice to "to match the fervor and ferocity of right-wing radio."

All the publicity was, quite literally, priceless. "It was off the charts in terms of how much ballyhoo and hoopla it generated, considering what it is," Michael Harrison, the editor and publisher of *Talkers* magazine, which tracks the talk radio business, told me at the time. "It's a modest start-up, and it was treated like some kind of revolution." In addition, the promotional nature of some of the coverage tended to obscure the fact that Air America was a tiny operation. At its debut, it was heard in just 5 of the 285 radio markets in the United States. Its stations—WLIB in New York, KBLA in Los Angeles, WNTD in Chicago, KPOJ in Portland, Oregon, and KCAA in Inland Empire, California—were mostly weak and rated near the bottom in their markets. Internet and satellite radio added a few more listeners. And that was it.

Finally, despite all the public statements of the company's executives, there was the lingering question of whether Air America was in business to be a business or in business to beat George W. Bush. "We're going to put it to Bush," Franken said in a conference call with reporters a few days before the network went on the air. "Bush is going down in November." On his first day on the air, Franken said, "This show is about . . . relentlessly hammering away at the Bush administration until they crack and crumble this November, because, don't get me wrong, friends, they are going down." And if there were any doubts about where he stood, Franken told the *Times*, "I'm doing this because I want to use my energies to get Bush unelected. I'd be happy if the election of a Democrat ended the show."

That was not exactly a long-term business plan. And in its early days, Air America did not seem like a long-term business. A dispute over contracts took the network off the air in Los Angeles and Chicago (broadcasts later resumed in L.A., but not in Chicago). Rumors began to circulate that the network had serious money troubles. The word was that Evan Cohen and his fellow investors had not brought in $20 million to $30 million, as they had claimed—the real number was far, far smaller. Mark Walsh resigned, saying he had been misled about the company's resources. Then everyone's paycheck bounced as Air America struggled to stay afloat. Finally, Cohen and his team were forced out. "It turned out that [they] did not have the financial where-withal that they represented, and those guys all went away," Jon Sinton told me.

At times it appeared the network might fold altogether. Certainly Air America was in desperate need of a savior. And then who should reenter the picture but . . . Sheldon and Anita Drobny. They formed a new company, called Piquant LLC, and bought back the assets of Air America. Other investors came in, too. Payrolls were met. Bills were paid. And Drobny favorite Mike Malloy, host of "What's Your Life Worth to the Bush Crime Family?", found a home at Air America. The network had made a full circle of sorts. And it was on the air.

But was anybody listening? In the first months of Air America's life, it was extraordinarily difficult to get an idea of the size of its audience nationwide. Even when it grew to include new affiliates—the list came to include stations in Miami, San Francisco, Atlanta, and several other cities—its reach was still so much smaller than that of established stars like Limbaugh and Hannity that it was impossible to compare programs on a nationwide basis.

It was possible, however, to look at how Air America performed in the nation's largest radio market, New York City. And in that blue-state bastion, the new network began well—or seemed to. Radio ratings, compiled by Arbitron Inc., the leading radio audience measurement firm, are kept on a quarterly basis. They come out in the first weeks of January, April,

July, and October and reflect an average of the preceding three months' ratings. Though they are the accepted standard in the radio business, executives often don't want to wait until the end of a quarter to see how their stations are doing, so they regularly make calculations during the ratings periods to estimate how big the audience is on a monthly basis.

Air America went on the air at the beginning of 2004's spring quarter. By May 1, it had been broadcasting for a month—a milestone of sorts, but by no means a statistically valid period for audience measurement. Still, in early May, network executives leaked word that in the New York City market Franken had actually beaten Limbaugh, who was broadcast on WABC. During the 10 A.M. to 3 P.M. time slot—the period that encompassed both Franken's and Limbaugh's programs—Air America claimed to have won a 3.3 percent share of listeners in the 25-to-54 age group, which is the demographic group most coveted by advertisers, compared to WABC's 2.8 percent share.

Franken was delighted. "We beat him," he said of Limbaugh during a television interview in early June. "The period we're opposite Rush, we—we beat WABC, so we think we beat Rush."

As it turned out, that was an overly optimistic assessment of events. When the spring ratings came out, the final results showed that WABC had won a 2.7 percent share of the 25-to-54 audience in the 10 A.M. to 3 P.M. time period; Air America's share was 2.2 percent. It was a clear victory for WABC, but still an impressive performance for the new network.

In the summer ratings period—July, August, and September—Air America improved a bit more, scoring a 2.3 percent share of the audience in the 10 A.M. to 3 P.M. time period to WABC's 2.7 percent share. "They're doing better than I expected," Phil Boyce, the longtime program director at

WABC, told me in September. "Obviously there is a market for this in New York. They've gotten a little bit better than they sounded to me initially. I'll give them credit."

One might have thought Air America would do even better in the fall, as the presidential race came down the stretch and political passions reached a peak. But when the ratings for the October, November, and December period came out in early 2005, Air America had slipped noticeably in the critical Al-versus-Rush time slot. WABC won a 3.6 share of the 25-to-54 audience, while Air America won only 1.6 percent. After a lot of hype, and a grueling political season, the long-established Limbaugh seemed to be pulling away from his new competi-tor. "Rush captured the election's excitement," Boyce told me in January 2005. "Franken didn't."

And that was in New York, a place Air America might be expected to do well. In some other markets, the numbers were still inconclusive. Still, the network's ability to gain a foothold, however small, in the world of talk radio pointed to a funda-mental difference between the politically charged talk radio business and the pure politics pursued by other liberal activists working to defeat George W. Bush. Simply put, unlike the activists, Air America didn't need to appeal to a majority of American voters to be a success. The base would do.

Remember the roughly 60 million people who vote for each side in a presidential election. If about 15 million of them are the hardest cores of their respective parties, one could preach to them all day and never affect the outcome of an election. But if one views them as a target audience—a way to make money— well, that's another matter. Limbaugh attracted about 15 mil-lion listeners each week—an audience that became the gold standard of radio success. Who was to say that at least some Air

America programs couldn't do pretty well by appealing to the core audience on the Left?

I asked Jon Sinton about the idea that with the electorate split fairly closely, one could appeal only to the hard-core believers on one side and still have a very big, very profitable business. "I think that's exactly right," he said. "There are plenty of people. If we only have our partisans listen, then we'll only be as successful as Rush."

Of course, the question remained of whether Franken and his colleagues had signed on to build a business or to defeat George W. Bush. As the fall of 2004 went on, the network showed signs that business was trumping the political crusade, or at least fighting it to a draw. In October, Franken took his program on the road for a week. At the time, it seemed as if everyone in the liberal activist universe was running around the swing states of Ohio, Pennsylvania, Florida, and the like. George Soros was touring swing states. Michael Moore was touring swing states. Bruce Springsteen was touring swing states. But Franken started his tour in California, a decidedly nonswing state. Why? Because Air America was welcoming new affiliates in San Diego and San Francisco, and Franken appeared in both cities to promote the new programming. It was an entirely routine thing to do in the radio business, but it took on special significance in the case of Air America. The itinerary of Franken's promotional road show suggested that the network was acting as a for-profit enterprise and not as a political campaign.

Of course, Air America did not abandon the political campaign entirely. After California, Franken's tour did head for the swing states. And when the network announced a deal to televise a shortened version of Franken's show on the Sundance Channel, it revealed that the program would run only through the November election. So it is perhaps most accurate to say that Air America was about both electioneering and trying to make money. "We are able to multitask," Sinton told me.

SENSITIVE AL

As I researched Air America, I wanted to discuss a number of things with Franken. Was he just doing the radio show to get rid of Bush? Did he really think he could be competitive with Limbaugh? And what about those "jokes" that the president was a "moron" and a "stupid schmuck" and an "idiot putz"? Were they examples of what he calls "kidding on the square"— that is, as he wrote in his book *Lies and the Lying Liars Who Tell Them*, "kidding, but also really meaning it"?

In September, about five weeks before the election, I called Franken at his Air America office. I said I hoped to interview him and perhaps come to Manhattan to watch him do his program. Franken, who had given dozens of interviews about his radio work, sounded reluctant. He told me he would have to discuss it with his publisher and his agent; he had signed a contract to do a new book, he explained, and at least part of it would be about Air America. His publisher might not want him publicly discussing topics he would otherwise save for the book.

Then Franken said, "I do have a couple of issues separate from this." He mentioned two articles I had written about a year earlier. One was a review of *Lies and the Lying Liars Who Tell Them,* and the other was a story about the liberal think tank the Center for American Progress, in which I described his performance at the group's opening party.

Franken seemed to have a detailed memory of the book review. His main objection, he told me, was that I had unfairly dismissed his assertion that George W. Bush had used cocaine. In the book, Franken had cited then-candidate Bush's answer to a reporter's question of whether Bush could have, in 1989 when his father was inaugurated as president, truthfully answered no on a federal form asking whether he had used drugs in the previous fifteen years. Bush affirmed that he could have said no but refused to answer any more questions. From that, Franken concluded, "it didn't take a genius to figure out that George W. Bush snorted cocaine sometime before 1974." In the review, I questioned that argument, writing that "Franken has no evidence [of Bush cocaine use]. And he certainly knows that during the 2000 campaign, reporters from major news organizations spent many hours searching—unsuccessfully—for proof of Bush drug use."

Franken didn't agree, to say the least. "You didn't actually include the inductive reasoning I used to arrive at this, which I think was pretty well argued," he told me. He mentioned a sketch he had written for *Saturday Night Live* many years ago called "The Amazing Colossal President"—he had also recounted the story in *Lies*—in which then-president Jimmy Carter visits a nuclear plant during an accident and begins to grow to an astonishing height. Reporters ask, "Is it true the president is over a hundred feet tall?" and a spokesman answers no. Then the question becomes, "Is it true the president is over ninety feet tall?" and the spokesman says, "No comment." It was a funny skit. By the same sort of reasoning, Franken said, one could view Bush's "no" and "no comment" as proof that he used drugs before 1974.

I protested that with an accusation so serious, reporters should have more than reasoning—some actual evidence, perhaps—before coming to a conclusion. Franken held firm: "What I'm saying is that in your effort to score one, I think you deliberately left out a pretty rock-solid logical case," he said, adding, "I think you're actually being unreasonable in not agreeing to my conclusion."

It didn't seem as if there was much point in continuing that discussion, so we moved on to the other instance that bothered Franken. At first, he said he was unhappy with what I had written about his speech to the Center for American Progress but could not remember exactly why. As we spoke, he looked up my article on the Nexis database and refreshed his memory. He said I had unfairly reported that his remarks included a tirade against Fox News—he had talked about "how shameless, how shameless, how SHAMELESS these people on the Right can be"—without explaining what it was about Fox that had made him so angry.

That was true. What Franken was saying at the event was that Brit Hume, the anchor of the network's program *Special Report*, had minimized U.S. casualties in a brief report in August 2003 in which Hume said that "statistically speaking, U.S. soldiers [in Iraq] have less of a chance from dying from all causes in Iraq than citizens have of being murdered in California, which is roughly the same geographical size." Asked about his statement, Hume later told the *Washington Post*, "Admittedly it was a crude comparison, but it was illustrative of something."

Franken's point—and he was correct—was that there were about 140,000 troops in Iraq and about 34 million people in California, and Hume's comparison, based on geographical size, wasn't valid. I had heard Franken make the case several times before—it was a standard part of his anti-Fox shtick and he carried around a dog-eared piece of paper with Hume's quotes on it. But I suggested to him that it had not been necessary for me to go into the details of it all because he certainly seemed to think that Fox was "shameless" for all sorts of reasons, and besides, the story was about the Center for American Progress, and not Al Franken's criticism of Brit Hume.

Franken insisted that I had missed the point of what he was saying and had been "deliberately unfair" to him. "I've been to Iraq, and I've been with those soldiers, and I've been with the parents," he told me. "I still to this day believe he [Hume] owes an apology to those people." As for me, Franken said he had a problem of trust. "I understand you," he said after I had tried to address his concerns, "and that's why I don't trust you." We left the conversation with Franken suggesting that I rethink my approach to the stories in question.

A short time later, I sent Franken an e-mail saying I had thought over his criticisms. I wrote that I still believed my criticism of his Bush/drugs accusation was fair. On the other story, I told him that "it would have been better if I had written that you were angry at Brit Hume for, you believed, minimizing the extent of U.S. casualties in Iraq." But I said I didn't think it was necessary to go into any greater detail because that would have taken the article far off course at the very beginning.

Franken responded—not to me directly, but to a mutual acquaintance, whom he asked to pass on word that he didn't want to do an interview. Hearing that, I waited a couple of months, until after the election was over and after Franken had made a December trip to Iraq to entertain American troops—his fifth USO tour—to get in touch one more time. Would Franken have time to do an interview now?

Franken was quite courteous and wanted to make sure that I had gotten his previous message—he didn't want me to think he had ignored my request. When I brought up the subject of an interview, he said, "Can we make some rules? Can I see the quotes that you use in the context that you use them?" That would have involved, in essence, giving Franken preapproval of portions of the book. I demurred, and Franken quickly turned the conversation back to those two articles that troubled him. He was still worked up about it.

"Here's my beef with you," he said. "I know you tried to address them, and I just disagreed with you. Like the cocaine thing with Bush. I think I did prove it by deduction that he did cocaine." Franken went back over the whole case, including "The Amazing Colossal President," to show that I was simply wrong. And then he went over the whole case on the Brit Hume quote, saying of Hume's comment, "It still makes me incredibly angry every day. It just drives me fucking crazy."

Franken said he felt "twice burned" by my articles. "I consider the review [of *Lies*] with the cocaine thing as a deliberate misrepresentation," he told me. "I consider the other thing also a deliberate misrepresentation by omission. I consider those things not to be lying as such, but lying by omission. . . . In both of those things a key thing was omitted in order to make your review more anti-me." For those reasons, he said, it was important that I show him the quotes I would use in the context I would use them. I told him I would think about it.

At that point, there seemed a real possibility that the exchanges could go on for quite a long time, and that Franken might talk endlessly about how he would not talk to me. And if I did agree to show him the portions of the book that included his quotes, I could foresee a protracted round of Kyoto-like negotiations over what to put in and what to leave out. In the end, I told him that I could not show him the quotes, and there was no interview.

But I had at least learned this: Al Franken could be very, very sensitive about what was written about him. Perhaps he shouldn't have been. He was, after all, the star of the most successful attempt yet to fight conservatives on talk radio (that wasn't saying a lot, but it was true). It still was not clear whether Air America would survive—at the beginning of 2005, the network was heard on about forty stations nationwide, compared to about six hundred stations for Rush Limbaugh's program— but liberal radio had at least gotten a start.

And, apart from *Fahrenheit 9/11*, Air America was the only part of the new left-wing activism that could measure its success by the amount of money it made. If it could make money, it would attract still more support. Since the network had proved it could actually put programs on the air—that had been an open question when the Drobnys were first looking for investors—it became more likely to attract people willing to put money into the company. Those investments were a kind of hybrid support, given partly for political purposes but also with at least the nominal hope of an actual return. Whatever the case, the money gave Air America the ability to stay on the air.

Will it ever prosper like conservative talk radio? Certainly there are enough potential listeners out there to make it successful. But the conservatives' dominance on talk radio took years to build, and did not grow out of just one company, or one set of investors, or one mindset. Air America was trying to create all that at once, which simply might not be possible to do. And more important, in creating the network, its executives relied on a caricature of what they believed conservative talk radio to be. Conservatives are mean? We'll be mean, too. Blowtorch? Wait'll you hear us. That's how Air America ended up with Randi Rhodes talking about killing George W. Bush. Maybe that will work, someday. But it didn't, as Al Franken had hoped, bring down George W. Bush.

CHAPTER SEVEN

"Our Goal Is to Win"

John Podesta and the Think Tank as War Room

On October 20, 2004, less than two weeks before the election, the new "progressive" think tank the Center for American Progress held a breakfast fund-raiser at its sleek headquarters near the White House. It wasn't a big-ticket event; you could get in with a donation of as little as $50, and there were none of the donors who had written five-, six-, and seven-figure checks to the organization. Still, John Podesta, the former Clinton White House chief of staff who founded and heads the Center, worked the crowd, thanking them for their support. When Podesta ducked outside to the lobby, I asked him whether it was possible to attract big donors to such a spartan event (it featured boxes of Krispy Kreme doughnuts laid out on a long table). Podesta laughed. "We save the big donors for the C-3," he told me.

Podesta's answer was pure Washington-speak—its meaning unclear to the uninitiated—but it said something important about his new organization. The Center for American Progress was actually two entities. One, the Center itself, was what is known as a 501(c)(3), which refers to the section and subsection of the Internal Revenue Service code under which it was organized. These 501(c)(3) organizations—usually referred to by the shorthand "C-3s"—are fully tax-exempt, nonprofit charitable organizations, meaning that donors can deduct contributions from their taxes. Because C-3s have that special tax status, the law forbids them from engaging in partisan political activity; they cannot, for example, advocate the passage of a particular bill or the election of a particular candidate. A think tank that is a C-3 simply can't go too deeply into electoral politics. Mindful of that, Podesta's mission statement began, "The Center for American Progress is a nonpartisan research and educational institute dedicated to promoting a strong, just and free America that ensures opportunity for all."

The other half of Podesta's organization was called the American Progress Action Fund, and it was what is known as a 501(c)(4) organization. Such organizations, called "C-4s," are tax-exempt and nonprofit but are allowed to engage in partisan political activity like lobbying or advocating the election or defeat of a candidate. The trade-off is that contributors to C-4s are not permitted to deduct contributions to those organizations from their taxes. Both groups can accept unlimited donations, but the tax advantages of giving to a C-3 are obvious. Therefore, Podesta chose to "save the big donors for the C-3." The breakfast fund-raiser, with the small donors, was for the C-4 Action Fund.

Beneath the arcana of the rules, the C-3/C-4 distinction meant that Podesta was trying to do two very different, and fundamentally incompatible, things with the Center for American Progress. With one hand, he was running a "nonpartisan" think tank. With the other, he was playing an aggressively partisan role in the presidential campaign.

It was an audacious idea. A number of political advocacy groups—from the National Rifle Association and National Right to Life Committee on the Right to People for the American Way and NARAL Pro-Choice America on the Left—maintain both C-3s and C-4s. To justify that, they claim that their primary, tax-exempt mission is to "educate" American voters, while on the side they engage in a bit of partisan politics. In fact, such arrangements are often little more than schemes to take in as much tax-free money as possible while engaging in as much partisan activity as possible. But in any event, those groups are clearly advocacy organizations. The Center for American Progress, on the other hand, was founded as a think tank, an organization ostensibly devoted to developing ideas. The institutions Podesta sometimes cited as his models—the conservative Heritage Foundation and American Enterprise Institute—did *not* have overtly partisan, C-4 arms. They were, well, think tanks. The same was true of the liberal Brookings Institution. ("We're 100 percent C-3," one Brookings official told me, surprised that I would even ask.) With the Center for American Progress, Podesta was trying to create something new: a think tank that doubled as a campaign war room.

His intentions were clear enough at the fund-raiser that October morning. The Center had advertised a "surprise call from a mystery guest," who, as it turned out, was Al Franken, calling in before his daily radio program. In the span of a few months' time, Franken had become a special friend of the Center. Among other things, he featured Christy Harvey, the woman who edited the Center's daily publication, *The Progress Report,* in a regular segment on his program. *The Progress*

Report, which Podesta called "one of our flagship products," was a compilation of the latest in Bush-bashing—all the day's anti-Bush headlines and analysis in one convenient package—which was sent out via e-mail to Democratic politicos, talking heads, and activists. Franken cited it often.

Over a speakerphone, Franken began by singing the song he usually performed to introduce Harvey's appearance on his Air America radio show, a crooning, *Saturday Night Live* lounge-lizard version of "Misty."

"Talk to me . . .

"Talk about the right wing's dishonesty . . .

"She's the Center for American Progress's deputy director for strategic communications . . .

"She is Christy . . . Christy Harvey is here."

Harvey blushed and laughed as Franken squeezed the words "She'stheCenterforAmericanProgress'sdeputydirectorforstrategiccommunications" to fit into the song. And then Franken became serious. "We at Air America, and my show particularly, get so much from *The Progress Report*," he said. But far more important, he continued, was that Air America and the Center had joined forces as part of an effort to create a new hub of power in American politics. "We're building an infrastructure incredibly quickly," Franken told the crowd. "We have to counter the right-wing machine that has been built up over the last forty years." When Podesta told him that "to see the growth of Air America and your show has been inspiring," Franken responded, "I feel like I'm part of a team. I'm just honored to be allied with you guys."

Franken was right. He and Podesta, and the supposedly nonpartisan Center, were indeed part of a team, a team dedicated above all to defeating George W. Bush and replacing him with a

Democrat in the White House. The think-tank chief and the radio host were going about their work in different ways, but Podesta's core ambition was the same as Franken's: whatever the talk about finding new ideas and sponsoring scholarly studies, the real purpose of the Center for American Progress was to win, and win now. The problem, for Podesta and his allies, was that their drive to win caused them to misunderstand what had made their role models, the conservative think tanks, succeed. The Heritage Foundation and the American Enterprise Institute had taken years to build an intellectual foundation for political success. Podesta wanted to do it immediately, and in the course of winning a passionate political campaign. In the end, trying to do both meant that, in 2004 at least, Podesta did neither.

THE COUNTER-COUNTER-ESTABLISHMENT

"Some of you may think that the last thing this city needs is another think tank," Podesta told reporters in October 2003, when he unveiled the Center at a National Press Club news conference. It was a good point. Why *did* Podesta believe another think tank was needed? The stated answer was that the Left—or the Center-Left, as Podesta would be more comfortable calling it—needed an institution to stand up to the power of the Right. But the deeper answer lay in the way in which liberals and conservatives view their place in the world of ideas and media. Put briefly, they live in almost precisely parallel universes, each seeing the other as virtually omnipotent.

Ask a politically minded conservative about the number of powerful intellectual and communications institutions that lean to the left, and he'll reel off an imposing list: the *New York Times,* which has not endorsed a Republican presidential candidate since Dwight Eisenhower; the *Washington Post,* which, like the *Times,* has endorsed only Democrats for president in the past half-century; a television network or two; pretty much all of academia; the Brookings Institution; and a host of other organizations, some of them financed by grants from institutions like the Ford Foundation and the Robert Wood Johnson Foundation. All in all, it's an impressive lineup.

Yet if you ask a politically minded liberal to assess his side's strength versus that of conservatives, he will list the powerhouses of the Right: Rush Limbaugh and other talk radio hosts, Fox News, the *Washington Times,* the Heritage Foundation, the American Enterprise Institute, and others, some of them financed by grants from places like the Scaife Foundations and the Bradley Foundation. He will then conclude that the Left is weak, outgunned, and overmatched. Former conservative David Brock—a favorite of Podesta's—has written that the Right has virtually taken over the political debate, while liberalism, which had once been quite powerful, now "seems a fringe dispensation of a few aging professors and Hollywood celebrities." And Al Franken was simply echoing the thoughts of many others when he said the Left needed to build a new infrastructure as quickly as possible.

In developing that viewpoint, Podesta and his colleagues were deeply influenced by a series of reports, the first appearing in 1997, by a group called the National Committee for Responsive Philanthropy. Analyzing the philanthropy of the Scaife, Bradley, and other conservative foundations, the report argued that conservatives had created a "vast and interconnected institutional apparatus" that had "shaped public consciousness and influenced elite opinion, recruited and trained new leaders, mobilized core constituencies, and applied significant rightward pressure on mainstream institutions, such as Congress, state legislatures, colleges and universities, the federal judiciary and philanthropy itself." Meanwhile, "mainstream"—meaning liberal—institutions starved for lack of support. To illustrate the point, the report included a graph in which a huge bar representing conservative giving stretched the length of the page, while a puny bar representing liberal giving barely rose above the base line. That idea of liberal weakness—almost an inferiority complex—was the subtext for the founding of the Center for American Progress.

It was also the subtext for much of the conversation when I visited Podesta at his office a few days before the election. For a man fighting an uphill battle, he was in a pretty good mood. Wearing a gray checked suit, cowboy boots, a white shirt, and a bright red tie on which "JK '04" alternated with tiny American flags, he told me he was feeling optimistic about the presidential race. It had not always been so, he said; he had only recently begun to believe that John Kerry would win. Democrats across the spectrum had put a lot of work into the election, he said; maybe this would be their time.

I had had trouble setting up the interview. Although he was unfailingly pleasant and polite, Podesta had at first declined my request for a talk, then accepted, and then canceled. As weeks, and then months, went by, I worried that I might not ever be able to sit down to talk with him—I especially hoped we would be able to do so before the election, because any conversation afterward would inevitably have a kind of postmortem quality to it, regardless of how the voting turned out. So finally I showed up at the Center's offices for the Action

Fund fund-raiser, wrote a check for $50, and made my way around the room. Seeing me, Podesta jokingly asked whether I had paid for my doughnuts and coffee. I assured him I had, although I viewed it more as a business expense than a political contribution. After we talked a bit more, he again agreed to an interview.

Sitting at a table in Podesta's office, near a framed caricature showing him standing astride the Capitol with a gun in each hand, ready for battle, I asked him how the Center came into being. Citing the Responsive Philanthropy reports, he told me that people on the Left had long envied the think-tank structure—primarily Heritage and the American Enterprise Institute—that had arisen on the Right a few decades earlier. But if those organizations were so powerful, I asked, and had no analogues on the Left, why hadn't the Left already created its own institutions to match them? The reason, he said, was that liberals hadn't really needed to, because they had always controlled at least part of the government. "At some point or another prior to 2002, you had leadership in one body or another—dominantly, during the Clinton years, in the White House, but also [at times] in the House or Senate," he told me. "Not just the political fight, but the intellectual fight, took place between [Democrats] in government and the voices from the intellectual milieu on the Right."

Democrats, Podesta was saying, were simply used to being in power *somewhere*. Republicans weren't. In 1976, for example, in the first presidential election after the founding of the Heritage Foundation in 1973, Democrat Jimmy Carter was elected to the White House, and Democrats won 292 seats in the House and a filibuster-proof 61 seats in the Senate. Republicans were so far out of power that they couldn't even see it on the horizon.

(They had no way of knowing that one of their favorites, Ronald Reagan, would rise to the presidency in just four more years.) Shut out of government, they built new institutions. Democrats never saw the need.

That began to change with the election of 2000, when George W. Bush won the White House, Republicans kept the House, and Republicans and Democrats fought to a 50–50 tie in the Senate (a tie that was broken in the GOP's favor by Vice President Dick Cheney). But Bush's victory was so narrow that many Democrats did not fully accept the reality of defeat. And within a few months of Inauguration Day, they were handed control of the Senate by the defection of Vermont's formerly Republican senator Jim Jeffords. That meant Democrats could still chair committees, still control the agenda, still face down the White House on a nearly equal level.

But even that was gone by November 2002. Bush, of course, remained in the White House, while Republicans won outright control of the Senate and remained in charge in the House. The gift from Jeffords had stopped giving, and the Democrats had nothing. The results seemed all the more devastating to Democrats because in the past, the party in control of the White House had almost always *lost* congressional seats in midterm elections. "I think it was clear, particularly by what I think was a disastrous strategy in '02, that something needed to be done," Podesta told me. "We're sitting there with no real power, a kind of weak voice in Congress, and the incapacity to put forward an alternative agenda, an alternative national security strategy. We were sort of for a little less than whatever the other guys were for."

But what to do? Even before the election, Podesta, who, after leaving the Clinton White House, took a post at Georgetown University Law School, had begun to accept the notion that for Democrats, having power had served as a substitute for coming up with new ideas. The Left, he told me, had built up "stovepipe institutions," meaning a number of parallel but unconnected organizations, often devoted to a single issue without integrating that issue into the spectrum of other Democratic concerns. The result was "no cohesion, no vision, really, about where the country could go," Podesta told me. "We got a little flabby intellectually, the ability to generate ideas, governing ideas, was weak."

At that point in our conversation, Podesta brought up a 1986 book by his friend Sidney Blumenthal, the former White House aide and arch–Clinton partisan, called *The Rise of the Counter-Establishment.* In it, Blumenthal traced the growth of institutions like Heritage and the American Enterprise Institute, which he collectively named the Counter-Establishment, because they arose as an answer to entrenched liberal power in government. Blumenthal attributed enormous power to those think tanks, and to the conservative foundations that financed them, arguing that they set the agenda in 1980s Washington. "The conservative networks that produce the various ideas are almost as important as the ideas themselves," Blumenthal wrote. "Once in place, the Counter-Establishment can constantly churn out agendas." Podesta told me that, among themselves, Democrats had been discussing the Right's agenda-setting power for a very long time. "People had been talking to no great effect for ten or fifteen years, maybe twenty years—go back to Sid's book," he said.

But nobody had done anything about it. So along with a few friends, Podesta wrote up a prospectus for a new institution, a think tank like the Heritage Foundation, that would be part of what might be called a Counter-Counter-Establishment. Sensing his party's precarious hold on power, Podesta actually began work in the months before November 2002, but the effort was casual and not terribly focused, much like all those conversations from years past. After November, it became much more serious.

Word of Podesta's planning got around. One of his colleagues at Georgetown was Robert Pitofsky, a former dean of the law school who was also a former chairman of the Federal Trade Commission. And one of Pitofsky's oldest friends was a man named Herbert Sandler, who, with his wife, Marion, founded the Golden West Financial Corporation, a hugely successful savings-and-loan based in Oakland, California. In recent years the Sandlers, who were friendly with House Minority Leader Nancy Pelosi, had become big donors to Democratic causes.

Pitofsky mentioned Podesta's project to Sandler, who was immediately interested. "Herb sort of showed up at my door at Georgetown one day," Podesta told me. "He didn't know me from Adam." But Sandler and his wife had studied the Responsive Philanthropy report on conservative institutions. "They had read about it, thought about it, and thought that something needed to happen on the other side to counterbalance it," Podesta said. The two men talked. Sandler said he and his wife were serious about wanting to start something new, and later Podesta flew to San Francisco for more discussions. "They talked me into it," Podesta told me. Once again, an outsider with deep pockets, not a member of the traditional Democratic establishment, provided the push to create a new political structure for the Left, just as George Soros did for America Coming Together. And the message was the same: The Left had to unite as it never had before.

Soros himself contributed to the Center for American Progress, just as he gave to MoveOn and America Coming

Together. He had two connections to the new group. First, he was friendly with the Sandlers. And second, one of Podesta's colleagues in starting the Center, Morton Halperin—a long-time hero of the Left who had been on Richard Nixon's ene-mies list, a top official of the American Civil Liberties Union, and a controversial (and unsuccessful) nominee for a position in the Clinton Defense Department—was, in 2002, working for Soros's foundation, the Open Society Institute. Before long, Podesta found himself talking with a very receptive Soros. A new think tank, Soros political advisor Michael Vachon told me, "was something that George had wanted to see for a long time, to counter the virtual monopoly that conservative groups had developed over the last thirty years over policy discourse." Soros pledged to give $1 million a year for three years. The Sandlers gave even more. The Center for American Progress was in business.

Why did everyone ante up so much money so quickly? I asked Podesta whether he was, in effect, surfing on the Bush hatred that came to characterize much of the Left between 2002 and 2004. "I think Bush really concentrated people's attention," he told me. Like nearly everyone else on the Left, Podesta spoke of the president's "radical" agenda, his suppos-edly wrenching departure from the norms of American behav-ior, especially in foreign policy. Without that—or at least, without that perception that Bush was "radical"—the donors probably would not have come forward. "It's what motivated Soros, it to some extent is what motivated a lot of the major donors, people who gave me money, people who gave America Coming Together money," Podesta said.

And give they did. According to forms filed with the Internal Revenue Service, the Center collected $11,731,782 in contributions in just the last few months of 2003 (it would not be required to file its 2004 contributions until late 2005). On the forms, Podesta had to itemize contributions but did not have to reveal the names of contributors. The biggest single contribution was $2.5 million—probably from the Sandlers, since Podesta told me they were the largest donors. There were three contributions of $1 million each—one of them Soros's, although Podesta told me that Soros "quickly lost interest in this, because he became preoccupied with getting rid of Bush." There were two donations of $500,000 each and three other donations, which were given not in cash but in stock, between $500,000 and $1 million. In all, contributions of more than $10,000 accounted for almost all of the Center's income. And the vast majority of the money went to the supposedly nonpartisan 501(c)(3), just as Podesta had told me at the coffeeand-doughnuts fund-raiser. When Podesta called and offered a tax-deductible way to defeat George W. Bush, wealthy Democrats answered.

THE TALKING-POINTS FACTORY

So the Left's long-held vision of a new think tank was becoming a reality. But what would it be?

"At its core, the Center for American Progress will be an incubator of new ideas," Podesta told reporters at the October 2003 news conference introducing the new institution. "We're not a mouthpiece, we're not an organ, we're not affiliated with any party, including the Democratic Party. In much the way that the conservative think tanks operate in a nonpartisan space, they have a point of view and we have a point of view. So while we operate in a nonpartisan space, we obviously have a point of view."

New ideas, with a point of view. But as the Center unveiled its work, it was not at all clear what those new ideas were. Did they have some deeply held guiding belief, as conservatives had had years ago with the ideas of deregulation and the beneficial effects of lower taxes? Not really. Instead, Podesta seemed to be devoted to the "idea" that George W. Bush should be defeated.

The Center's debut came at a conference called New American Strategies for Security and Peace, held in late October 2003 at the Wardman Park Marriott Hotel in Washington. The conference featured speakers like retired general Wesley Clark, who six weeks earlier had joined the field of candidates for the Democratic presidential nomination, and Joseph Wilson, the former ambassador who had become a full-time Bush antagonist over the CIA/Niger/uranium affair. Clark, speaking to the conference by satellite from his campaign in New Hampshire, got things off to a rousing, nonpartisan start by blaming President Bush for the September 11 terrorist attacks. "There is no way this administration can walk away from its responsibility for 9/11," he said. "You can't blame something like this on lower-level intelligence officers, however badly they communicated memos with each other. . . . The buck rests with the commander in chief, right on George W. Bush's desk." Clark's speech made headlines for days—and got the Center's name into the newspapers and on television.

Other speakers included former Clinton national security officials Sandy Berger and Richard Holbrooke, who would play major roles in the Kerry campaign. Senator Hillary Rodham Clinton, meanwhile, praised Podesta by saying he had the "warrior spirit," as well as the "strategic mind" to run a new enterprise like the Center. The conference featured one Republican, sometime maverick Nebraska Senator Chuck Hagel, who delighted the crowd by ridiculing those in his party who were suspicious of his appearing before the Center at the request of the "dreaded John Podesta, that tricky, wily fellow that he is, [who] hoodwinked the flat-footed senator from Nebraska into speaking before you Communists."

Perhaps some of the hard-edged politics came from the fact that the purpose of the first conference was not so much to present scholarship as to offer a broad discussion of foreign policy issues. But nearly a year later, the Center held another conference on national security, and it appeared that little had changed. In September 2004, Podesta brought his national security team—Clark was there again, this time as an ex-candidate—to the Mayflower Hotel in downtown Washington to release a new report entitled "Failing Grades: America's Security Three Years After 9/11." The study consisted of a slickly produced brochure made to resemble a report card grading the Bush administration's efforts in a number of areas of national security. Podesta did not give the Republican team very high marks. The study even included an actual report card, small enough to fit in one's pocket, which read like this:

CLASS	GRADE	COMMENTS
Terrorist Threat	C–	Needs strategy, focus on Afghanistan
Homeland Security	D+	Good intentions, weak follow-through
Nonproliferation	F	Increased threat, paid no attention
Military Power	D	Stretched too thin, need to honor troops

The sixty-six-page report elaborated on some of those themes. But it would be difficult to call the work scholarship. The report was written in a kind of newsbite style, and its 207 endnotes cited a mix of press accounts, the September 11 Commission report, a few General Accounting Office reports, and other readily available material—all in all, not much more in-depth than might be found in a series of newspaper articles.

Other reports produced by the Center were in much the same vein. There was, for example, "Are We Better Off?"—a joint production of the Center and the leftist-fringe magazine *Mother Jones,* in which Podesta presented the results of a *Mother Jones* survey, conducted by Democratic pollster Stanley Greenberg, which purported to show that under George W. Bush, rich Americans had become very happy while, in Podesta's words, "millions of middle-class families are seeing the American dream slipping through their fingers." There was "Understanding the Impact of the Bush Administration's Economic Policy: A View from the States," which featured Iowa's governor, Tom Vilsack, who at the time was vying for the vice-presidential spot on the Democratic ticket, denouncing the Bush administration for pursuing "the most shortsighted, breathtakingly misguided economic policy of any in my lifetime" and "mortgag[ing] our future with an astonishingly reckless tax policy." And there was "Special Interest Takeover: The Bush Administration and the Dismantling of Public Safeguards," which featured former Clinton administration officials charging that under President Bush, "special interests have launched a sweeping assault on protections for public health, safety, and the environment."

The rhetoric used in these reports and in the conferences that unveiled them was indistinguishable from the rhetoric coming, at the same time, from the Democratic National

Committee or the party's candidates for president. And that was the *nonpartisan*—the C-3—side of the Center. What was coming from the Center's partisan side—the C-4—was even more overt and even less characteristic of a think tank.

The Progress Report was the heart of the Center's work. A daily compilation of anti-Bush articles and info-bits, it was sent out via e-mail to more than 60,000 subscribers. It was produced by a twenty-seven-year-old named David Sirota, who had attracted notice on Capitol Hill when he was the energetic spokesman for Democrat David Obey on the House Appropriations Committee, and before that, for Vermont Representative Bernie Sanders, best known as the only social-ist in Congress. Christy Harvey, Sirota's deputy and the object of Al Franken's lounge-singer act, joined the Center after spending five years doing research for the liberal columnist Al Hunt. (Harvey took over the report full-time in the fall of 2004, when Sirota took a leave to work on a friend's campaign in Montana.)

Podesta told me his inspiration for *The Progress Report* was *The Note*, a daily online political analysis sheet written by Mark Halperin, the political director of ABC News (and the son of Morton Halperin). *The Note* took an often cynical, deeply inside-baseball approach to politics, and was read almost reli-giously by politicians, political operatives, and media alike. In Washington and New York, it was an important part of the daily conversation about the presidential campaign—what it said could affect coverage not only on TV but in newspapers and magazines as well—and it was that kind of agenda-setting voice that Podesta hoped to create with *The Progress Report*.

"I know Mark from the White House," Podesta told me. "I'm reading *The Note*, it was coming in my e-mail every day, and it struck me that a sharp, policy-oriented analysis could get people— You could deliver a product, you could do it early, and you could try to help drive stories, you could help people have a perspective on the news, as long as it didn't become a sort of DNC-like *Pravda* publication."

That was the important thing, Podesta told me: to write something from the Center's perspective that would catch the eye of reporters, producers, and editors without sounding as though it was coming from Democratic Party operatives. "You know, the stuff that was coming out of truly party organs was horseshit," Podesta continued. "It was never going to get better. It was always going to be what it was. And that's not anybody's fault, I don't think, it's just like that's the nature of— If you're writing propaganda, it reads like propaganda. My purpose was really different."

So *The Progress Report* was born. But Podesta's desire to avoid becoming *Pravda* soon proved more difficult than he originally envisioned. Sirota had not spent years speaking for David Obey and Bernie Sanders without developing the habit of sounding like a partisan. And *The Progress Report*, right from the beginning, became a kind of tipsheet of the day's anti-Bush spin. Should Democrats blast the president for his "Mission Accomplished" appearance on the aircraft carrier *Abraham Lincoln*? *The Progress Report* would help get out the word. Should Democrats blame "neoconservatives" for virtually everything that was wrong with President Bush's foreign policy? *The Progress Report* would give them the talking points. Should Democrats praise filmmaker Michael Moore and defend *Fahrenheit 9/11* in the face of widespread questions about its accuracy? *The Progress Report* would tell them how.

None of that was what might be called sharp, policy-oriented analysis. And it was so overtly partisan, so overtly anti-Bush, that it raised concerns among the Center's lawyers about whether the daily stream of attacks might violate the Center's standing as a "nonpartisan," 501(c)(3) institution. So in July 2004, after nine months of blasting the president—and as the presidential campaign entered its most intense phase—Podesta moved *The Progress Report* from the C-3 side of the Center to the more openly partisan C-4 side. "The campaign was getting going, and we thought that from a legal perspective, if we wanted to continue to critique both [the administration's] policy and the direction the president was taking the country, and to do it from an ideological perspective, that we needed to do that activity through a C-4 and not through a C-3," Podesta told me.

And so the Center took a giant step toward complete politicization. *The Progress Report* took the gloves off—such as they were—and became one long, uninterrupted attack on the administration. A look at headlines issued each weekday during October shows what the *Report* had become by the end of the campaign:

October 1: "Bush Administration Suppresses Facts, Spreads 'Good News'"

October 4: "Rationale for War Goes Down the Tubes"

October 5: "[Cheney] In Bed with the Axis of Evil"

October 6: "Cheney Has No Response to Halliburton Charges"

October 7: "White House 'All Wrong'"

October 8: "Bush's Jobs Record Is an Embarrassment"

October 12: "Low Wages Even Lower, Pensions Disappearing"

October 13: "Bush Can Run, but He Can't Hide"

October 14: "President Makes Promises He's Already
   Broken"

October 15: "Republicans Running Scared"

October 18: "Bush Will Say Anything to Avoid
   Responsibility"

October 19: "Major League Deception" ("Bush brazenly
   misled the American people . . .")

October 20: "Bush Hoses Firefighters"

October 21: "Ashcroft's Partisan Assault"

October 22: "Bush Administration Fights Loans for Poor"

October 25: "Halliburton Gets Special Treatment"

October 26: "Administration Pushes Bogus Theory"

October 27: "Leave No Republican Operative Behind"

October 28: "All the President's Excuses"

October 29: "Not Enough Troops to Guard Facilities"

And that was not all. The Center's website also posted a
daily "Talking Points" section, which gave more anti-Bush tid-
bits for its readers to use on television, in articles, and in daily
conversation. Here are topics from the "Talking Points" from
the month of October:

October 1: "President Failed to Make Case on National
   Security"

October 4: "Bush Case on War Collapses"

October 5: "Iraq Fantasy Unraveled by President's Own
   People"

October 6: "Cheney Fails to Advance Administration's Case"

October 7: "Administration Committed a Colossal Error by
   Invading Iraq"

October 8: "President Ignoring Reality on Jobs"

October 12: "'Ownership Society' Is a Sham"

October 13: "President's Domestic Agenda Laid Bare"

October 14: "President Fails to Offer Agenda for the
Future"

October 15: "A Progressive Agenda on Offshoring"

October 18: "Wealth Gap Widens for African Americans
and Hispanics"

October 19: "GOP Ramps-Up Voter Suppression Efforts"

October 20: "No Flu Vaccine Shortage in Congress"

October 21: "Bush Administration Limits Voting Rights"

October 22 "Former CIA Director Says War on Iraq
'Wrong'"

October 25: "Post-War Failures Endanger Americans"

October 26: "American Taxpayers Foot Huge Bill for Mess
in Iraq"

October 27: "GOP Targets New Voters"

October 28: "Excuses on Iraqi Explosives Don't Hold Up"

October 29: "'Game, Set, and Match'—President Left Iraqi
Explosives Unguarded"

There was more still: "The Daily Outrage" (of the Bush administration, that is), the Center's political cartoons, and other grist for the anti-Bush mill—dozens of attacks on Bush each day, five days a week, fifty-two weeks a year. By October 2004, the Center for American Progress had come a long way from being the "nonpartisan research and educational institute" promised by Podesta just a year earlier. His think tank— once the hope of many Democrats seeking intellectual renewal— had become, instead, a talking-points factory.

THE PERMANENT CAMPAIGN

What went wrong? From Podesta's point of view, probably nothing; it was never clear just how serious he was about founding a real think tank, as opposed to a Democratic communications shop. But others, outside the Center, had different views. I asked a well-known Democrat in Washington, one who keeps close track of the ideas and think-tank business, how he would assess Podesta's performance. He asked that I not use his name—he had to live with his fellow Democrats—and then delivered a long, and apparently heartfelt, diagnosis of a party in deep trouble. The Center, he told me, had pretty much made itself "part of the Democratic attack machine, packaging the arguments for firing Bush and generally reinforcing the Democratic assault." In that sense, he continued, Podesta's group had "merged with the 527s and other organizations focused single-mindedly on getting rid of Bush, which is a curious role for a think tank to play, but not for a Democratic advocacy group."

The problem for Podesta and others in the Democratic Party, this Democrat told me, was that they had misunderstood—almost willfully misunderstood—what made conservative ideas succeed. "When I looked at the conservative resurgence," he told me, "what I saw was a definite sequence. They began with ideas, because they understood that no amount of marketing would overcome a governing view that didn't appeal to most Americans, one that seemed reactionary. They understood that to become politically competitive, they'd have to become intellectually competitive. In the process, they raised the quality of conservative thinking and made their critique of liberal programs more compelling. The sequence was first they developed the ideas, and then came the conservative amen chorus that drives liberals so crazy—talk radio, Rush Limbaugh, Fox News, the *Washington Times.* I think Democrats tried to leapfrog the essential first stage of idea development and the hard work of honing a coherent governing philosophy. They wanted to leapfrog that stage and go on to building a vast liberal echo chamber as powerful as the conservatives'. But the problem is that just getting bigger amplifiers doesn't make the music any better."

That was the view from one of Podesta's allies. I also asked someone on the other side of the ideological divide, Heritage Foundation president Edwin Feulner—whose work building that institution had been one of Podesta's inspirations—what he thought of the Center. As it turned out, Feulner followed Podesta's group pretty closely; he was on the e-mail subscription list for *The Progress Report* and could tell me what was in that morning's edition. He also kept up with press reports about the Center, as well as with gossip going around on the grapevine. The differences between the founding of the Center and the beginnings of the conservative institutions Podesta wanted to emulate, Feulner told me, were enormous.

Feulner pointed to an article about Podesta that had appeared in the *New York Times Magazine* in October 2003, when the Center opened. The piece began with Podesta meeting a group of Democratic donors in a private home in the Washington suburbs. The donors were a frustrated lot, wanting the new think tank to wage the daily sound-bite battle with Limbaugh and Fox. But Podesta told them Democrats first needed to come up with some new ideas. "We've got to fill the intellectual pail a little," he said, according to the *Times*. To do that, the article continued, Podesta had convened a number of focus groups around the country in search of new thinking.

Feulner recited the story up to that point and then stopped suddenly. "Gotcha!" he said. "John, you've got it exactly backwards. You start a think tank because you've got certain ideas you want to propound. You don't start a think tank to find out what your ideas are. You've got it exactly bass-ackwards.'"

And there was another thing, Feulner said. Heritage's ideas were *conservative*, as opposed to *Republican*. Sometimes those were the same thing and sometimes they weren't. Heritage championed many of the ideas that Ronald Reagan governed by, but when his successor, George H. W. Bush, came to office, the think tank spent much of its time fighting a Republican president. ("I can remember how critical lots of Heritage people were of George Bush the first," my Democratic source told me. "[Former Heritage official] Burton Pines said to me that to President George H. W. Bush, 'idea' is a four-letter word.") After George W. Bush took office, Heritage opposed the White House's position on steel quotas, the farm bill, the education bill, and the Medicare prescription drug entitlement. Heritage opposed congressional Republicans on those issues, too. "Tom DeLay wouldn't speak to me for weeks because of what we did on Medicare," Feulner told me.

The point, Feulner said, was that "we are properly principled conservatives. And the 85 to 90 percent of the time that Republicans on the Hill are that way, that's great, but the other 10 percent, we're going to tell it like it is, and if they're uncomfortable and don't like that, then that's too bad." It was simply not possible to imagine Podesta or the Center acting in a similarly independent, and sometimes ornery, way. If there was a Democrat of whom the Center disapproved in 2004—other than Zell Miller, the Georgia senator who supported Bush and thus provoked the Center's wrath—that disapproval remained unspoken.

A final difference between the Center and the Heritage Foundation was that Heritage—a C-3, not a C-4—produced studies that more closely resembled true scholarship than anything produced by Podesta's group. If one looks at the Foundation's output in October 2004, some of the reports had a clear partisan edge—one was entitled "Tax Hypocrisy: Kerry Makes the Case for Fundamental Tax Reform"—but most of the others were the actual stuff of Washington think tanks:

October 4: "Pressure Sudan to Halt Oppression in Darfur"

October 4: "A Conservative Vision for U.S. Policy Toward Europe"

October 4: "The Sociological Origins of 'White-Collar Crime'"

October 4: "The Balanced Budget Amendment: The Wrong Answer to Runaway Spending"

October 6: "Revising the Payroll Survey Benchmark: What to Expect"

October 7: "The Real News in the Duelfer Report"

October 7: "Framing the Economic Debate"

October 8: "China's Orwellian Internet"

October 8: "Improving Trade with Uruguay: Cementing Economic Reforms and Advancing a Hemispheric Pact"

October 8: "Jobs: The Ultimate Pocketbook Issue"

October 12: "Details Matter: A Closer Look at Senator Kerry's Health Care Plan"

October 12: "An Examination of the Bush Health Care Agenda"

October 13: "Anything but Avoidance: Citizens for Tax Justice's Blundering Corporate Tax Report"

October 13: "Insource More Jobs by Raising the H-1B Visa Cap"

October 14: "Homework: Congress Needs to Return with a Better Plan to Reform Homeland Security Oversight"

October 15: "The Battle for Fallujah Is Crucial for Iraq's Future"

October 15: "The U.S. Should Oppose Dictatorship in Belarus"

October 19: "Defense Transformation and the New Allies"

October 19: "The Principles of Immigration"

October 19: "Kofi Annan's Shrinking Credibility"

October 19: "The Senate and House 9/11 Reform Bills Both Miss the Mark"

October 19: "Why the Budget Deficit Should Not Stop Tax Reform: The Ensuing Struggle over 'Neutrality'"

October 20: "Bush and Kerry: Stark Contrasts on National Security"

October 20: "Intelligence Reform: The Heritage Foundation's Research"

October 21: "Powell's Trip to Northeast Asia: Reaffirming Alliances in Tokyo and Seoul and Talking Straight in Beijing"

October 21: "Intelligence Reform Needs to Enhance Our Legal Capacity to Combat Terrorism"

October 21: "Scorecard on the Economy: A Guide for Policymakers"

October 22: "Google v. Microsoft: Trustbusters Not Needed"

October 25: "Dividend Policy and the 2003 Tax Cut: Preliminary Evidence"

October 25: "U.S.-Russian Security Cooperation After Beslan"

October 26: "Broadband by 2007: A Look at the President's Internet Initiative"

October 26: "The British Iraq Troop Redeployment: Why It Is Necessary"

October 27: "Global U.S. Troop Deployment, 1950–2003"

October 27: "Pro-Life Policy: Does It Make a Difference?"

October 27: "Secretary Powell Must Not Change U.S. Policy on Taiwan"

October 27: "Is the U.N. Meddling in the U.S. Presidential Election?"

October 28: "Tax Hypocrisy: Kerry Makes the Case for Fundamental Tax Reform"

October 28: "Putting Off 9/11 Reform Law Is the Right Answer"

October 29: "Past. Present! Future? Economic Growth in America"

One could even find criticism of Republicans, and of the Bush administration, in that list—all in the final weeks before a crucial election. And Heritage produced no *Progress Report.* Perhaps it came closest with its creation of the website Town-hall.com, a compendium of writings by conservative colum-nists (including some anti-Bush commentaries). But the website was not the product of Heritage scholars; in operating Townhall, Heritage served more as a common carrier than anything else.

None of that is to say that Heritage was not committed to selling its ideas. Back in 1986, Sidney Blumenthal wrote that the Foundation thrived by marketing its policy analyses to lawmakers and key aides on Capitol Hill, as well as to the "opinion-making elite," who would then disperse the ideas among the larger population. It wasn't enough just to produce a study; a think tank had to get it out to the public, too. "We don't just stress credibility," Feulner told Blumenthal in 1986. "We stress timeliness. We stress an efficient, effective delivery system. Production is one side; marketing is equally important."

Podesta's mistake was that he began the marketing campaign before he had a product to sell. When he unveiled the Center, he promised a "muscular effort" to "inject" progressive ideas "directly into the public debate." In practice, that meant little more than booking the Center's talking heads in the media. The Left, he told me, envied "not just the intellectual capacity" of the Right but also the Right's "capacity to train people and put them on television, put them on radio."

Media became an obsession at the Center. Podesta hired a full-time television booker, a former producer of the CNN debate show *Crossfire,* and he also retained the services of Michael Sheehan, one of the premier media consultants in Washington. Sheehan had advised presidential candidates John Edwards, Joseph Lieberman, Bob Graham, and others before making a heroic (and unsuccessful) effort to make John Kerry more likable on television. At the same time, Sheehan was working with the Center, training the new staff to have the right touch on TV.

It was an effort of which Podesta was quite proud. In June of 2004, when he took part in a panel discussion sponsored by the liberal organizing group Campaign for America's Future, he stopped in the middle of a thought to tell the crowd he had just received a message from the office. As it happened, CIA Director George Tenet had resigned that morning, and Podesta said the Center's people would be all over the story. "I just got an e-mail, we're doing four cable shows tonight on Tenet's resignation," he told the group. "That comes with communications scale, the ability to be out there." Somewhere, the donor who wanted Podesta to take on Fox was smiling—and the Democrat who hoped his party would truly rethink its ideas was groaning.

A BUMPER STICKER ON A LEMON

When he speaks around the country, Podesta often tells audiences that the work of the Center is more difficult than the work done by conservative think tanks. The reason, he explains, is that conservatives have simple ideas, which are easy to communicate, while liberals have complex, nuanced ideas, which are difficult to communicate. (This, of course, is the same argument that many liberals have used to explain their lack of success in talk radio.) In the *Times* article that caught Ed Feulner's eye, Podesta put it this way: "Conservatives have their eight words in a bumper sticker: 'Less government. Lower taxes. Less welfare.' And so on. Where's our eight-word bumper sticker? Well, it's harder for us because we believe in a lot more things."

It was, for many Democrats, a comforting thought, because it seemed to say, "We haven't succeeded at the ballot box

because it's harder to communicate our excellent but complicated ideas, which are far better than the simplistic slogans
used by conservatives." The bottom line was that Podesta was
arguing that his party's problems were mostly related to communications, not content.

Back in late 2003, as the Center was getting organized, I got
in touch with a centrist Democrat source—not the one quoted
earlier in this chapter—to assess Podesta's prospects. He was
aghast. The Democratic Party had yet to grapple with serious
problems with its governing philosophy and why that philosophy was not winning voters on a national level, he told me.
That was tough work, not sloganeering. "Podesta keeps saying,
'What's our bumper sticker?'" my source said with more than
a little frustration in his voice. "The problem is not the bumper
sticker. The problem is the car."

In the end, Podesta's quest for a slogan was just one of the
mistakes he made as he guided the Center in its first year. The
first big mistake was that he paid little attention to the fundamental problems of his party. The second was that he emphasized media over scholarship, reversing the relationship that
should be found in a true think tank. And the third was that he
adopted a partisan stance far beyond the limits of propriety for
the head of a tax-exempt, charitable foundation. When Podesta
said he wanted to make the Center for American Progress "something very different" from other think tanks, he undoubtedly
succeeded, although in a way that might not be in the institution's best long-term interest.

Back in November 2003, at the Center's coming-out party—
it featured the premiere of Robert Greenwald's *Uncovered,* which
had been cofunded by the Center and MoveOn—Podesta

gave the crowd his standard speech about finding "new ideas." But while he suggested that that was important, he also made it clear that it was not *all*-important. "We respect the need for debate," he told the cheering audience. "But our goal is to win."

CHAPTER EIGHT

From Fringe to Mainstream

The Strange Life of the Theocratic Conspiracy Theory

On Wednesday night, September 1, 2004, as Democratic Senator Zell Miller and Vice President Dick Cheney spoke to the Republican National Convention in Madison Square Garden, a New York University professor named Mark Crispin Miller was onstage at a small theater just a few miles away in Manhattan's East Village, telling an entranced audience that supporters of George W. Bush planned to do away with the Constitution and impose, all across the United States, a theocracy based on the first five books of the Old Testament. He wasn't kidding.

"Our common law will be based on Leviticus, okay?" Miller said in a performance of his monologue/play *A Patriot Act*. "You read your Leviticus lately? There's a long catalog in Leviticus of the things that are forbidden on pain of death."

At that, Miller's sidekick, a comedian and magician named Steve Cuiffo, began to read a list.

"Adultery. Homosexuality. Premarital sex . . ."

"Only the woman gets killed for that," Miller interjected.

"Bestiality . . ."

"They kill the animal, too," Miller said.

"Dishonoring your father and mother . . ."

"Everyone in analysis is *fucked.*"

The crowd laughed, perhaps a little nervously. Cuiffo resumed.

"Idolatry. Astrology. Blasphemy. Witchcraft. Apostasy. Heresy."

It was stern stuff, and at times Miller seemed to sense that even his sympathetic East Village audience was a little skeptical. Of course they believed George W. Bush was awful; of course he had to be defeated. But was he really planning to impose Levitical law in the United States? They hadn't heard much about that. Miller anticipated their doubts.

"A few names and faces, very quickly, so you don't think I spend my leisure time in a tinfoil hat, okay?" he said. With that, he projected a series of pictures on a screen behind him and began reading off a list of names most people had never heard of, names like R. J. Rushdoony and Howard Ahmanson, who, according to Miller, were leaders of the American theocratic movement. Unless one spent much time surfing the websites and publications of the farthest fringes of the Left—sites like AlterNet and BuzzFlash and articles with titles like "Slouching Toward Theocracy" and "The Islamic Republic of America"— much of what Miller said seemed more than a little strange.

Yet just a few months later, in the days after George W. Bush won reelection, the word "theocracy," and the question of whether the president and his supporters actually intended to impose religious law in America, burst into the mainstream. Suddenly a lot of serious people were talking seriously about theocracy.

On NBC's *Meet the Press* the Sunday after the election, host Tim Russert raised the subject with presidential advisor Karl Rove, saying, "One Democrat said to me, 'Are we on the verge of a theocracy . . . ?'" In *Time* magazine, columnist Michelle Cottle wrote, "You can't even have a beer with a rank-and-file liberal these days without the conversation degenerating into paranoid fantasies about how evangelical leaders are at this very minute hunkered down in Bush uberadvisor Karl Rove's office plotting to institute an Old Testament theocracy overseen by Attorney General Jerry Falwell." A regular columnist in *USA Today*, DeWayne Wickham, wrote that Bush's approach to religion, along with that of House Majority Leader Tom DeLay, "runs the risk of turning our democracy into a theocracy."

The *New York Times* was particularly concerned. Writing in the paper a few days after the election, former senator Gary Hart warned of the Bush administration's "disturbing tendency to insert theocratic principles into the vision of America's role in the world." In a television interview, *Times* columnist Paul Krugman worried that "what [Bush] is actually doing is he's managing to convey to one part of his base the fact that, 'Well, just give me a chance. Let's get this election behind us and I will ram a theocracy down the throats of the people,' while at the same time conveying a message to the swing voters that 'I won't.' And then the question is, which is the real Bush?" And on the op-ed page, historian Garry Wills, while not using the T-word, wrote that the election represented the triumph of "fundamentalist zeal, a rage at secularity, religious intolerance, fear of and hatred for modernity"—a reasonably good description of the foundations of a theocratic state.

Such talk had to come from somewhere. And indeed, beyond AlterNet and BuzzFlash, a small group of left-wing authors and researchers had been writing about the subject for years. But in the summer of 2004, *A Patriot Act* offered perhaps the most accessible and most penetrating treatment of the subject that had ever been produced. It was so hard-core—Miller actually predicted the execution (by stoning) of homosexuals and adulterers—that the people who, after November 2, began to muse about the idea of a theocracy might well have been embarrassed to associate themselves with it. But *A Patriot Act* was important, not because it revealed the full extent of conspiratorial theorizing that characterized a certain corner of the Left—although it did that very well—but because the days after the election revealed how quickly those theories could race, largely unexamined, from the political fringe to the mainstream.

A CONSPIRACY SO VAST

For Mark Crispin Miller, the story always begins with George W. Bush's words. And of all the verbal miscues and mangled phrases the president has ever uttered, perhaps the most famous came in a speech Bush delivered on September 17, 2002, at the East Literature Magnet School in Nashville, Tennessee. The president was speaking to an audience of students and teachers, explaining why the nation was at war. It was a good speech, at least after all the thank-yous and glad-you're-heres; Bush's words were simple, clear, and meaningful. "You've got to understand there are some in this world that simply do not adhere to the ideals we believe in," he told the children. "In Iraq, they don't put their hand over their heart and say, 'Liberty and justice for all.' They don't believe in liberty. The dictator who runs Iraq doesn't believe in justice. He only believes in liberty and justice for those who he decides get liberty and justice."

So far, so good.

Then, discussing how Saddam Hussein had repeatedly deceived the United Nations, Bush said, "There's an old saying in Tennessee—I know it's in Texas, it's probably in Tennessee—that says, 'Fool me once, shame on you. Fool me . . .'" Bush paused. An odd look crossed his face. "'Fool me . . .'" Bush began again. Clearly lost, he paused for another moment before finally blurting out, "can't get fooled again."

The moment was excruciating or hilarious, depending on one's feelings about the president. But there is no doubt that Bush's enemies loved it. Michael Moore used the clip as the closing scene of *Fahrenheit 9/11,* and Mark Crispin Miller used it in the opening scene of *A Patriot Act.* At the performance I attended, the audience laughed at Bush's gaffe, but Miller, seated in a large brown leather armchair on a sparsely furnished set, quickly shushed them. Bush's misstatement, he explained, wasn't really funny.

"That's a good one, but I suggest it's a mistake for us to make fun of Bush for his stupidity when he says things like that, because when Bush says things like that, it is not stupidity talking," Miller argued. "It's only on certain subjects that he loses contact with the mother tongue." Bush, Miller explained, stumbled when he tried to express empathy, or idealism, or altruism. On the other hand, he was able to speak quite clearly about topics like war and revenge: "When he speaks as a punisher, he's as coherent as any other politician."

From the very beginning, listening to Miller's presentation

required a certain amount of suspension of disbelief. By almost anyone's standard, George W. Bush had made more idealistic speeches than any president in recent memory. (Indeed, had there ever been a chief executive more idealistic about the capacity of freedom to improve conditions in the world?) Nearly all of those speeches were delivered in a perfectly normal fashion, without any major miscues; Bush seemed completely comfortable speaking about empathy, idealism, and altruism. But Miller, who has written two studies of Bush, *The Bush Dyslexicon* and *Cruel and Unusual,* was laying the predicate for his theory that the president was part of a theocratic conspiracy, and he began, in effect, by asking the audience to share his assumptions. A relaxed and often engaging performer—he teaches something called "media ecology" at NYU—he pulled the crowd into his story, and they seemed happy to go along.

The most important feeling that Bush could not express, Miller continued, was remorse: "Apologizing, admitting fallibility—I mean, this guy could just as easily say 'shame on me' as he could improvise a sonnet." The audience laughed as Miller played the Tennessee video one more time. "Watch it again, and you'll notice that it's when he sees the phrase 'shame on me' hovering on his mental horizon that he gets this deer-in-the-headlights look and he decides he better quote the Who instead."

Having established, at least for the sake of his argument, that Bush was incapable of expressing remorse, Miller next argued that the president lived in a world of imagined demons. "When reasonable people look at their adversaries, they see other people," Miller said. "They see human beings. Mistaken, maybe; wrongheaded; possibly insane—but human beings nonetheless. When Bush and company look at their adversaries, they don't see human beings. They see creatures of an entirely different order. What they see is demons—hateful, sex-obsessed, unpatriotic demons."*

Who made up Bush *and company*? No one in the audience could have been surprised when Miller listed the Reverend Jerry Falwell, Rush Limbaugh, Ann Coulter, and a number of other usual suspects. Miller read Falwell's famous statement, made during an appearance with fellow televangelist Pat Robertson two days after September 11, that the terrorist attacks were God's punishment for the sins of "the pagans, and the abortionists, and the feminists, and the gays and the lesbians who are actively trying to make that an alternative lifestyle, the ACLU, People for the American Way—all of them who have tried to secularize America."

"So those three thousand deaths downtown were a good thing, right?" Miller said. "I mean, God willed it. He knows what He's doing. And it doesn't take a huge leap of the imagination to infer that all those demonic subgroups of our population—you know, the pagans and the lesbians and the civil libertarians—they should be wiped out because they're evil-doers. . . . Remarkable how easily a man of the cloth can talk genocide."

Miller was asking his audience to make another one of those assumptions necessary to reach the end he wanted to achieve. Was Falwell really talking about genocide? Even if one agreed

---

*Although I was scribbling notes furiously in the dark as Miller spoke, I wasn't able to get everything down verbatim; I have taken some of these quotations from the DVD of *A Patriot Act*, released in the fall of 2004, so some of the words might differ slightly from those spoken during the performance I attended.

with everything Falwell said—something very few people seemed to do, since his remarks were widely condemned at the time—it would still take a huge leap of the imagination to infer that pagans and lesbians and civil libertarians should be exterminated. And it would take a bigger leap still to infer that Falwell was speaking the mind of George W. Bush, who in the days after September 11 expressed feelings that were precisely the opposite of Falwell's, and who criticized Falwell's remarks as "inappropriate." But Miller moved on.

He played another clip of Bush speaking, also from September 2002, a few days after the Tennessee speech. Bush called Saddam Hussein a "man who would use weapons of mass destruction at the drop of a hat" and outlined a scenario in which Iraq might supply terrorist organizations with weapons of mass destruction. "We will not allow the world's worst leaders to threaten us with the world's worst weapons," Bush declared.

"No problem with his grammar there, did you notice?" Miller said. "I mean, as a verbal construct, this was flawless." Of course, Miller added, Bush's statement was also "demented" and "insane." And yet the president's audience—he was speaking at an Army National Guard aviation facility in Trenton, New Jersey—applauded enthusiastically. Why was that?

"What they were applauding was his anger," Miller said. "That's the secret of Bush's popularity, insofar as he is popular. It's all about the rage. Millions, several million of our fellow citizens admire in this president precisely those qualities that terrify the rest of the world. His temper, his self-righteousness, his inflexibility. Now, what's the reason for this appeal? Well, obviously, as we've seen before in history, you've got the masses, you've got a lot of have-nots. They feel themselves somehow empowered by the fantasy of kicking ass along with the big guy. It explains the appeal of most action heroes. I mean, this is what the Germans liked about Hitler."

That statement marked a critical moment in *A Patriot Act.* Once an anti-Bush presentation reaches the Hitler analogy, it comes to a dividing line of sorts. People in the audience either find such comparisons extreme, and somewhat repellent, or they don't. The audience at *A Patriot Act* didn't; there were no boos, no hisses, no *c'mons*, no walking out, not even any murmuring. So Miller continued. Did all of that rage felt by Bush supporters result simply from have-nots resenting the haves? No, there was another factor at work, Miller said. And the other factor was sex.

Miller showed a famous photo from a Marlboro cigarettes ad featuring a cowboy in a kind of half-crouch, apparently in the act of roping an unseen but wild animal. The rope twisted around the man's upper thighs and waist. Miller directed a light cursor at the man's crotch. "Check out his package," he said. Then Miller quickly changed the slide to a photo of Bush, during his May 2003 visit to the aircraft carrier USS *Abraham Lincoln,* in which the president's parachute harness wrapped around his upper thighs and waist.

Miller said that a few days after that heavily publicized event, he was watching the television program *Hardball,* which featured the talk radio host and former Watergate felon G. Gordon Liddy as a guest. Miller read Liddy's words: "Here comes George Bush. You know, he's in his flight suit, he's striding across the deck, and he's wearing his parachute harness, you know—and I've worn those because I parachute—and it makes the best of his manly characteristic. . . . He has just won every woman's vote in the United States of America." In the theater, the flashlight pointed to Bush's crotch.

"There's something here worth following up," Miller said. "I suggest to you that it will help us to grasp this anger that I'm talking about, because there's something far more mysterious about this rage that now basically runs the country." On the screen, Miller flashed a series of pictures. There was Pennsylvania Senator Rick Santorum, the conservative Republican who once made an infamous comment musing about "man on dog" sex. There was confrontational radio host Michael Savage. There was conservative opinionmeister William Bennett, who famously had a penchant for gambling, and Limbaugh, who even more famously became addicted to prescription painkillers.

"Now, are these people, all these people, the whole pack of them, are they hypocrites?" Miller asked. Someone in the audience shouted out that yes, of course they were. "No," Miller answered. "I would suggest to you that they're not really hypocrites. To call them hypocrites is to improve the picture somewhat." The typical hypocrite's hypocrisy is usually benign, Miller argued, while "these people have to have, as if to reconfirm the fact that they are not evil themselves, they have to have some object for their projection, some object whom they can blame for everything they hate in themselves." That explained the Right's opposition to Bill Clinton, Miller said— it was "pure projectivity" by sexually repressed conservatives. But now, "What those [right-wing] figures did, all of them, on the domestic front throughout the '90s, our president does globally. I mean, our foreign policy is based on projectivity. Bush, you could say, is our Projector-in-Chief."

"Everything Bush says about Saddam Hussein is true of

him. He's talking about *himself*," Miller continued. When Bush said that Saddam had defied the world, he was talking about himself. When he said that Saddam had continually lied, he was talking about himself. When he said that Saddam had made the United Nations look foolish, he was talking about himself. "I'm suggesting that there is a weird convergence here, that this intense, hostile, angry, fearful loathing is not about Saddam Hussein," Miller explained. It was really about George W. Bush and a right-wing "projective movement."

"It's about Republicans who liken John Kerry to Hitler," Miller said with clear indignation in his voice. (Perhaps ten minutes had passed since Miller himself had compared Bush's appeal to Hitler's.) "It's about Republicans who call Democrats the 'coalition of the wild-eyed.' It's about Tom DeLay claiming Ted Kennedy has indulged in hate speech because Kennedy criticized our policy in Iraq. Hate speech!

"Now, on the grand scale, this is a movement full of rage against the other, because the other is filled with rage. This is a movement full of bloodlust, eager to wipe out the bloodthirsty other, kind of a mirror image of Osama bin Laden. This is a deeply uncanny and very troubling development. It is a movement. It exists. And it wants to take us back. I mean, I'm talking way back. I mean, sure they want to go back before the '70s and '60s to the '50s. No doubt about that. They also want to go back before the New Deal to the '20s. Well, they also want to go back before the Progressive Era to the Gilded Age. Well, not quite. They also want to go back before the Emancipation Proclamation to the days of slavery. Not even. What they want to do is take us back to a moment prior to the Enlightenment. They want to take us back to a moment when faith registered more than reason."

The screen behind Miller filled with a medieval print of a heretic being broken on a wheel. "They want to take us back to an imaginary age of absolute moral clarity, when good was good and evil was evil and everybody could see the difference," Miller explained. "They want to take us back to an imaginary Manichean age when you were either with us or against us, which means you either are us, or we'll exterminate you, because we can only tolerate ourselves, we can only tolerate those who share our values."

And there it was. In the course of a half-hour or so, Miller had gone from George W. Bush's verbal stumbles to his flight suit to an imagined Manichean age in which all dissenters will be exterminated. The audience seemed spellbound as Miller moved to the centerpiece of his theory.

"Is it just a lone megalomaniac in the White House?" he asked. "No, no. We're talking about a theocratic movement that was instrumental in placing him there." Miller then read a statement from the website of an obscure organization called the Chalcedon Foundation, founded in 1965 by a radical theologian named R. J. Rushdoony, which was devoted to a theocratic doctrine known as Christian Reconstructionism.

"'We believe that the whole word of God must be applied to all of life,'" Miller read. "'It is not only our duty as individuals, families, and churches to be Christian, but it is also the duty of the state, the schools, the arts and sciences, law, economics, and every other sphere to be under Christ the King. Nothing is exempt from His dominion. We must live by His word, not our own.'"

"Now, what this means programmatically is that the United States should be transformed officially into a Christian republic, where non-Christians are disenfranchised," Miller told the audience. "It will also mean replacing the Constitution, which the theocrats still hate, with the first five books of the Bible." At that point, he launched into the list of sins punishable by death that began this chapter.

Miller projected a lineup of photographs on the screen behind him. The men in the photos were, he said, leaders of the theocratic plot. In the upper left was Rushdoony. Next to Rushdoony was conservative California philanthropist Howard Ahmanson, who has funded a number of conservative causes and once served on the board of the Chalcedon Foundation. Next was Marvin Olasky, the academic who coined the phrase "compassionate conservatism" used by the Bush campaign in 2000, and who is a friend of Ahmanson's and a sometime beneficiary of Ahmanson's funding. Then came Senator Trent Lott, televangelists Falwell and James Robison, the Reverend Louis Sheldon of the Traditional Values Coalition, and finally, and somewhat inexplicably, Iran-contra figure Oliver North, now the host of *War Stories* on the Fox News Channel.

Miller argued that the men acted under the cover of something called the Council for National Policy, which he described as a super-secret group of politically active conservatives. The Council does, in fact, exist; it was founded in 1981 by a group of well-known conservatives, including Richard Viguerie, Paul Weyrich, Howard Phillips, Morton Blackwell, Phyllis Schlafly, and others. Because one of its founders was Tim LaHaye, author of the apocalyptic *Left Behind* novels, and because the Council does not make public what goes on at its meetings, some on the Left have theorized that the organization is a front for a theocratic initiative.

"In 2000, Governor Bush addressed the CNP behind closed doors," Miller said. "The campaign never released his remarks.

We don't know what he told them, but is it really so difficult for us to see the theocratic drift of every single one of the administration's policies? . . . It's hard to understate the extent to which this administration is driven by the theocratic agenda.

"Let's take this war, for example, this mysterious war, this gratuitous war right in the middle of the War on Terrorism. Why do that? Why go there? I mean, is it all Halliburton? Is it all oil? Can economic motives explain this whole thing? Well, no. There's another dimension to this." Miller cited a quote in a somewhat sympathetic study of the Bush family, *The Bushes: Portrait of a Dynasty* by Hoover Institution scholar Peter Schweizer and his wife, Rochelle. "George sees this as a religious war," the book quoted an unnamed family member as saying. "He does not have a PC view of this war. His view of this is that they are trying to kill the Christians. And we the Christians will strike back with more force and more ferocity than they will ever know." From that single anonymous quote, Miller concluded, "That's a projective movement, exactly like Islamism. They're trying to wipe us out. We must exterminate them."

And with that, Miller came to the end of his theory. He had a few more points to make—he said Bush's theocratic impulse rippled through domestic policies like those pursued by the Office of Faith-Based and Community Initiatives and the administration's stands on the environment—but he had laid out his best case. "This is kind of a grim picture I'm painting, isn't it?" he asked the crowd. Of course they agreed. And who wouldn't—if it were true?

ARE YOU NOW, OR HAVE YOU EVER BEEN, A THEOCRAT?

A few weeks after seeing *A Patriot Act,* I got in touch with Miller, who said he would be happy to answer my questions by e-mail. I began with a practical one: How would his nightmare vision actually come to pass? "How would the Constitution be done away with?" I asked. "Would the president simply declare his own law, and the legislative and judicial branches just go along with it? What about the military? And the population at large? I'd like to get a better idea of how you think such a change might actually occur."

I had misunderstood things, Miller answered. "As you'll find when you read through the literature," he wrote, "the U.S. theocratic movement is not based, as far as I know, on any simple plan for swift takeover. It is a gradualist movement, based on the assumption, or expectation, that America will naturally evolve into theocracy, primarily through the rise of a committed generation of young [Christian] Reconstructionists at work throughout the government, both federal and local. . . . The strategy is *incremental* change."

"Do you see that happening right now?" I followed up. "Are there some events that you would characterize as milestones that we have already passed on the way to a theocracy? And when you write [in the book *Cruel and Unusual*] that 'These Christian nations would be just as tolerant and democratic as Iran under Khomeini, or Afghanistan under the Taliban,' do you mean that you would envision the kind of chopping off of hands and soccer-field executions in the United States that we saw in Afghanistan?"

"Yes, I see it happening right now," Miller responded. "I see it in a White House that uses federal revenues to support religious groups—nearly every one of them Christian—that proselytize. I see it in an army whose troops pray collectively to Jesus, and some of whom get baptized, just before they hit Fallujah. I see it in the recent legislation (in the House) meant to keep the federal judiciary from having any say on faith-based matters. I see it in a government that pushes programs without any scientific basis, but that have the full approval of the Christian Right: abstinence-only school programs for teens, an abstinence-based AIDS policy, 'intelligent design,' etc. . . .

"You seem to want to ridicule the whole idea by reference to atrocities committed by *Islamist* theocrats," Miller continued. "Well, Islam is Islam, not Christianity. So, no, we won't be seeing women in the U.S. forced to put on burkas, or the public chopping-off of hands. But there are Christians out there arguing for other punishments no less atrocious. Death by stoning for adultery, for instance, or for children who dishonor their parents. If you have trouble finding such examples, let me know, although I'm certain that a journalist of your abilities can find them easily enough, as they are commonplace on theocratic Web sites."

Granted, there are kooky religious websites in the world. But Miller's answer seemed to convey a deep hostility to religion itself; some of his answers did not seem to make sense in any other context. For example, if I were a soldier about to hit Fallujah, I would certainly be praying my heart out, and I wouldn't be surprised if the guy next to me were doing the same. On another of Miller's points, the federal judiciary seems to have an enormous say in faith-based matters, at least to the extent of determining where such activities can and cannot take place. That seemed obvious. But where some people—like me—saw normal American life, Miller saw the beginning of a theocratic takeover.

I wondered whether the people and institutions that Miller had identified as committed theocrats in fact lived up to the name. First there was the Chalcedon Foundation. Miller had not misrepresented the group; a look at its statements and positions suggested that it was indeed devoted to promoting a theocratic view of the world. But Miller had exaggerated Chalcedon's importance by quite a bit. The foundation was virtually unknown and relatively tiny; its 2003 federal tax filings listed total contributions of about $576,000. Chalcedon took in another $216,000 that year by selling a piece of property, and $96,000 more from selling books and tapes. In all, the foundation's assets were about $1 million—roughly one-thirtieth of what George Soros alone contributed to pro-Democratic causes in the 2004 election. Perhaps Chalcedon's devotees were committed, as Miller said, but they were not particularly powerful.

Then there was R. J. Rushdoony, the theologian and founder of Chalcedon. Rushdoony died in 2001, so there would be no asking him about his beliefs. Howard Ahmanson, the next link in Miller's theocratic conspiracy chain, was famously reclusive, speaking very seldom with the press (he suffered from Tourette's syndrome as well as a general suspicion of reporters). It would be difficult to speak to him. But Marvin Olasky, the third link in the chain, was an open and accessible man. I called him up.

Olasky has been all over the map spiritually and intellectually. Born and raised a Jew, he became a Christian. Once a Marxist, he became a libertarian. Whatever his beliefs, he managed to establish himself in the worlds of academia and journalism. A longtime professor of journalism at the University of Texas at Austin, he was invited to Princeton University to serve as a visiting professor in the 2004–2005 academic year, and since 1992 he has edited a Christian-oriented news magazine, *World*. When we spoke, I asked him about the first two links in the chain. First, was Rushdoony, the founder of Chalcedon, a theocrat?

"Yeah, I think so," Olasky said. "He was in favor of putting biblical law into practice." There really wasn't any question about it; Rushdoony's massive book *The Institutes of Biblical Law* was essentially a three-volume guidebook to theocracy. "The mistake I think he made is that modern America is not ancient Israel," Olasky told me. "Israel was a holiness theme park. America is a liberty theme park."

What about Ahmanson? The answer to that question was a bit more complicated. Olasky told me that in the 1980s Ahmanson "was heavily influenced by Rushdoony" but that he later distanced himself, ultimately leaving Chalcedon's board of directors. "I don't know how far Howard went," Olasky told me, "but I know Howard is no longer connected with Rushdoony's organization."

That didn't really answer the question. I wanted to ask Ahmanson himself, and Olasky agreed to help me get in touch with him.

Through Olasky, I asked Ahmanson, via e-mail, "What do you say to critics of the Left like Miller who accuse you of planning to impose a scheme of biblical law in the United States?" Ahmanson answered quickly, sending me a one-page statement headlined "Why I Am Not a Theocrat."

"In one sense, the term 'theocracy' has often been used of societies politically governed by priests and religious leaders," he wrote. "Obviously I do not favor this." A few of the other things he wrote seemed to have the flavor of theocracy—"I hold that the biblical law is the highest form of the natural law"—while others did not. For example, Ahmanson said that it was "highly debatable" whether there should be government-run public schools, but since there were, "I am opposed to organized prayer or Bible reading in them." Why? Because "God is not necessarily pleased with it . . . and because the 'God' prayed to is quite likely to be something other than the Trinitarian God of the Gospel." Ahmanson also told me that he did not favor Old Testament penalties, like stoning, for violations of the Ten Commandments.

It seemed that every reason Ahmanson gave for not being a theocrat was a biblical one. It still wasn't clear whether he had serious theocratic leanings or not. I wrote Ahmanson another note, asking three more questions: The first was, "Can you say, simply and directly, that you support the Constitution as the foundation of the United States government?" The second was, "Do you believe in and support the First Amendment, Second Amendment, etc., and the protections contained in them?" And finally, I asked, "If you were to serve in the federal government, could you take an oath to 'preserve, protect, and defend' the Constitution?"

"I do support the American founding and find it not contrary to the Scriptures!" Ahmanson wrote back. "I'm on the board of a think tank called the Claremont Institute that is devoted to the American founding. I quote the Bible first because I consider it to be the higher authority, and the founding documents to be authorities ordained by God for this nation. But if I'm going to argue against 'theocracy,' I'm going to do it on the basis of *logos tou Theou,* if you know what I mean."

It was a clever answer; *logos tou Theou* is Greek for "the word of God." And it did seem perfectly reasonable for Ahmanson to believe, as many of the Founders did, that the Constitution does not grant us rights but rather safeguards those rights given to us by a higher power. What did that make Ahmanson? I really didn't know. He seemed to occupy some sort of middle ground between the theocratic impulse and the modern democratic one.

So Miller had been right about one man, Rushdoony, and perhaps partially right about a second man, Ahmanson. But *A Patriot Act* described a large and powerful conspiracy. Olasky was allegedly the third man in the chain of conspiracy, so I asked him where he stood. "As for me, I can say in one sentence: I am not a theocrat, and I believe in the Constitution," he told me. Elaborating, he said, "I tend to be something of a Christian libertarian. On just about everything, whether it's schools or social welfare programs, I'm pro-choice—not on abortion, because that's the killing of human beings. But I am very, very, very far from being a theocrat."

I asked Olasky about the actual vehicle of Miller's conspiracy theory, the Council for National Policy. What did he know about that? Olasky told me he had been with the group only once, when he delivered a speech at its meeting in 2003. Olasky said he spoke about education—school choice, vouchers, the Christian school that he and his wife started in Austin, Texas, a few years ago. Most of those attending seemed to him to be wealthy midwestern donors visiting Washington to hear briefings on a number of subjects—not exactly a rare occurrence in the capital. "The biggest reaction I recall was someone who asked a question about how I'd come to be a Christian, coming out of my Marxist background in the early 1970s," Olasky told me. "That seemed to interest the audience quite a bit. If that's what Mark Crispin Miller thinks is the center of power, he's way off." I asked Olasky if he had been sworn to secrecy about anything that went on at the Council meeting. He said no.

Of course, one wouldn't seriously expect Olasky to say, "Why yes, as it happens I am involved in a secret plot to impose theocratic law on the United States." But Olasky seemed open about it all, and, more important, Miller, for all the innuendo and six-degrees-of-separation theorizing, had never presented any evidence that even suggested, much less proved, that Olasky was a theocrat. So I went back to Miller.

"I still have some questions about Olasky," I wrote. "You say he was a protégé of Ahmanson and has in general espoused the [Christian] Reconstructionist agenda. But all you cite is Olasky's having thanked or acknowledged Reconstructionists a few times in the past; the only quote you have from Olasky himself is his statement about the Bible and slavery, which seems more odd than anything else. [Olasky had once written, "While Scripture makes defense of slavery in some modes impossible and in other modes difficult, it does not simply ban all of its modes."] It seems to me that, given what you have cited, saying that he favors the replacement of the Constitution with law based on the Pentateuch is going too far."

"Olasky is a cagey guy, but his work makes quite clear that he's committed to a Christianized republic," Miller responded. "This is manifest throughout [Olasky's book] *Compassionate Conservatism*, although the pitch is very subtly made: his denial of the Establishment Clause, for example, is, as a rhetorical device, far more effective than, say, urging the adoption of Levitical law could ever be. Olasky's theocratic views are more explicitly expressed in *World*, the publication that he edits. If you regard the general thrust of *World* as moderate, Byron, you and I inhabit different planets."

With that, Miller's story had changed; he moved from the specific to the general. Olasky expressed his theocratic ideas "subtly." The "general thrust" of Olasky's magazine, *World,* was theocratic, although Miller did not cite any examples, either in his note to me or in *A Patriot Act* or *Cruel and Unusual.* And Miller shifted the terms of the debate; one would have to live on a different planet, he said, to view *World* as moderate. But the question was not whether *World* was moderate. The magazine was, in fact, mostly conservative, and based on religious principles, but the question was whether it was theocratic. And Miller offered no evidence that it was.

At that, Miller's conspiracy chain seemed to fall apart. Like many conspiracy theorists, he had begun with a little bit of truth—Rushdoony really was a theocrat—and built an enormous edifice on a rather tiny foundation. By the time he got to Olasky, it was all over. And no one else down the line even seemed to matter. Pat Robertson had been losing influence for years among conservatives. The same was true of Falwell. And Trent Lott? He had worked within the constitutional system for decades and had been both a Democrat and a Republican. If ever a man was a politician to his very core—with a flexible belief system that one would never find in a theocrat—it was Trent Lott.

And anyway, in the end, what did it all have to do with George W. Bush? I called Michael Cromartie, who knows many of the people involved and who studies evangelicals in his role as vice president of the Washington-based Ethics and Public Policy Center. "To try to tie all this straight back to the president is utterly illogical and absurd," Cromartie told me.

"The president comes out of sort of an evangelical therapeutic ethos, of small men's Bible study groups talking about how they got over their problems. It's what Terry Eastland [of the *Weekly Standard*] calls the 'love-thy-neighbor presidency.' That's the extent of his public philosophy."

ONE LAST THEORY

Before the election, I was undecided on whether to include a chapter in this book on *A Patriot Act* and the Bush/theocracy theories. For the most part, the idea seemed, well, too far out there, and not really representative of a significant strain of thinking on the Left. But that changed after November 2, with the words of Garry Wills and Gary Hart and Paul Krugman and the assorted Democrats who expressed their concerns to Tim Russert and Michelle Cottle. Theocracy was hot, and yet few people knew the full extent of the conspiratorial theorizing that supported the idea.

Miller would probably say that was because the right-wing media—in his mind, that meant institutions like the *New York Times* and the *Washington Post*—didn't want people to learn about it. At one point in *A Patriot Act* he said, "I don't know if you've noticed, but we in essence have lost our civil liberties." Toward the end of our correspondence, I asked him whether he was talking about himself. "You have a play that is performed in New York and which drew a packed audience during convention week and at other times," I wrote. "It is extremely critical of George W. Bush and some of the people who support him. You have two successful books that are also extremely critical of Bush. And yours are not nitpicking criticisms; they are very big and very serious charges about the president. You express your views in all sorts of media interviews. You are a professor at a major university. So the question is: Do you believe your rights of free expression have been hindered or limited in any way?"

"I didn't say, '*I* . . . have lost *my* civil liberties,' " Miller answered. "I said that *we* have lost *ours*—as *we* have lost all those civil liberties that can now be denied to *any* of us." Miller went on to discuss the USA Patriot Act and what he believed were various threats to freedom of the press. "As to my own free speech rights," he continued, "I'm both flattered and amused that you would use my case to demonstrate that I enjoy the same unfettered liberty as, say, Ann Coulter or Sean Hannity." Miller conceded that *A Patriot Act* drew good audiences—although it played far off Broadway—but said he created the play in the first place because of "sheer frustration at my total inability to speak, in public, critically about the president. After 9/11, I could give no bookstore readings, nor appear on radio or TV shows to talk about my work. (I was allowed on some small lefty shows, but that was it.)" Miller said he was not charging that the White House had worked to silence him. But he added, "I have no doubt whatsoever that the corporate media was very careful not to let me on the air to talk about either of my books on Bush."

Miller also complained that his books were not widely reviewed. "The national print media largely ignored *The Bush Dyslexicon*—although the *Washington Post* attacked it," he wrote. "*Cruel and Unusual* has received a total of three reviews, two negative and one noncommittal." One of those reviews, in the *New York Times,* compared Miller to Coulter. That really stung.

"That's the way things work here, by and large," Miller told me. "As 'censorship' refers to blunt suppression by the state, I cannot accurately claim to have been censored outright. On the other hand, insofar as one does exercise one's free speech rights primarily through the media, and as the media system here is very cozy with the state, I *can* say that my free speech rights *have* 'been hindered or limited' by the arrangement." He again pointed out the attention given to Coulter—her success really seemed to bother him—"while I, and others similarly critical, are kept off in the margins."

And there we ended the conversation. Miller seemed to be describing a corporate conspiracy to control the media, and a media conspiracy to ignore critics of George W. Bush; and if those critics had not been ignored, they would have revealed the theocratic conspiracy the president headed. That was a lot of conspiring. In years past, others had believed in the "October Surprise," or in the theory that the CIA had introduced crack cocaine into Los Angeles, or, going further back, in the gunman on the grassy knoll. Now, it was the grand unified theocratic scenario.

In *A Patriot Act,* Miller said that reasonable people see their adversaries as essentially human. Perhaps those adversaries are mistaken, and perhaps they are insane, but they are nevertheless human beings. Bush and his fellow theocrats, on the other hand, see their adversaries as demons—"hateful, sex-obsessed, unpatriotic demons"—who are engaged in all sorts of dark plotting. That idea was at the very heart of Miller's theory. And yet in *A Patriot Act,* Miller portrayed *his* adversaries as hateful, sex-obsessed, unpatriotic demons who are engaged in all sorts of dark plotting. The irony was so obvious that it virtually slapped him in the face, yet he appeared not to notice it.

But the bigger issue in Miller's story was not about Miller himself. The larger point was that some very serious liberals and Democrats had, in the days after the election, almost instantly embraced his ideas, and some prestigious media outlets had given the theocracy question real prominence. After November 2, 2004, some mainstream commentators threw around the word "theocracy" as easily as Miller and the writers on BuzzFlash and AlterNet had done a few months earlier.

Perhaps that was the end result of all the incredible energy that had been thrown into the effort against George W. Bush, in movies and on radio and in political organizations and on the Internet. By the end of the presidential campaign, Bush had been so demonized that his adversaries—not the kooks on the fringes, but intelligent, respectable people—were ready to believe almost anything about him. It was as if, in the 1990s, the *New York Times* had decided to become a forum for those theories about Bill Clinton having committed murders in Arkansas. Of course, that didn't happen; back then, that kind of stuff was mostly kept on the edges of the political conversation. In 2004, with a different president in the White House, it *became* the conversation.

"We Bought It, We Own It"

The Lessons of 2004 for the Future

On the day after George W. Bush was reelected, the team at MoveOn sent a wrenching e-mail to members around the country. "We'll admit to being heartbroken by the outcome of yesterday's election," wrote Wes Boyd, Joan Blades, and Eli Pariser. "It's a dark day."

Just six months earlier, Blades could barely contain her enthusiasm as she exclaimed, "We're going to win by a landslide." Now, she and her colleagues were looking for bright spots. There was Wisconsin, where they said MoveOn volunteers had turned out more than 27,000 voters, far more than Kerry's margin of victory. There was New Hampshire, a state won by Bush in 2000 but by Kerry in 2004, "where we turned out 9,820 of the people on our list and Kerry won by 9,171 votes." And there was Colorado, where they claimed to have helped Democrat Ken Salazar win election to the Senate.

There were also inspiring stories of volunteers who

responded to last-minute calls to join the Democratic get-out-the-vote effort. In Ohio, MoveOn put out a mass e-mail just three hours before the polls closed, and in rushed two dozen volunteers. "One volunteer whose car broke down ran home, grabbed her bike, and biked from house to house in the thunderstorm, knocking on doors and reminding people to vote," they wrote.

Such tales of determination just made "the loss more painful in some ways." But Boyd, Blades, and Pariser wanted everyone to know they were determined to keep on. "Our journey toward a progressive America has always been bigger than George Bush," they wrote. "The current leg is just beginning—we're still learning how to build a citizen-based politics together. . . . Today, we'll take a breath. Tomorrow, we'll keep moving toward the America we know is possible."

The letter combined the shock of defeat with a touch of humility. Both were gone just a few weeks later, when the MoveOn team addressed the question of who should be the next chairman of the Democratic National Committee. "We can't afford four more years of leadership by a consulting class of professional election losers," Pariser wrote in another e-mail to members. "Now it's our party. We bought it, we own it, and we're going to take it back."

It wasn't the kind of talk one might expect from an organization trying to regroup after a devastating loss. And it certainly wasn't the voice of an organization searching its soul to find out what had gone wrong. After the election, MoveOn was in no mood to look back.

They weren't alone. The group's biggest benefactor, George Soros, also seemed disinclined to ask whether his approach to the campaign had been productive. He sent out no "heart-

broken" letter—to whom would it have been addressed?—
nor did he make any substantial public statement in the days
after the election. Instead, the blog that Soros had started during his twelve-state tour to defeat Bush simply stopped on
November 3, with the brief statement: "I hope, but don't trust,
that the second Bush administration will have learned something from the mistakes of the first." With that, Soros announced
he was off to Europe for work related to his foundation; by the
Friday after Election Day, he was in Budapest, receiving an
award from the president of his native Hungary.

Indeed, if Soros was pondering anyone's mistakes, it was
not his own. Days before the election, Soros had said, in a
speech to the National Press Club in Washington, "Frankly, if
President Bush is reelected, I shall go into some kind of
monastery to reflect." The audience laughed; they instantly
assumed he was joking that if the election turned out badly, he
would have to engage in some sort of penance and meditation
on his own actions. But Soros meant nothing of the sort. "I've
been blaming the Bush administration for the policies followed by this administration, which really took America off
the rails," he said, "but if we now endorse him, then my next
question will be: What's wrong with us?" Soros seemed genuinely perplexed. Over and over, he had told his fellow American voters what they should do, and there seemed a good
chance (which indeed came to pass) that they would not listen. What was wrong with them?

At the offices of America Coming Together in downtown
Washington, there was, likewise, no appetite for self-
examination. The organization had helped turn out more
Democratic voters than ever before, and Ellen Malcolm and
Steve Rosenthal were not inclined to call that a failure. ACT did

launch a meticulous review to find out which of its tactics had worked and which had not. But it was a technical approach, to find out where tinkering would be needed, rather than a general assessment of the group's strategy. Shortly after the voting, a reporter from the left-leaning website *Salon* pressed Malcolm repeatedly to speculate on the group's failure. "What went wrong?" the reporter wanted to know. "Why had ACT failed?" Malcolm insisted that ACT had been very successful and had met its goals. When the reporter persisted, Malcolm cut the question short. "You're not listening to what I'm saying," she said.

A month after the election, Steve Rosenthal took to the pages of the *Washington Post* to defend ACT's work. The ideas going around that George W. Bush won Ohio because Republicans were able to turn out more religious voters, or more exurban voters, or that GOP volunteers did a better job than ACT's paid staff—those were all myths, Rosenthal argued. The real problem for Democrats was that voters trusted Bush more than Kerry to handle national security issues, and Kerry was unable to exploit economic issues enough to damage Bush. In short, Rosenthal's message was: Don't look at ACT. We did our job. The candidate should have done his.

Michael Moore began Election Day on a hopeful note. "We are hours away from what we hope will be the good news about President-elect Kerry," he e-mailed supporters in the early hours of November 2. He opened the day in Florida, hoping his camera teams would somehow catch voter fraud in action. When that didn't happen, he moved on to Ohio. "I am in Cleveland, and the turnout is huge," he e-mailed as evening approached. "I've been getting early tracking results from across the country, and things are looking good—very good."

And then, silence. Moore was not heard from again until

November 4, when he sent an e-mail to supporters headlined "My first thoughts about the election." The message was simply a list of the names of every American serviceman and woman who had been killed in Iraq. "May they rest in peace," Moore wrote, closing the letter. "And may they forgive us someday."

The next day, Moore was in a better mood, sending out the message "17 Reasons Not to Slit Your Wrists." Among them: Bush's victory was not all that big, Republicans didn't win a filibuster-proof majority in the Senate, and "88 percent of Bush's support came from white voters. In 50 years, America will no longer have a white majority. Hey, 50 years isn't such a long time!"

Then it was back to promoting *Fahrenheit 9/11*. Moore intensely wanted his film to be nominated for an Academy Award in the Best Picture category, but by the end of 2004, the movie was overtaken by more powerful forces. First, a number of Oscar-contending pictures, like *The Aviator* and *Sideways,* grabbed the attention of the movie industry. And then a vague sense of embarrassment about Moore's excesses seemed to take hold among some in the entertainment business. It did not take them long—just hours—after Bush's victory to begin speculating that Moore had energized the president's support-ers at least as much as Kerry's. In the end, there would be no Oscar nomination.

As might be expected, Robert Greenwald kept a much lower profile, not making any public statements after the election. Instead, he kept on keeping on. In December, he joined up with a number of organizations—MoveOn, David Brock's Media Matters for America, AlterNet, and others—to protest the Sin-clair Broadcast Group, which during the campaign had stirred controversy when it considered airing a segment of an anti-Kerry documentary (in the end, the piece did not air). Also, with Moore out of the picture for a Best Documentary Oscar, Greenwald hoped that *Uncovered* might sneak into the nominations; according to a report in *Daily Variety,* he pulled the movie from a scheduled television run so that it would be eligible. But the Academy ignored him, too.

On Air America, less than nine months after his "Bush is going down! Bush is going down!" debut performance, Al Franken began his first postelection program with a bitter comedy routine. Kerry had made mistakes, Franken conceded. For example, it was a mistake when Kerry announced, in the first debate, that he would put U.S. national security in the hands of other countries. And then there was his decision to announce that he would ban the Bible, which Franken called "a huge mistake, especially in very Christian areas." And then there was Kerry's pledge to build an enormous health-care bureaucracy and place the health of American patients in the hands of doctors in France.

It was kind of funny, but not really; Franken's anger came through in every word. The only reason American voters had misconceptions about Kerry, Franken said, was that George W. Bush and his campaign had spread lies about Kerry's true positions. "I guess what I'm leading to is, I don't mind losing an election if it were over an honest disagreement based on facts," Franken said. "But that's not what happened."

He mentioned a poll, done by the University of Maryland, which he said showed that many Americans still believed that Iraq had weapons of mass destruction. "What [the poll] showed is that a large majority of Bush supporters are delusional," Franken said. "Literally are delusional." And why were they delusional? "It is because there has been a systematic campaign over the years by the right-wing media . . . to lie to the American people," Franken explained. For that reason, Franken said, liberal talk radio had to keep going. "Air America was never intended to stop here, win or lose," he said. "We won't go away."

A few weeks later, Franken made good on his word when Air America announced that he had signed a new contract to stay with the network for at least two years. His original contract had been for a relatively brief term, set to end just months after the election. Many observers believed Franken was interested in appearing on Air America only until the race was finished and then, whoever became president, he would go on to other things. But it turned out he liked having a daily platform, and his decision to stay, along with some new investors, brightened Air America's future somewhat.

At the Center for American Progress, the mood among Franken's colleagues and support team was one of determination. There was no *Progress Report* on November 3, but the group had gotten itself back together by the next day, when *The Progress Report* began with the headline "The Fight Goes On." To lighten things up, the *Report* quoted a scene from *Animal House* that has become a favorite of losing sports teams everywhere. When Bluto, John Belushi's character, was told that his fraternity had lost its battle with the college dean, he yelled, "Over? Did you say over? NOTHING is over until WE decide it is! Was it over when the Germans bombed Pearl Harbor? HELL, NO!"

Then it was back to work. In the months leading up to the election, John Podesta had been one of the few people on the Left trying to stake a claim to moral issues as part of the campaign. After the election, when some commentators attributed

Kerry's loss to a deficiency on "values" issues, Podesta redoubled those efforts. The Center's first detailed statement after the voting was "Reclaiming Morality," which outlined ways in which the Left might define issues like poverty, health care, the environment, and even the deficit in terms of moral values.

And finally there was Mark Crispin Miller. At the end of *A Patriot Act,* after he spent a great deal of time outlining the Bush theocratic conspiracy, Miller offered a ray of hope. "We do have the right to vote, don't we?" he said. The audience agreed, happy to hear something positive after more than an hour of conspiracy talk. And then Miller doused that hope by saying that the Bush campaign had an elaborate scheme—Plan A, he called it—to rig the election using Diebold electronic voting machines. And if that didn't work, Miller said, a conveniently timed terrorist attack—Plan B—might rally support for the president just before the election.

After the voting, Miller saw Plan A in action. "This election was definitely rigged," he wrote in *Salon*. "I have no doubt about it." Bush got eight million more votes in 2004 than in 2000, Crispin said, and there were simply not enough "right-wing Christians" to account for that increase. "There is no way in the world that Bush got eight million more votes this time," Miller wrote. "I think it had a lot to do with the electronic voting machines. Those machines are completely untrustworthy, and that's why the Republicans use them." (In fact, when the final results came in, Bush won about eleven million more votes than in 2000, a fact that Miller would have said just made his thesis stronger.)

Miller argued that the news media were "obliged" to make Republicans account for the votes, because "simply to embrace this result as definitive is irrational." Miller recounted how he had "worked and worked and worked" to get the voting-machine story into the media, but it simply did not attract the attention it deserved.

And then he told a story that revealed something about himself and about his corner of the Left. Before the election, Miller said, he was so alarmed about the potential for widespread fraud that he discussed it with John Kerry himself. "I actually got invited to a Kerry fundraiser so I could talk to him about it," Miller wrote. When he got his chance to talk to Kerry and wife Teresa Heinz Kerry, Miller said, Mrs. Kerry became "really indignant" and "really concerned" about the possibility of fraud. But the candidate himself was a different story. "Kerry just looked down at me—he's about nine feet tall—and I could tell it just didn't register," Miller wrote. "It set off all his conspiracy-theory alarms, and he just wasn't listening." In the end, Miller seemed to see himself as the character in the movie who tries to tell everyone that disaster is coming but can't get anyone to take him seriously. Of course, in the movie, the Cassandra turns out to be right. But in real life, sometimes he's just a nut. And so Miller seemed—at least until after the election, when commentators began to echo his theocracy allegations.

A VASTER, BETTER CONSPIRACY

The liberal activists had organized historic numbers of people, raised historic amounts of money, even made historically profitable documentaries in the drive to defeat George W. Bush. And yet they failed. Why?

The simplest reason is that they just did not represent the

"real majority" of Americans, despite their deeply held belief that they did. In the end, MoveOn's radical antiwar beliefs, and Michael Moore's radical economic beliefs, and Robert Greenwald's radical beliefs on the media were, well, radical. The activists were on the fringes of American political life, even though they thought they were near the middle.

Why did they believe that? Because it was an easy mistake to make. The country is so big that its political fringes are big, too. About 59 million people voted for John Kerry. If one-third of them were the truest of the true believers, that was more than 19 million people. Or perhaps it was just one-quarter—still nearly 15 million. Whatever the case, the numbers make it clear that one could have a large following—say, 2 or 3 million people—and still be firmly on the fringes. But it doesn't look that way from the inside. If you are running a website or an advocacy group, the sheer size of your membership—imagine having 2 million people respond to your every utterance—might convince you that your influence is enormous.

In effect, a number of the groups in the Vast Left Wing Conspiracy were closed loops: circles of like-minded people who appealed almost exclusively to other like-minded people, but who at the same time exhorted one another into thinking that their appeal stretched far beyond the circle. Before the election, living inside their closed loops, they were not able to scan the horizon to see that they were, in fact, outnumbered by the other guys.

MoveOn was a 2.5-million member closed loop; when Pariser said, "We're the majority," he believed it. George Soros was a one-man closed loop; before the election he was convinced that a majority of Americans agreed with him, and after the election he believed that they had somehow gone crazy. The core audience for *Fahrenheit 9/11,* while vastly larger, was another closed loop, made up of people who disliked George W. Bush reaffirming their passions by participating in the group exercise of attending a movie. Even America Coming Together was a closed loop of its own, made up of like-minded organizations, all talking mostly to one another.

Making matters even worse was that the closed loops, rather than spreading edge-to-edge across the political landscape, tended to overlap. People who belonged to MoveOn watched *Fahrenheit 9/11* and contributed to America Coming Together and listened to Air America. The sheer variety of those activities—often described admiringly in the newspapers—seemed to be evidence of a broad, heterogeneous movement. It wasn't. Or, at the very least, it wasn't broad and heterogeneous enough to win an election.

And things were even worse than that; in some cases, the new activists on the Left didn't really understand their own side. For example, they almost completely bypassed black Americans, certainly the most loyal Democrats in the electorate. I went to lots of events during the campaign, hosted by MoveOn and the Center for American Progress and the Campaign for America's Future and others, and often noticed how extraordinarily white the audiences were. One could literally go to a gathering with several hundred people and find not a single black face, or perhaps one or two black faces. Smaller events, like the MoveOn house parties, also tended to be all white—just look at the photos of hundreds of such events posted on MoveOn's website.

At one point in the late summer of 2004, I brought up the subject with Donna Brazile, the Democratic strategist who ran Al Gore's 2000 campaign. She had a lot to say, none of which she wanted made public until after the election. "Remember, that sector of the liberal progressive movement has always been predominantly white," Brazile, who is black, told me. "It's a clique." And members of the clique, who prided themselves on their commitment to civil rights, didn't want to be told that they weren't terribly inclusive, as Brazile discovered when she pointed out that all of Kerry's top advisors were white. "When I took on the Kerry campaign early on about diversity, I got the crap beat out of me by the Left," Brazile told me. "I said, 'Hello—if the Republicans danced around with an all-white team, an all-white inner circle, you guys would be telling us to go out and beat them up.'"

In the end, as impressive as its accomplishments were, the Vast Left Wing Conspiracy just wasn't quite vast enough. And given its failures—the closed loops, the inability to appeal beyond the base—it would be easy to dismiss the liberals' political efforts as doomed to failure. After all, Republicans made substantial gains in 2004, and Democrats ended up further out of power than they had been in generations.

But some of the liberals' failures came as a result of entirely understandable—and perhaps one-time-only—factors. One was the simple fact that they were starting out, and they were in a hurry. They built their new infrastructure in a remarkably short period of time—not much more than eighteen months. The impressive thing is not that it wasn't fully completed but that it was as advanced as it was. In the next few years, they will keep building—new organizations, new donors, new ways to reach voters—in ways that might make the 2004 effort look primitive.

Their haste, which was the product of the anger they felt at George W. Bush and the desperation they felt at being out of power, also led them to make mistakes that might be corrected in the long run. For example, the urgency to win elections *immediately* caused John Podesta's Center for American Progress largely to abandon its role as an "incubator of new ideas" that could provide an intellectual foundation for liberalism. Now, with no election in the immediate future, the Center might get to the real work of a think tank.

Similarly, America Coming Together, which in a very short time threw tons of money—not always very efficiently—at the problem of voter turnout, will probably refine its methods now that the immediate pressure of an election is off. It might also forgo what might charitably be called the ethical shortcuts it took in the way it accounted for its finances—or at least come up with more sophisticated ethical shortcuts to deal with future campaign finance restrictions.

Meanwhile, all the organizations will still have their favorite target: George W. Bush. The president began his second term determined to achieve big things. The liberal groups will likely busy themselves with trying to stop him from doing those big things. In the process, they will also be practicing and improving their techniques of political organization.

And the key elements of the Vast Left Wing Conspiracy will remain in place. MoveOn will doubtless find another issue around which to organize, just as it has at various times pivoted on the Clinton impeachment, the 2000 recount, the Bush administration's response to 9/11, and the war in Iraq. Ellen Malcolm and Steve Rosenthal will come up with a new and improved version of ACT. God knows Michael Moore will still be around and, master promoter that he is, will find a way to make his next project a political cause. Air America, if it can attract enough listeners and actually make some money, could play a role in future campaigns. Robert Greenwald will still be turning out documentaries. The Center for American Progress will be Talking-Points Central. As for George Soros, during the campaign his political advisor, Michael Vachon, insisted to me that Soros "does not plan to be involved in future election cycles" and is "eager to get out of partisan politics." But after the election came reports that Soros had gotten together with Peter Lewis and Herbert and Marion Sandler in a new, multi-million-dollar venture to promote their policy ideas. It seems a sure bet that Soros will stay in the game.

Finally, lest he be forgotten, Mark Crispin Miller will almost certainly find a new conspiracy that threatens the Republic. Word of it will be spread by BuzzFlash and AlterNet and will eventually make its way to the op-ed pages of the *New York Times*.

Years from now, we might well look back on the 2004 election as a turning point in American political history. When MoveOn's Eli Pariser said of the Democratic Party, "We bought it, we own it, and we're going to take it back," he was being typically hyperbolic—Pariser was, after all, only twenty-three years old and given to great enthusiasms. But the angry pronouncement contained a kernel of truth, for MoveOn and other left-wing groups *had* figured out ways to bypass the traditional political party structure in order to reach voters and raise money. As a result, they transformed how campaigns are waged in this country.

The year 2004 might also be a turning point for the Democrats, the moment when left-wing coalitions united as never before to rebuild the liberal movement. Some observers might scoff at the idea, but consider the remarkable transformation of the conservative movement in recent decades. Compared to the Left today, the conservative movement in the 1960s was much further removed from power, much less organized, and not nearly as well financed. In 1964, Republican Barry Goldwater was routed by Democrat Lyndon Johnson, losing by more than 22 percentage points, whereas in 2004, John Kerry lost to Bush by a mere 3 points. The Left could rebound much more quickly than the Right did.

Indeed, some factors suggest that the Vast Left Wing Conspiracy might have better luck in 2008 than in the last election. Beyond the liberal groups' own failings, they lost in 2004 because of one key factor they could not control: The country was at war, and voters did not trust the Left's candidate to conduct that war. In 2008, things might be different. Also, by that time, the country might simply be tired of Republicans and ready to change leadership. But even if the planets align in their favor, the activists of the Left will still be entirely capable of defeating themselves, unless they emerge from their closed loops and see that their views are not necessarily shared by all Americans—and that those voters who disagree with them are not necessarily delusional. Then, and only then, will the Vast Left Wing Conspiracy—Boyd and Blades and Soros and Podesta and Moore and Malcolm and Rosenthal and all the institutions they built—be ready to win.

ACKNOWLEDGMENTS

This book had its beginning in January 2003, when I attended an antiwar rally in Washington staged by the radical group International ANSWER. The organization's leaders were old-style communists—they actually called one another "comrade"—and were (or, at least, should have been) too far out for anyone to take seriously. But as I began writing about the antiwar movement, my reporting moved on to the larger and more important groups on the Left devoted to opposing the war and, later, to electing a Democrat in 2004.

Special thanks go to my editor, Jed Donahue, who saw some of my pieces and called me out of the blue one day. Within fifteen minutes, the idea for this book was shaped. I also owe a big debt of gratitude to my agent, Joni Evans, who has steered me through the zillion things I didn't know about writing and publishing a book.

I would like to thank my editors at *National Review*, Rich Lowry, Kate O'Beirne, Jay Nordlinger, and Kathryn Jean Lopez, along with the rest of the staff, who showed great forbearance as I spent my time going to antiwar protests, Bush-bashing plays, "Take Back America" conferences, and left-wing documentaries.

Thanks also go to John Corry, who read the manuscript through its various stages and offered me his usual straight-to-the-point thoughts. Terry Eastland helped me through the theocracy question. Hugo Gurdon, editor of *The Hill*, allowed me to try out ideas in my column there. And Derek Willis, late of the Center for Public Integrity, was always helpful on campaign finance issues.

Particular thanks go to some of the subjects of this book, among them John Podesta, Ellen Malcolm, Michael Vachon, Joan Blades, Sheldon Drobny, Cecile Richards, Mark Walsh, Jim Gilliam, Jon Sinton, and Mark Crispin Miller, who graciously agreed to talk to me. There were also some people who helped me on the basis that their names not be used, and my (anonymous) thanks go to them, too.

My parents, Tom and Helen York, and my sister, Karen Moore, were always optimistic and, even more important, refrained from asking the sometimes-painful question: "How's the book going?"—even when that was what they really wanted to know.

Finally, my wife, Marty, is the reason this book was written. I have read hundreds of acknowledgments in which authors thank their wives or husbands for the love, support, and understanding that made it all possible. I thought I would find a better way to say it. I haven't. In the end, the truth is I couldn't imagine writing a book—or doing anything else—without her.

INDEX

ABOUT THE AUTHOR

BYRON YORK is the White House correspondent for *National Review*. He also writes a regular column for *The Hill*, a newspaper about Congress, and has written for the *Atlantic Monthly, Wall Street Journal, Weekly Standard,* and *New York Post,* among other publications. A frequent guest on television and radio, he has appeared on such programs as *Meet the Press, The NewsHour with Jim Lehrer, The O'Reilly Factor, Tim Russert, Special Report with Brit Hume,* and *Hardball* and has contributed occasional commentaries to National Public Radio. He lives in Washington, D.C.